This Book Belongs To:

John and Sharon Voss
(303) 833-3333

Voss and Associates
Financial Services

*After you have savored
the pearls of this book,
please return it to
John or Sharon*

Enjoy!

THE
LAST CHANCE
MILLIONAIRE

ALSO BY DOUGLAS R. ANDREW

MISSED FORTUNE

MISSED FORTUNE 101

THE
LAST CHANCE
MILLIONAIRE

It's Not Too Late to Become Wealthy

DOUGLAS R. ANDREW

WARNER
BUSINESS
BOOKS™

NEW YORK   BOSTON

Warner Business Books
Hachette Book Group USA
237 Park Avenue
New York, NY 10169
Visit our Web site at www.HachetteBookGroupUSA.com.

Warner Business Books is an imprint of Warner Books, Inc.
Warner Business Books is a trademark of Time Warner Inc. or an affiliated company. Used under license by Hachette Book Group USA, which is not affiliated with Time Warner Inc.

Printed in the United States of America

First Edition: June 2007
10 9 8 7 6 5 4 3 2 1

Library of Congress Cataloging-in-Publication Data
Andrew, Douglas R.
   The last chance millionaire : it's not too late to become wealthy / Douglas R. Andrew.
       p. cm.
   Includes index.
   ISBN-13: 978-0-446-58053-3
   ISBN-10: 0-446-58053-8
   1. Finance, Personal. 2. Finance, Personal—United States. 3. Investments.
4. Financial security. I. Title.
   HG179.A5598 2007
   332.024'01—dc22

2006037667

Book design by Charles Sutherland

To my Family and Posterity

May the principles and insights
Contained in this book
Bring you
Clarity, Balance, Focus, and Confidence
To help you accomplish
Your Greatest Dreams
And create a
Meaningful Transformation
In your lives.

Contents

ACKNOWLEDGMENTS   xi

PREFACE   xv

CHAPTER I   1
From Broke Boomer to Blazing Bloomer
Remove the Obstacles to Your Future Financial Well-Being

CHAPTER 2   19
Baby Boomer Blunders
Ten Financial Mistakes You Can Correct Before It's Too Late

CHAPTER 3   41
Take Ownership of Your Retirement
Make Social Security the Bonus, Not the Basis, for Income
and Find the Right Lead Advisor to Lodge Your Money Safely

CHAPTER 4   59
Understand the Three Marvels of Wealth Accumulation
Let Compound Interest, Tax-Free Savings, and Safe Leverage
Boost Your Net Worth

CHAPTER 5   85
Liberate Yourself from IRAs and 401(k)s
Why Uncle Sam's Savings Plans Should *Not* Be Yours

CHAPTER 6   **113**
Harness the Power of Safe, Liquid Equity
How Tax-Deductible Debt Works in Your Favor

CHAPTER 7   **133**
Learn How to Become Your Own Banker
Put Other People's Money to Work on Your Behalf

CHAPTER 8   **155**
Locate the Key to Your Retirement: It's Sitting
Under Your Own Roof
How to Find the Home Mortgage That Works Hardest for You

CHAPTER 9   **191**
Sprint to Retirement Wealth via Tax-Smart Alternatives
Prepare a Strategic Rollout of IRAs/40I(k)s to Save Taxes

CHAPTER 10   **221**
Establish an Individual Retirement Abode (IRA)
How to Invest in Your Second-Home Dream and Retirement
Savings—At the Same Time

CHAPTER I I   **239**
Choose Investments That Pass the Liquidity, Safety,
and Rate of Return Tests
A Scorecard for Stocks, Bonds, Money Markets, Mutual Funds,
Annuities, and Maximum-Funded Insurance

CHAPTER 12   **273**
Insure That Your Retirement Income Lasts as Long as You Do
How Maximum Tax-Advantaged Life Insurance Contracts
Pay for Your Retirement

CHAPTER 13 301

Make "At-Retirement Planning" Different from
"For-Retirement Planning"

How to Approach Retirement with 50 Percent More in Savings
and Create an Income Stream That Will Last as Long as You Do

CHAPTER 14 317

Redefine Yourself for a Future of Abundance

Optimize *All* of Your Assets—Financial, Core, Experience, Contribution

APPENDIX A 327

What You Need to Know About TEFRA, DEFRA, TAMRA, and Internal
Revenue Code Compliance

APPENDIX B 335

State Individual Income Taxes

INDEX 337

ABOUT THE AUTHOR 347

Acknowledgments

An author's work can be unique only in the expression of ideas, which rarely, if ever, claim just one originator. Ideas are the result of countless interactions with people who influence the path one takes.

I wish to express sincere gratitude for the wonderful people who have helped and inspired me to create *The Last Chance Millionaire*.

To my incredible literary agent, Jillian Manus, thank you for your excitement and encouragement in the creation of this work. You are so generous with your time and talents to help others. You have so much good in your heart, energy in your soul, and passion for life!

I give special thanks to my chief editor at Warner Books, Rick Wolff, for a wonderful working relationship. You have believed in my message and the power of delivering it to the world. And thanks to all of the great people, especially Sean Jones, at Warner Business Books who have helped to make this book a success.

To my wife and loving companion of more than thirty-three years, thank you for your love, compassion, patience, and understanding as I pursue those things that I am passionate about. You have been by my side rendering assistance and encouragement with every project I have undertaken. I love you dearly!

I offer gratitude for my two sons, Emron Andrew and Aaron Andrew. Thanks for carrying the baton while I worked on this book. Special thanks for helping with all of the charts and graphs, as well as the case studies in this work. I feel so fortunate and blessed to be your father.

Special thanks to my entire family, especially to my daughters, Mailee, Adrea, Mindy, and Ashley, for all of your help and support in our mutual endeavors. Thanks to Harmony, my daughter-in-law, and Scott and Brian, my sons-in-law, for your incredible talents and help in our business development. My greatest love and joy are found in my family.

Thanks to Mahesh Grossman, Grace Lichtenstein, and the Authors Team for their help in organizing this work. Grace, it was a delight to work with you closely throughout this project as you helped capture so many of the ideas and expressions that I flooded you with for hours and hours. Thanks for holding me to the task at hand.

I am grateful for Heather Beers, a wonderful friend and editor. I sincerely appreciate your special talents and your encouragement. I also extend special thanks to Toni Lock at tmdesigns for her help with the layout of the charts, graphs, and illustrations in this work. I express sincere gratitude to Kristin Varner for her unique and professional artwork. Amid your busy schedules, you all came through beautifully using your incredible talents.

I express special appreciation to Lee Brower, Marshall Thurber, and Mark Victor Hansen for your encouragement, inspiration, and advice that have contributed to the successful completion of this book.

I appreciate the many teachers and mentors in my life: Thanks to my coaches: Dan Sullivan, Lee Brower, Adrienne Duffy, and Leo Weidner. Thanks to Don Blanton, John Childers, Mike Midlam, Marv Neumann, Philip Bodine, Jerry Davis, and Philip Tirone for the brainstorming and ideas that we have shared, created, and enhanced together.

I express gratitude to my talented and dedicated unique-ability team for the countless hours of help and assistance you all render in our mutual endeavors. Special thanks to Michael Larkins for managing the operations of our company while I was heavily engaged in my writing and speaking endeavors.

Finally, I feel overwhelming thankfulness for our TEAM network of professional financial advisors and many alliances who have invested time, energy, and money to support our cause in helping people optimize their assets, manage their equity, and empower their true wealth. Together we are better—and we can turn this world right side up!

Preface

About eighty million Baby Boomers (those born between 1946 and 1964) are approaching retirement in the next twenty years. The crisis? Most Boomers will not have enough accumulated for retirement to meet their needs, let alone their wants.

The problem? The average Baby Boomer has less than $50,000 accumulated for retirement (which means many have less than that), primarily due to bad habits. Many will become "Broke Boomers" if they don't quit consuming so much. I have found that most people simply need direction on how to begin conserving their resources and putting them to work. The solution? Social Security isn't the answer. Taking ownership of your financial future *is* the answer. This book will empower you with the knowledge to achieve a greater degree of financial independence while there is still time left—it's not too late! You can become a "Blazing Bloomer" by creating tremendous wealth and financial security for yourself!

If you are concerned about preparing for retirement, this book is for you. I will reveal ten financial misconceptions—what I have nicknamed "Baby Boomer Blunders"—that most Boomers have made or will likely make. Boomers who labor under these misconceptions will learn dynamic strategies on how to cure or overcome their mistakes. Those who think they are safely headed toward retirement will gain invaluable insights on how to prevent or avoid making blunders. This book will help retirees understand that the planning they do *at* retirement is different from the planning they did *for* retirement. Those who are fearful that it is too late to prepare adequately for a comfortable retirement will experience new hope. Those who are already in a state of financial independence will experience a meaningful transformation as they are enlightened by opportunities they didn't know existed.

As a financial strategist, lecturer, and consultant for more than thirty years, the asset optimization, equity management, and wealth empowerment strategies that I teach have enabled clients nationwide to dramatically increase their financial independence. You will benefit from years of research and practical application of proven tax strategies, as well as extensive experience in financial planning and unorthodox insight that has proven an invaluable asset to thousands of individuals. I will introduce contrarian but proven strategies—as demonstrated in my first two books, *Missed Fortune* and *Missed Fortune 101*—that have empowered people throughout America to dramatically enhance their financial net worth. Thousands of financial services professionals are now using these books to help their clients understand these dynamic concepts and strategies that can help them achieve financial freedom. It's not too late for you to become wealthy!

Unlike other books written for Baby Boomers that tend to offer up the same old traditional retirement planning strategies that get people only so far, this book will offer new ideas that are built on sound principles. As for this book's differentiation from my previous works, *The Last Chance Millionaire* clearly stands apart—taking the underlying principles examined in the *Missed Fortune*™ series to the next level. My hope is that this book will serve as a wealth enhancement handbook—outlining specific, actionable steps that you can take now.

This book will help you realize you don't need to start from scratch to begin accumulating money for retirement. Instead, you can utilize three marvels: 1) compound interest, 2) tax-favored accumulation, and 3) safe, positive leverage. The greatest asset that most people have to prepare for a comfortable retirement and alle-

"My heavens, I have never thought more clearly about all of my options." Their body language suggests they are infused with energy.

When you get *balance*, you eliminate the wobble in your life. When you have a car out of alignment or whose tires aren't balanced, it can rumble down the street, weaving this way and that. Get an alignment and balance those tires and you get rid of the wobble. You get it to run precisely and your car gains speed in a hurry. In the same way, your finances may be wobbly. Learn how to balance your finances (and the priorities in other aspects of your life) and you suddenly gain velocity toward financial independence and peace of mind. It won't matter that you started late; you'll zoom ahead of the others who are still wobbling along without much direction.

When you find your *focus*, it brings accuracy. I'll help you focus on the important opportunities and activities that will help you most at this stage of your life.

Clarity, balance, and focus generate *confidence* that you can achieve all the good things you want for yourself and your family. In fact, increased confidence attracts new opportunities.

It is my sincere hope that reading this book will empower you with enough clarity, balance, and focus to give you the confidence to creatively deploy my strategies to manage your money successfully. You will discover a new path that will lead you beyond just getting along—leading you toward wealth, comfort, and a life of abundance. Yes, your last chance may indeed be your best chance to becoming a millionaire!

Douglas R. Andrew
Fall 2006

viate unnecessary income tax on their IRAs and 401(k)s is sitting under their own roof—their lazy, idle home equity! This book will teach you how to become your own banker, take ownership of your future, and how to achieve financial independence and retire in dignity. You will be able to turn on the afterburners to prepare for a comfortable retirement for maximum results with minimal risk.

Most of my clients are Boomers and retirees. I'm a Boomer—born in 1952. I understand why Boomers often feel confused, isolated, and powerless. My goal is to help you overcome the greatest barriers you face and to employ the best strategies possible by utilizing your greatest abilities. I have found that the three greatest barriers to progress are: 1) a lack of knowledge, 2) a lack of confidence, and 3) a lack of money. With the new knowledge you will attain, you will gain confidence. And I will help you find and make money.

I've been privileged to be affiliated with Lee Brower, president and founder of Empowered Wealth, LC for several years. I am an executive committee member and one of the founding quadrant living architects of the Brower Quadrant Living Experience™. In his system there are four categories of assets: Human, Intellectual, Financial, and Civic. Human assets are your *Core* assets. Intellectual assets come from your *Experiences*. Financial assets are usually measured monetarily. And Civic or Social assets are the *Contributions* we give back to society. I prefer to call this strategy a holistic approach to optimizing all of the assets on your personal and family balance sheet.

When we meet with clients, we start by talking about four essential mental adjustments everyone should make in order to clear away confusion and achieve their dreams: Clarity, Balance, Focus, and Confidence.

When you get *clarity* in your vision, it gives you energy. When people get a grip on what they are trying to accomplish and where they are headed, it sweeps away many mental roadblocks to action. I watch people listen to us describe the four different kinds of assets they have (human, intellectual, financial, civic) and I can almost hear them say,

THE
LAST CHANCE
MILLIONAIRE

CHAPTER 1

From Broke Boomer to Blazing Bloomer

Remove the Obstacles to Your Future Financial Well-Being

© Cartoonbank.com

*"If we take a late retirement and an
early death, we'll just squeak by."*

IS THAT SCENARIO A LITTLE TOO close to home to get a laugh out of you? If so, you've got plenty of company. Whether everyone will have enough money to retire is a question that looms large today for 78 million Americans—the Baby Boomers born between 1946 and 1964. If you're among the oldest Boomers, those born right after World War II, you will have to face this issue sooner rather than later. After all, according to the U.S. Census Bureau, 330 of us are turning 60 every *hour*.

I say "us," because I am one of you. I was born in 1952, and like you I am part of the largest population explosion in history. So we're in this arena together. As a financial strategist and retirement specialist, I know it's one thing to talk about the game, but another thing to play it.

It's likely we've all carried a common dream throughout our lives—achieving financial independence. Creating wealth. Maybe even obtaining that elusive status: "millionaire."

Well, here we are, with retirement just up ahead. Have you arrived?

Magazine articles and television news sometimes suggest that Boomers all have bundles of money, as well as a nice big home, and retirement IRA and 401(k) accounts that are growing steadily in value.

Unfortunately, it's not that simple.

To begin with, even the oldest Boomers may not expect to quit working on their 65th birthday. Whether it's out of financial necessity or lifestyle preference, many do not anticipate retiring in the traditional sense.

It has been well documented that unlike our parents' generation, we are less interested in "playing golf every day." We are more active, more likely to work beyond the traditional retirement age of 65, and, unfortunately, less financially prepared than our parents were for the "golden years."

According to the Bureau of Labor Statistics, the average age of retirees is 68. The life expectancy for a normal, healthy male age 65 is another twenty years, to age 85. If a person stops earning income at age 68, there is now a seventeen-year gap to cover with retirement resources, rather than the five-, ten-, or twelve-year gap that existed just one to two generations ago. Based on the better health and mortality (life expectancy) of the upcoming Baby Boomer retirement force, "retirement" in the traditional sense should now be at age 73! For many Boomers, retirement planning needs to provide adequate resources to last thirty years or longer. This book will help prepare you so you don't outlive your money.

Beyond whatever size nest eggs we may have nurtured, Social Security is often something Boomers expect to incorporate into their retirement. But there are conflicting statistics and studies about how much money we will be able to collect in Social Security, as more and more of us begin dipping regularly into that wellspring of dollars established by the federal government some seventy years ago.

In fact, the national Social Security Trust Funds could be headed for serious trouble. The 2006 Trustee's Report projects that the Social Security Trust Funds will totally run out of steam by the year 2040 unless there is serious reform.

I maintain that Social Security benefits should be viewed as a supplement to your retirement, not as your primary source of income. It should become a bonus *for*, not the basis *of*, your planning.

WHAT MAKES YOU ANXIOUS ABOUT RETIREMENT?

Are you concerned about the possibility that, like the pair in the cartoon, it's too late to plan for a comfortable retirement? Do you believe you have not saved enough—or anything substantial at all—and must start from scratch? Do you fear that not only will you never become a millionaire, but that you may end up a Broke Boomer?

Many of your fellow Boomers have the same concerns.

- DO you think it's too late in life to catch up with wealthier friends, customers, or business associates in your circle who seem to have it all—a great house, a second getaway home, a plan for making their money last?
- ARE you worried that even if you do have enough, you

might outlive your money and wind up dependent on charity or your children when you are old?

- DO you believe you are powerless to reverse the course of your personal financial history?

At age fifty-four, when I sit down and project myself into the future ten or fifteen years, I ask myself, "What has to have happened in my life leading up to age sixty-five or seventy, both personally and financially, for me to be happy with my progress toward my golden years?"

When I visualize how I want to live during retirement, I know that realistically I need to focus *now* on eliminating the barriers that would prevent me from realizing my vision. I also need to determine which strategies, resources, and opportunities I can use *right now* in order to achieve my goals. Lastly, I need to harness and direct my best abilities and strengths to *optimize* all of my assets.

A wonderful friend and entrepreneurial coach, Dan Sullivan, taught me to have a conversation with my clients framed around their greatest dangers, opportunities, and strengths. I use this framework with my clients to understand where they are and where they want to go. Inasmuch as most of my clients are Boomers and retirees, allow me to outline what they have shared. When I have these enlightening conversations, it's apparent that people are confused. They feel isolated. They feel powerless.

How about you? Do you share any of the following concerns? Do you want to learn how to employ some of the strategies listed? Do you have any of the abilities outlined below?

GREATEST *BARRIERS* TO OVERCOME:
- Not having enough money accumulated for retirement
- Outliving your income after retirement
- Losing your ability to earn and save

- Consuming instead of conserving retirement resources
- Losing your health and mobility
- Dying too soon and leaving others without adequate resources
- Having resources dwindle due to taxes and inflation
- Using up resources to pay for long-term health care
- Having to work to make ends meet
- Not having enough resources to care for your parents physically and financially as they age

GREATEST *STRATEGIES* TO EMPLOY:

- Tapping into one of your greatest assets—your home equity
- Realizing that it's not too late to become wealthy—there's still time
- Turbocharging your retirement savings
- Employing the three marvels of wealth accumulation
- Taking full ownership of your retirement
- Overcoming or avoiding Baby Boomer Blunders
- Initiating a strategic rollout of your IRAs and 401(k)s
- Repositioning assets for greater liquidity, safety, and rate of return
- Becoming your own banker
- Redefining yourself at retirement

GREATEST *ABILITIES* TO UTILIZE:

- Possessing a good work ethic
- Having one to two incomes with more discretionary dollars to set aside
- Having home equity available to use for safe leverage
- Still having enough time left to accomplish retirement goals

- Dispelling myths from parents who grew up in the Great Depression era
- Having the capacity to live longer and more healthfully
- Having the ability to work longer and contribute value far beyond age sixty-five

If you feel you have some of the same barriers that are blocking the path to your financial security, this book is meant for you:

- It can help you overcome and alleviate the greatest barriers you are facing.
- It can provide you with refreshing and proven strategies.
- It can reveal and harness your best abilities that need to be utilized to succeed in reaching your goals.

HOW *THE LAST CHANCE MILLIONAIRE* WILL HELP

I know many of you are feeling the "darkness of night" as you look toward your retirement years. You have probably already realized that if you keep doing what you've always done, you'll keep getting what you've always gotten. Rather than letting you stay in that rut, I want to bump you out of it to reveal the "brightness of day"— your brilliant future—full of peace, abundance, and prosperity.

This book will give you new direction. It will instill greater confidence for your future. Through the creative strategies, you will be endowed with new capabilities. You will feel empowered to prepare adequately for a comfortable retirement. You *can* achieve financial independence, and you can do it *now!*

The most important thing I want to give you is an insight-based experience. When you have insights that are yours, you are able to make a change for the better. You will experience epiphanies— those moments when you go, "Ah hah! I get it!"

There's still time to become a "last chance millionaire," or what I also call a Blazing Bloomer! You can still get your act together, even though it's late in the game. But it is going to take work on your part. I don't have a get-rich-quick scheme. I have a system, but it requires that you optimize your assets and discipline your spending—that you conserve rather than consume.

I ask that you abide by three ground rules as you read this book:

- First, I would like you to keep an open mind about my system, even if some of the strategies I suggest sound counterintuitive.
- Second, be willing to suspend your disbelief until I present my full arguments in favor of certain ideas that might be different from the conventional retirement financial planning wisdom you have heard up until now.
- Third, I want you to avoid justifying why you have not taken certain financial steps. By the time I connect all the dots, you will understand how you can make major improvements in your financial future.

DISCARD OUTDATED INFORMATION AND CLEAR THE PATH TO NEW IDEAS

First, I will introduce you to common misconceptions about money and the blunders many Baby Boomers have made with their money. You've always been told that the way to get ahead is to buy a home, get a cheap mortgage, and pay it off as quickly as you can. You have also been told to sink as much money as possible into an IRA or 401(k) plan, and to make sure they produce a high rate of return. For years you've been bombarded with this constant stream of conventional wisdom.

But I am about to prove to you that old, conventional wisdom in this case is wrong. Just because for thousands of years most of humanity thought the world was flat, it didn't make it that way. In my previous book, *Missed Fortune 101,* I wrote that, "All the dogs barking up the wrong tree doesn't make it the right one." *I will es-*

tablish my case that socking away money into IRAs and 401(k)s and making extra payments on your mortgage are both counterproductive.

I will show you a different and totally revolutionary approach. I believe it is possible to cure your mistakes, to avoid making new blunders. There is a better way to gain financial independence.

Yes, my strategies go against the current of traditional financial planning. In fact, most of the tactics I will offer you are contrary to popular belief. Yet all my advice is based on fact, tax law, and the practical application of thousands of very wealthy people.

But I'm giving you fair warning. These strategies are not for financial jellyfish. These strategies are for forward-thinking, disciplined people who are ready to examine their own roadblocks to wealth. They are for people willing to buck the trend of misguided, typical financial wisdom and instead make the most of proven, yet less familiar, methods to create a personal plan for true wealth.

My suggestions are for the majority of hardworking families with husbands and wives who have reached a degree of financial stability by working most of their adult lives. However, if you are among the few who are already financially independent, I will show you how to experience *a meaningful transformation* as you are enlightened by opportunities you didn't know existed. I will show you how to develop a proper PLAN—an acronym for Perpetual Life of Asset Nurturance™. When we learn to nurture all of our assets properly, we create a new life for them that will live on into perpetuity.

In short, I will give you direction, confidence, and capability to achieve your dreams.

MY "ELEVATOR SPEECH"

Once again, I must warn you: Do not expect me to show you how to get rich quickly. Be prepared to study, listen, learn, and do basic homework. This book is not entitled *Super-Quick Wealth Enhancement and Asset Optimization for Dummies*. Also, please don't get the idea that this book is just for those people who are already wealthy. I want to empower families at every income level and in every tax bracket.

To give you the ultra-brief version of my system, let's pretend we are in an elevator in an office building. You've heard about this book and you ask: "What exactly do you do, Doug?"

Here's my "elevator speech" reply:

You know how most people save for retirement by socking away money in IRAs and 401(k)s, and also try to pay off their house by sending extra principal payments to their mortgage company? Why get a tax break when you put money in a qualified retirement plan, expecting that you'll be in a lower tax bracket when you retire, only to get clobbered by taxes on the back end? To me, that's like driving on the highway with one foot on the gas pedal and the other on the brake. You may get to your destination eventually, but it's a pretty jerky ride.

How about your home? We all know market values fluctuate. What I do is assure people that if their houses go down in value, they will not lose their equity—not one penny.

What's more, if you are sending extra principal payments to the mortgage company, you're killing your partner, Uncle Sam, *by depriving yourself of one of the best tax deductions we have as Americans: home mortgage interest.*

As you approach retirement, you painfully come to the realization that you've increased your tax liability by postponing it to a time when you no longer have significant deductions. I can show you how to dramatically enhance your net worth and your net spendable retirement income, and never outlive your money, by *not* doing what most people do.

We've reached your floor. The elevator door is about to open. Do I have your attention yet?

WHAT ARE THE MAIN ISSUES I ADDRESS?

I will show you how to grow wealthy steadily, utilizing three marvels: compound interest, tax-favored accumulation, and safe, positive leverage. Now, you may be sitting there thinking, "Oh, I already understand those three concepts!" Don't put this book down!

Every month, I have a new group of financial services professionals (often comprising more than 100) come through my intensive three-day asset optimization, equity management, and wealth empowerment training. Many are sophisticated, veteran financial planners, CPAs, and tax attorneys, and the vast majority are surprised when they discover that they didn't know what they didn't know—especially about compound interest, tax-favored accumulation, and safe leverage. Over 80 percent of them flunk a simple, but tricky, three-question math quiz. After the training, they usually admit they have been advising their clients the wrong way.

Please don't get me wrong. These are well-intentioned advisors pointing their clients toward conventional saving and investment strategies that are *good*. What I want to do is show you that what I teach them is the *better* or *best* way to optimize assets and accumulate wealth. A friend once taught me a ditty: "Good, better, best; never let it rest! Never let it rest, till good gets better and better gets best!"

Whatever you've done up until this point, don't worry. It was probably good. But you can begin now to reposition assets—to turbocharge your wealth accumulation. As I often say, *It's not what you begin with that counts; it's what you end up with.*

Your greatest asset, the one most people already have, is sitting under your own roof. That asset is your home equity. I will show you how to manage it to alleviate unnecessary income tax on your IRAs and 401(k)s. I will teach you how to become your own banker, take ownership of your future, achieve financial independence, and retire in dignity.

I will show you strategies to turn on the afterburners during retirement to dramatically enhance your financial situation, with maximum results at minimal risk. I will teach you a new way to look at tax-favored investments that can offer you predictable asset accumulation and tax-free spendable income.

This is a book for you—a mature person—but there is no reason you can't also hand it to your thirty-year-old children, or newlywed son or daughter, and say, "We've made some mistakes, but here is a way you can avoid them. Learn how to maximize your assets in a tax-favored environment for the next thirty years, and you'll be further ahead."

YOU, TOO, CAN BE A THRIVER

Lee Brower, president of Empowered Wealth, LC, of which I am a national advisory board member and founding architect, origi-

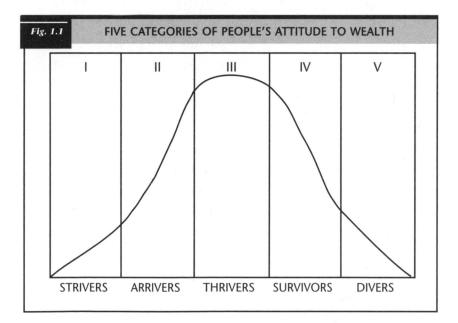

Fig. 1.1 — FIVE CATEGORIES OF PEOPLE'S ATTITUDE TO WEALTH

I II III IV V

STRIVERS ARRIVERS THRIVERS SURVIVORS DIVERS

nated the model of *Strivers, Arrivers, Thrivers, Survivors,* and *Divers,* depicting a bell curve of financial phases people may go through as they mature (Figure 1.1). Here is my interpretation of these five categories of people:

Strivers are the masses of people who may want to manage their money better, but who don't understand the dynamics of money. They are often financial jellyfish. They live in the here-and-now. All they want to figure out is how to make money and spend it. These are people who, when they need cash, go to a check-cashing store and pay 3 percent to collect some of their own money. They are consumers who spend their savings rather than conserving it for the future.

Arrivers are the former Strivers who, with knowledge and discipline, graduate to the next levels of true wealth transformation. They understand that there are three marvels of wealth accumulation: compound interest, tax-favored growth, and safe leverage using other people's money.

Thrivers are further up the ladder. They are Arrivers who know how to repeat the marvels of wealth accumulation over and over again—with their house, their second home, with other real estate, with all of their assets (Human, Intellectual, Financial, and Civic).

Survivors, on the other hand, are those Thrivers who become more fixated about the return *of* their money instead of the return *on* their money. They stop taking the steps that grew their wealth, and it begins to taper off. They say, "I've just got to hang on." These are the people who think Social Security is enough to see them through their retirement comfortably.

Soon Survivors can become *Divers*, who, with their retirement money taxed on the back end and their asset accumulation models abandoned, run the risk of outliving their money.

How do the Thrivers of the world do it? Stay with me and you will find out how to free up cash and apply it toward achieving financial independence—learning how to put lazy, idle dollars (money you might not even know you have) to work.

I will show you proven methods of building your assets to

achieve greater net spendable retirement income and to increase the value of your estate, all in a tax-favored environment. I will also help you figure out which other assets, such as CDs, stocks, bonds, and annuities, you ought to reposition in order to get more zing out of your money.

A PERSONAL, INSIGHT-BASED, LIFE-CHANGING EXPERIENCE

My wife, Sharee, and I have six wonderful children—four daughters and two sons. Our family loves to work hard, and we love to play hard.

We plan and carry out a family vacation with a specific purpose every six months involving our entire family, including my children's spouses. I'll share more about the power of this concept in Chapter 14. For now, I want to share some insights we gained on a family vacation several years ago.

One summer when school was out, we were able to pick up an inexpensive scuba-diving package in the western Caribbean. After our children were certified to scuba dive, we enjoyed a wonderfully relaxing week on Cozumel Island in Mexico. Each day we would venture out to a different scuba dive site and take in two dives of forty to sixty minutes in duration. The famous Palancar Reef located off Cozumel is touted as the third best scuba diving site in the world (behind the Great Barrier Reef and the Red Sea). It is a protected underwater park. The visibility is often 100 to 150 feet and the water temperature in the summertime often stays between 78 and 82 degrees up to depths of eighty feet. We would arrive back at the resort hotel in time for lunch and enjoy the rest of the day lying in hammocks, reading books, and talking about what we observed and learned that day.

Wherever we dived along the expansive reef, the plant and animal life was beautiful. We observed hundreds of varieties of fish, including jacks, triggerfish, angel fish, snappers, sting rays, barracuda, and giant groupers. Occasionally, if we searched hard in small underwater caves and small canyon walls, we would discover crabs, lobsters, octopi, and large eels. The colors of the fish, coral, and plant life were brilliant.

Toward the end of the week, we opted for a special night diving excursion. The night dive took place just a few hundred yards from the resort pier. We didn't have to travel far to experience what has remained one of our family's favorite dives.

It was a calm, clear night. The moon was shimmering over the gentle tide as we entered the dark water. Two barracudas curiously accompanied us as we descended slowly to a depth of about sixty feet and knelt on the white sandy ocean floor. Looking up toward the surface of the ocean, we could clearly see the moon and stars from our underwater vantage point. We quickly gained an appreciation of the immensity of the earth and space above as well as below the surface of the sea.

Our dive master signaled for us to turn off our flashlights for a few minutes. In awe we observed a scene of hundreds of tiny fish that were illuminated by their own energy source and by the reflection of the moon's light. They looked like tiny, colored neon Christmas lights flickering around us—we were mesmerized by this peaceful scene. Then our dive master directed our attention to the ocean floor that lay ahead of us and signaled for us to turn our flashlights on.

We had been preoccupied with looking behind us—at where we had been. Across the ocean floor, as far as our lights could penetrate, the sea seemed to have come alive. We observed more crabs, lobsters, octopi, and eels creeping, crawling, and slithering in one pass of our flashlights than we had discovered in five days of daytime diving. The ocean floor seemed almost animated, reminding me of the "Under the Sea" musical scene in *The Little Mermaid*. More colors emanated from these creatures than we had ever before seen. It was the same ocean—in fact the same spot—we had dived earlier in the week, but now it was transformed, shimmering with life. It dawned on me that the abundant life had been hidden until the timing was right and a different light brought things out of obscurity.

So it is with the financial strategies contained in this book. An entire ocean of opportunity is there waiting for you. A life of peace and abundance can be yours—as you look forward, rather than behind you. You are about to see new opportunities, new paths, that may have been obscured until the timing was right and someone could shed light on concepts that have been hiding—maybe right under your own roof!

SO HOW DO I GET ON THE SMART TRACK TO MILLIONAIRE STATUS?

Only about 5 percent of all American households have a financial net worth in excess of $1 million. But you, too, can become a millionaire or multimillionaire within just a few years by employing the strategies contained in this book. However, unless you overcome the barriers, employ these strategies, and harness your best abilities, your potential wealth will not come to fruition. This might be your last chance to become a millionaire, safely, and just in time to establish a nest egg that will last as long as you do.

The strategies in this book are designed to help you make up for lost time. It's not too late to become wealthy. But I need to restate once again, it will not happen overnight. If you want to accumulate a million dollars or more in retirement assets as soon as possible, you'll need to pay close attention to ways that you can get a great head start, methods that will have you sprinting past some of your peers.

If this is your last chance to become a millionaire, you'll want to do it right and ensure that you *will* achieve the financial independence that you desire. Are you interested in having *more* money? How about a *lot* more money? Then I implore you to read the entire book.

(As a token of appreciation for investing in the purchase of this book, I also invite you to listen to a special audio CD I have recorded for readers of *The Last Chance Millionaire* entitled "Secrets of Wealthy People." Please go to www.MissedFortune.com/Secrets to hear this enlightening information.)

THE BENEFITS OF FINANCIAL INDEPENDENCE AWAIT YOU

I've been a financial strategist for more than thirty years, helping people optimize their assets, manage their equity, and empower their wealth. Thousands of people have implemented these strategies and are now on the right path. I have interviewed many of them throughout the world. Here are some of the most mentioned benefits people enjoy (and you can also enjoy) as a result of employing the strategies I disclose in this work:

- You will be able to overcome the greatest dangers and conquer your greatest fears about having enough retirement resources—whether it's money for prescriptions and medical care, or money for golf, cruises, and visiting your grandchildren.
- Have you ever been told you have no hope because you don't have enough money? You will feel greater hope as you embark on a new beginning toward a secure future, able to fight against inflation and taxes gobbling up your hard-earned savings.
- You will be able to prove to yourself and to others that you *can* become financially independent and savvy. You will be totally accountable and responsible for your own future—fully independent from others—free from any reliance on the government to help provide for your retirement.
- You will be endowed with true wealth—a feeling of peace and abundance—that will allow you to give back to society, especially any family and friends that may need help. You may want to set up your own charitable

family foundation or outreach program to help bless the lives of others in need. Your passion and purpose will be able to live on as you freely give to your favorite charities.

- You will enjoy richer and more meaningful relationships with your loved ones. With the proper perspective and priorities in your life, you will find the relationships that matter most will be enhanced when your financial house is in order. Marriage relationships become stronger and more intimate than ever when partners are on the same page, working together to achieve financial independence as a team for a long and fulfilling retirement.

I hope I've convinced you to continue reading. Consider *The Last Chance Millionaire* as your nick-of-time road map to a retirement future free of financial traps and full of promise. This is your time. You can do this. And you can begin right now!

REMEMBER THIS:

- No matter what your age, it is not too late to examine the current status of your retirement plan—even if you feel behind the curve—to take steps to catch up.
- Be willing to suspend judgment about unconventional financial concepts and try to remain open to brand-new revolutionary strategies.
- Learn the best strategies for optimizing your assets to enhance your retirement income.
- Recognize this key element: Your greatest resource is most likely the equity trapped in your house that can be tapped to fuel retirement savings.
- Build your wealth by joining the Thrivers who get the message, act, and who repeat their successes.

CHAPTER 2

Baby Boomer Blunders

Ten Financial Mistakes You Can Correct Before It's Too Late

WHY ARE MANY BOOMERS FACING A crisis as they approach retirement? Because we have all had plenty of time to make every financial blunder under the sun. The biggest blunder for some is not squirreling away enough money during the prime of our work life so we can relax and enjoy that bounty later on.

"As many as 40 percent have saved almost nothing," one expert told a congressional panel recently.[*] These people will not have enough to meet their needs in their golden years, let alone their wants.

While my clients tend to be more affluent than the average Boomer, it surprises me when I hear reports that, in 2005, the average Boomer had only about $30,000 accumulated in retirement savings.

How did this happen? It's usually because of a mixture of bad habits and one-size-fits-all financial advice.

As my friend Dan Sullivan, author of *The Laws of Lifetime*

---

[*]Gail Russell Chaddock, "Baby Boomers Face Retirement Squeeze," *Christian Science Monitor,* February 27, 2004.

Growth, teaches, "All progress begins by telling the truth." So, how many of what I call Baby Boomer Blunders apply to you?

- I have saved only 1 to 3 percent of my income, instead of 10 to 20 percent.
- I have borrowed to consume, rather than to conserve.
- I have paid off my house by sending extra principal payments to the mortgage company.
- I would love a vacation condo or cabin, but I can't afford one yet—I'm waiting until I retire to buy it.
- I have bought and sold investments at the wrong time.
- I have not matched the right investment vehicles with my objectives.
- I am at risk *in* the market, rather than linking my investment returns *to* the market to preserve safety of principal.
- I have paid too much for insurance, rather than letting Uncle Sam pay for it.
- When I focus on my comprehensive balance sheet, I concentrate on the least important category—money—versus the most important assets: my family, health, and values.
- After working for forty years, I'm wondering what it was all for.

Let's spend a bit more time on the background behind most blunders.

BOOMERS ARE DIFFERENT FROM THEIR PARENTS

Raised after World War II, Boomers bring to their mature years a different set of experiences than those of their parents. Whereas many of their parents grew up during the Great Depression, where they learned hard lessons about how money could disappear in a flash, Boomers have lived through an era of unprecedented prosperity, easy credit, and quick gratification. Most never really felt they had to put a nest egg away. They tend to have the attitude: "If I want something, I buy it. If I can't pay cash, I'll finance it. I'll worry about tomorrow when tomorrow comes."

Contrast that way of thinking to my father, for example, who was a member of the Depression generation. From the time he was young to well beyond his official retirement, he worked hard, saved, and lived a relatively simple life.

When he was starting out, my dad delivered newspapers and then got a job as a stock clerk working at Woolworth. My mother was a sales clerk at the same Woolworth store. When he asked her out on a date, he was fired because it was against company policy for employees to date one another. Of course I'm grateful he was able to find other work and continue the courtship! They were married in 1938.

My mother and father never really talked a lot about suffering during the Depression. My dad had watched his father struggle, but his family didn't lose their home. To them, life was simple because they didn't know anything different. Soon my dad sought security in working for a large company and spent much of his career in management at the Geneva Works of U.S. Steel in Utah.

My father was deferred by the military draft because he was employed in a defense-related industry. Like many, he was enticed by the giant steel industry with company benefits. While many of those who worked for him were union members whose take-home pay was larger due to overtime, he opted for a predictable salary, health insurance, and a pension.

When he finally retired as superintendent of a division, he did collect that stable pension—but inflation made it worth less and less with each passing year. He lived twenty-five years past his retirement and even started a gift and candy distribution company immediately after retiring—not only for the extra income, but also because he knew the importance of staying in motion to keep himself healthy and occupied.

WHY BOOMERS ARE LAX ABOUT PLANNING FOR RETIREMENT

Much has changed since my father's day. Unlike their parents, who had to confront joblessness and world turmoil early in life, many Boomers want to live life as it comes—every day, every month, every year. They don't worry the way their parents did about putting something aside for the future. The concept of having "something to fall back on" does not grip them in the same way. Having witnessed how the government bailed out failures such as Chrysler and the savings and loan industry, they figure government will always be there to bail them out.

This false sense of security is the reason that it comes as such a shock when entire communities find themselves without jobs because of the shifts in the global economy or the mistakes of big business.

Older Boomers have been brought up short by scandals, downsizing, outsourcing, and economic upheaval. Younger Boomers are beginning to realize security is not in their job—it's in the unique skills of an individual and in an individual's ability to stay marketable.

The result is that older Boomers think it might be too late to catch up, while younger Boomers think there is still going to be enough time to save something. (In theory there is still time.) However, for too many Boomers, spending is a way of life; saving is not.

HELP! I'M RUNNING OUT OF TIME!

Like it or not, time does catch up with all of us. Perhaps you are among those who, at age forty-five or fifty, insist: "I'll worry about retirement later." Or perhaps you think that putting $500 aside each month or $6,000 each year is too much of a sacrifice to your present-day lifestyle.

If so, listen closely. However great a sacrifice $500 a month may seem, it is not going to cut it. Indeed, you really don't have the time to sock away $1,000 a year for thirty-five years like young people do.

Instead, I want to help you find $100,000 or more. You probably think you don't have that much money. You don't realize it, but you do—and it's sitting right under your own roof!

Using safe leverage—which is what banks and credit unions do—can be the answer to your search. Separate $100,000 of equity from your house, put that $100,000 to work for you safely, and it can grow into a sizable retirement nest egg. Let it sit for just 7.2 years at 10 percent, and it can grow to $200,000. (That's the rule of 72 that I will talk about in detail in Chapter 4.) If you are age fifty, the $100,000 could double twice before age sixty-five, blossoming into a $400,000 nest egg!

My point is, you can't set aside the same money you are earmarking for a boat, a new truck, or a vacation in Hawaii. You have to allow it to accumulate in a systematic way. *You need to conserve, not consume.*

Now let's dig a little deeper into the psychology that drives specific blunders.

MISCONCEPTION #1: SHORT-TERM INVESTMENTS FOR LONG-RANGE GOALS; AND LONG-TERM INVESTMENTS FOR SHORT-RANGE (LESS THAN FIVE YEARS) GOALS.

This may be the biggest mistake I come across in well-intentioned families.

Numerous people come to me holding retirement funds in certificates of deposit, money market accounts, and other short-term investments, earning a dinky interest rate. Yet they don't plan to touch this money for five, ten, or even fifteen years. Savings vehicles such as CDs and money market accounts are short-term investments, best used like those short-term parking lots at the airport—convenient places to park your money for a brief stay.

If you get 3 percent on a taxable investment like a CD or money market fund, you will probably net about 2 percent; even if you get 5 percent, you net about 3.5 percent. That's fine for money you plan to access in less than five years, but it is not a great idea for your retirement nest egg.

Conversely, in the 1990s people were tucking away huge amounts of money in mutual funds. It seemed to make sense because returns were very good, over time. Mutual funds are long-term investments.

You could have thrown a dart at a dartboard made of mutual fund newspaper listings in 1990, bought the first ten you hit, held them for ten years prior to the market crash of 2001, and you could have achieved 12.9 percent average annual return on those mutual funds. However, the average investor did not get 12.9 percent; he or she actually got 2 or 3 percent for those years, because people held them for only 2.9 years. According to Dalbar and Morningstar, two of the leading ranking services for the mutual fund industry, the average mutual fund investor gets antsy after a few years and pulls money out of what is really a long-term investment to buy a car, RV, ATV, or Jet Ski.

Too many people use a long-term investment such as a mutual fund as if it were a drive-up window at the bank or credit union. They're using put-and-keep accounts for put-and-takes, and vice versa.

After reading this, if you just muttered, "Oops," please don't get too upset with yourself, your spouse, your parents, or your friends. Everybody commits this blunder at one time or another. As you make your way through this book, I'll show you that neither this blunder nor these other common misconceptions need to cast a permanent shadow over your retirement.

MISCONCEPTION #2: I WILL PROBABLY LIVE FOR ONLY FIFTEEN OR TWENTY YEARS AFTER RETIREMENT.

The fastest growing new segment of American society today is those people over the age of 100. People in every segment of American society, no matter what the race, ethnicity, or gender, are living longer than they thought they would.

When Social Security first started, the average life expectancy for someone already age 65 was about another twelve and a half years. Now it is over seventeen years.* Your parents might have lived into their 70s or 80s, and often that conditions a person to think of themselves as having the same life expectancy. Mention the age 85, 90, or 95 to people, and they might think: "I'll be dead by then."

Well, I have a lot of clients who are still alive and kicking, even though they assured me they would be dead by now. And these are not even Baby Boomers!

If this is true for my 70- or 75-year-old clients right now, imagine what's going to happen among Boomers who are just around the corner from 60. A longer life expectancy is on the horizon for them, and even longer for their children and grandchildren. The mortality experts are saying that a baby girl born right now has a possible life expectancy of 137 years!

Life insurance companies have had to revise their mortality tables. Once upon a time in the not too distant past, they assumed that very, very rarely would anybody live beyond age 95. As a result, life insurance policies endowed at age 95, and anyone living beyond that triggered a taxable event. Eventually, not only were the mortality tables revised, but so was the tax code. Recently the mortality (life expectancy) table was updated to protect the tax-favored treatment of life insurance, allowing life insurance policies to endow at age 120. There is already talk of increasing it to 140!

In a couple of Goal Cultivator™ groups that I have organized among family and friends, I conducted an exercise outlined in a curriculum developed by Dan Sullivan, called The Lifetime Extender™.** It's the same issue we're getting at with clients. The Kore-

---

*Social Security Administration, "Basic Facts," February 2, 2006.
**Goal Cultivator and The Lifetime Extender are trademarks of The Strategic Coach.

ans call it *kop-jocki,* meaning "suddenly—without previous thought." Try it, and it will help you approach your life expectancy in a more realistic way. Thanks to Dan, it did for me.

Here goes.

Spit out the first number that comes in your head when I ask this question: "At what age are you going to die?" Now write down the number.

Invariably Boomers write down numbers between seventy-five and eighty-five. Why? Either that's when your father or mother passed away, or you are adding five or ten years to the age at which he or she died, figuring you might make it a little further down life's road because you exercise more regularly, eat better, or have given up bad habits like smoking. Even if a parent lived longer than this, you tell yourself: "I don't want to live any longer than that because I won't be healthy."

Next, ask yourself: "If I were to die at eighty-five, what condition would I like to be in—physically, mentally, emotionally, and financially—at age eighty-four?"

The near-universal reply: "I would like to be sharp as a tack. I want to have enough money. I still want to be capable of taking care of myself; I don't want to be a burden to anyone."

In other words, everyone wants to be healthy until the day they die.

Then picture yourself in that state and ask, "What am I doing to make sure that happens?" People usually reply: "I'm eating better. I'm getting more exercise. I've been planning my finances so I won't be penniless," and so on.

Then ask: "If I'm really in that kind of shape at eighty-four, how much longer will I likely live?" Like most, I answered, "Well, if I'm *really* in that good of shape at age eighty-four, I'll probably live another ten or twenty years."

The next question: "And if I'm going to live another ten to twenty years, what would I start doing?"

"I'd probably play golf more; I'd travel; I'd pay more attention to my civic duties," and so on.

At this point, ask yourself, "Okay, why don't I start doing some of those things now?"

There's more, but you get the idea. When Dan does this exercise, he discovers that most people will psychologically extend their lives at least another ten, fifteen, even twenty-five years. I myself extended my life to age 105 almost instantly.

Now here's the importance of this exercise; by changing your mind to live to age ninety, ninety-five, or 100, you boost the likelihood that you will actually live that long. Change your mind to live longer, and most likely you will.

The truth is that within the bounds of reason, most people die when they think they are going to die. In my practice, I find that people almost program themselves to shut down at a certain stage. If you give them a new viewpoint, people live longer, unless something crops up that's unexpected or out of their control, such as cancer or a heart attack.

From a financial standpoint, this means that if your spending habits are designed to cover you up to age eighty-five, but you are conditioning your mind to think in terms of living longer, you will need to incorporate the strategies in this book so you don't outlive your money.

MISCONCEPTION #3: I BELIEVE THAT FINALLY PAYING OFF MY HOUSE MORTGAGE WILL GIVE ME PEACE OF MIND.

The concept that a house must be paid off is one we have learned from parents who went through the Depression, when loans and mortgages were called due even though they weren't delinquent. In those days, it was important to get rid of mortgage interest. People were so happy when they made the final payment, they would throw a party and burn the mortgage.

Perhaps you have heard echoes of this from the previous generation. What you don't hear is that once you pay off your mortgage, you won't have mortgage interest to deduct from your income taxes. The result is that you lose a crucial tax break, and you kill your best partner, Uncle Sam.

Instead of peace of mind, you have a new worry—because you have lost this deduction, you jump to a higher tax bracket. Yes, you have an immediate addition to your spendable income if you are not writing a check each month to the bank. But there's a hitch. Uncle Sam offers that deduction to encourage home ownership. *If you don't pay that interest anymore, you'll now pay a bundle of money in extra income tax as April 15 rolls around.*

Those who pay off their mortgage begin to realize within a year or two that they could use a new tax break. They also discover that by handing over all that money to the bank, there's a lot of lazy, idle cash stashed away in that paid-off house.

In the past few years, as the cost of homes shot upward, many of my clients have had an epiphany without me having to prod them. "I don't care if it's paid off when I die," they say. "My money is trapped in my house."

Later on, I will show you how to put those lazy, idle dollars to work for you in a tax-favored environment. For now, keep in mind that the money you use for home mortgage payments creates a major, legal tax deduction.

"But what about leaving the house to the kids?" you ask. "Isn't that our legacy? Shouldn't we bequeath them a paid-off home?" I say, the kids who really care about you want *you* to enjoy your money. Those kids concerned about getting the house after you die are, more often than not, the ones who probably would sell it and spend all the money they get for it within six months.

MISCONCEPTION #4: MY $100,000 TO $300,000 NEST EGG IS GOING TO CUT IT AT RETIREMENT.

This is the flip side of the people who have saved almost nothing. I have clients who start out thinking: "We're set—we've saved up $300,000." The problem is that at 65, you can quickly begin to deplete that nest egg if it is parked in an investment or bank account that is earning only 6 percent.

That 6 percent amounts to only $18,000 a year, or $1,500 a month. Chances are, you're going to need more than that. Perhaps you need at least double—say, $36,000 a year—and you now realize you probably will live to age eighty-five or ninety. You will be dipping into your principal almost immediately. When you do the math, you realize your nest egg will dwindle rapidly.

Consider this. Even though half a million dollars may seem like a ton of money, at 6 percent interest, it is going to provide only eight and a half years of income for someone used to living on earned income of $6,250 a month ($75,000 a year). Suddenly that nest egg looks more like one laid by a parakeet than by the golden goose.

MISCONCEPTION #5: I'LL BE IN A LOWER TAX BRACKET WHEN I RETIRE.

There's a nasty surprise awaiting those who think this way. If you are expecting a pension, and you add Social Security and a piece of a qualified plan such as an IRA or 401(k) to it, your taxable income as a retiree will be as high as it was before you retired. But you will have fewer tax deductions to offset that income, because you will no longer be putting money into those tax-deferred IRAs or 401(k)s.

In addition, you may no longer have dependents at home, for whom you were entitled to a tax deduction. If you insisted on paying off your mortgage, you no longer can deduct its interest payments either.

Add it all up. If your income stays the same, or even if it drops from $75,000 to $60,000, you don't have the $15,000 in deductions that you used to get. So you remain in the same tax bracket you were in before retiring—but because you must pay the extra tax, you wind up with fewer dollars to spend.

If you think this sounds wrong, go ask your retired mom, dad, or friend whether their taxes dropped once they left their jobs. A business acquaintance did this, and his mother, a former teacher, replied, "Son, I am paying taxes up the wazoo. I pay more in taxes now than I ever did, and my income is less."

MISCONCEPTION #6: DEFERRING TAXES ON RETIREMENT FUNDS SAVES ME TAXES.

For years tax consultants have said if you use 100-cent dollars on the front end—that is, if you put the money you earn as a younger person into tax-deferred plans such as IRAs or 401(k)s— you'll have a bigger nest egg on the back end, when you retire. However, if that nest egg is taxable you can still run out of money!

It's true that $150,000 in pre-tax money can double in a tax-deferred account to $300,000 in ten years at 7.2 percent. It looks as if that's better than using already taxed dollars (66.7-cent dollars, if you are in the 33.3 percent income tax bracket). If you take the same $150,000 and pay tax on the front end, it amounts to only $100,000 of seed money, and when that doubles, it grows to only $200,000 to harvest on the back end. So the illusion is that you have $100,000 less in an account that is funded with after-tax dollars.

What the consultants often don't explain is that you will have to pay taxes on the full $300,000 tax-deferred nest egg on the back end. Once you do, you net the same amount of money. *That means that $300,000 less 33.3 percent in tax will net you $200,000.* There is no difference between funding a retirement account with after-tax dollars or pre-tax dollars, assuming the same tax bracket and provided that the account funded with after-tax seed money accumulates tax-free and stays tax-free when you withdraw the gain. But people have the misconception that because it grows to a bigger number in a pre-tax account, that's better. The mentality is: "Get a tax break today, and we'll have more money."

If you have already understood Misconception #5, you realize that it is fallacious to think that in retirement you will be in a lower tax bracket. If that is not true, why postpone taxes? Get paying them over with by paying on the front end.

Actually, when you set aside 100-cent dollars on the front end and take out 100-cent dollars on the back end, your nest egg can last into perpetuity. Don't think that's possible? I will show you, a bit later on, that by marrying several concepts and strategies together that are explained in Chapters 3 through 12, you can create a retirement fund using 100-cent dollars (tax-advantaged dollars) on the front end and then withdraw 100-cent, tax-free dollars from it on the back end. I will prove that this strategy will give you 50 percent more net spendable retirement income than traditional retirement accounts. Or, it would allow you to take an income stream into perpetuity compared to traditional accounts that would probably run out of money—long before you die—based on the same income distributions.

MISCONCEPTION #7: IRAS AND 401(K)S ARE THE BEST WAY TO SAVE FOR RETIREMENT.

The retirement savings vehicle that can last into perpetuity that I just hinted at is *not* an IRA or 401(k). I want to demolish the myth that tax-deferred plans such as Individual Retirement Accounts (IRAs) and 401(k) company retirement plans are the best kinds of strategies to use in saving for retirement. They're okay, but they're likely to crash and burn (become depleted) before you die.

Yes, these plans offer tax-deferred savings. But tax-deferred does not mean tax-free. What it usually means is that while you don't pay income tax on that money when you first put it away, you're going to get clobbered on the back end.

If you were a farmer, and you had this choice, which would you rather do: *Save taxes* on the seed you bought in the springtime and *pay tax* on the sale of your harvest in the fall? Or would you rather *pay tax* on the seed and sell your harvest *without any tax* on the gain?

I would rather pay for the seed with after-tax money, and then reap the harvest tax-free. Yet millions of otherwise prudent Americans are choosing to save taxes on their seed—their contributions to IRAs and 401(k)s—and then they are faced with a huge tax hit when they want to reap the harvest from it (as they start to withdraw money when they are retired). Please refer to Figure 2.1.

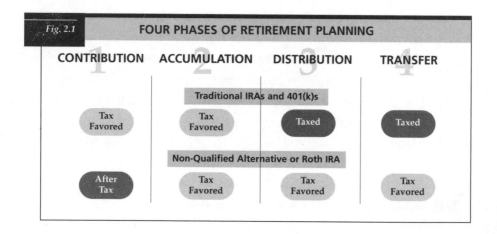

Uncle Sam now offers you another choice—Roth IRAs and Roth 401(k)s. Using these plans, you contribute the seed money with after-tax dollars, watch your contributions grow, and then harvest the gain in retirement tax-free. I believe Roths are a step in the right direction, but there are still too many strings attached.

In later chapters, I'll go into considerable detail on these often misunderstood and confusing retirement plans. In the meantime, I hope you will keep your mind open to the possibility that there might be smarter alternative advice about IRAs and 401(k)s than you have received from your CPA, your investment advisor, or your company benefits department.

MISCONCEPTION #8: IF I REACH THE AGE OF 59½ OR 70½ AND DON'T NEED MY IRA AND 401(K) MONEY, I'LL JUST LET IT SIT THERE.

People tend to think they should postpone pulling money out of tax-deferred accounts. They believe they really will have much more money if they let most of their money stay there rather than transferring it out somewhere else. Postponing tax to future beneficiaries is often referred to as a "stretch" IRA. Most financial advisors recommend you take out only the minimum amount at the age of 70½, which is the deadline before Uncle Sam starts charging you a big penalty. *If you don't take minimum distributions based on their formula, the IRS assesses a 50 percent penalty on top of the income tax!*

I think taking only the minimum out of IRAs, whether at your first opportunity when you reach 59½ or postponing until age 70½, is a bad idea. It's like refusing to change the oil in your car when it could have cost you $30 to $50—maybe less—and driving it several thousand more miles until you pay big-time with a major engine repair. You are delaying the inevitable and making the problem worse. You can either pay the IRS now, or you can pay them considerably more later.

Those financial advisors don't understand that they can reposition retirement money so it's tax-free from today forward. I will prove it can be far more advantageous to withdraw the money, get the tax over and done with, and put the funds into something tax-free from that point forward.

They also don't understand that you can strategically counterbalance your tax and get money out with substantially reduced or totally offset tax by using mortgage interest offsets (see Chapter 9).

MISCONCEPTION #9: I VIEW RETIREMENT AS A TIME FOR FINALLY DOING WHAT I'VE ALWAYS WANTED TO DO.

Activities such as cultivating hobbies, visiting the grandchildren, or working part-time are among the rewards of retirement.

Wouldn't it be better to do the things you want to do sooner, rather than later? I have watched a lot of clients who spend so much of their lives scrimping and saving so that when they arrive at retirement, they have a hard time letting loose and spending it.

Whatever their dreams were, they continue to harbor a conservative attitude when they retire. They are simply afraid they won't have enough money. They feel guilty about spending and enjoying what they earned. Or they finally reach retirement but have lost their good health and can't do the things they promised themselves. Do keep in mind that as you get older, you may lose the energy or the desire to go globe-trotting and to do all the other things on your list. I am big on stopping to smell the roses along the way.

MISCONCEPTION #10: I THINK OF RETIREMENT AS A TIME TO COAST.

I think too many people have the attitude: "I can't wait until I can coast." The word "retire" means to put out of use. I don't ever want to be put out of use, and I want to dispel the idea that at retirement you will be put out of use.

Boomers need to prepare themselves to redefine their lives so when they retire, they are simply shifting gears—not putting the transmission into neutral. In fact, if Boomers start preparing for retirement in the right way, they can shift gears into the most profitable growth stage of their lives.

Colonel Harland Sanders, who was the founder of Kentucky Fried Chicken, didn't open his first franchise until age sixty-five—and it wasn't in Kentucky. The first KFC opened in Salt Lake City, Utah, in partnership with Pete Harman, who owned and operated the Dew Drop Inn restaurant. By the time Sanders was age eighty, he was wealthy and famous with franchises all over the world.

My wife, Sharee, and I have a tradition of spending a week celebrating our wedding anniversary every February in Maui, Hawaii. A "must do" on every visit includes getting a macadamia nut ice cream cone from a Lappert's Ice Cream shop. Walter Lappert tried to retire quietly on Kauai at age seventy, but ended up starting a bonanza of an ice cream business. The first batch was produced on December 21, 1983, and today tens of thousands of gallons are made monthly with over 100 flavors. Walter Lappert passed on in 2003, but his ice cream legacy lives on and is managed by his son Michael.

People need to realize that their usefulness is not just assembling widgets. Start now to discover your marketability. A lot of people I know have become consultants, creating a market for their hard-earned wisdom. I have a friend who was an excellent oral surgeon, but he developed a tremor and could no longer practice. He became a consultant to other oral surgeons. Another, a cosmetic dentist, teaches numerous other dentists how to add value to their practices. Another who worked for a major company became a part-time consultant to businesses. During the last five years, his former employer and others are paying him more than when he worked full-time. He spends half his time riding around the country in a motor home. He's happier and healthier than ever, making himself necessary every day, with less stress.

If you can figure out how to continue to contribute to society—to keep creating value—the world will reward you for that usefulness. Whether it's your business acumen, or your life experiences, or even a simmering talent for music or art that have been on the back burner—this is the time to share what you have within.

"UH-OH. I'VE DONE EVERYTHING WRONG! I WON'T BE ABLE TO CATCH UP."

If these blunders and misconceptions sound familiar, you're definitely not alone. But one aim of this book is to reassure you that it's not too late to learn how to make course corrections and start navigating in the right direction. *You can overcome or prevent these blunders.*

By way of illustration, let me tell you about a close friend who is a barber.

Carey is a Vietnam War veteran with a small shop in a strip mall in San Diego.[*] Having cut people's hair for more than thirty years, he has a loyal group of customers and makes a decent living. Carey is not a big spender; he likes nothing more than to spend his days off fishing and hunting. But he had saved very little money, and figured he would have to keep working the rest of his life.

Periodically, I urged Carey to come and listen to my equity management/asset optimization seminar. After I wrote *Missed Fortune 101*, I suggested he read it, but like many fellows, he's not much of a reader.

Then a few years ago, the spot where his small home stood was rezoned from residential to commercial, which dramatically increased its value. A company made him an offer he couldn't refuse, and he sold that home previously valued at $200,000 for $550,000. His first inclination was to buy his "dream home" for cash using most of that money and put the rest in the bank.

"I'm set," he told me.

Sitting in Carey's chair, listening to his plans, I could hardly contain myself. "No, no, no! You want to mortgage your new home to the hilt, and, if you qualify, take out a home equity line of credit for the difference," I said.

"How can I afford the payments?" demanded Carey.

"You'll get more than enough money from the interest you'll be earning on the cash you did not put into the house to make your mortgage payment," I insisted. "The point is, this is your key to a financially secure future."

That got Carey's attention. He came to one of my seminars and sat in the front row. Afterward I said to Carey half in jest, "Every month you put off applying these concepts will probably cost you $50,000 down the road." He thought I was kidding.

---

[*]His name and his location have been altered to protect his privacy.

The next time I taught a seminar in San Diego, he returned, this time with his wife. She listened and said, "I've always been taught to first pay off my house. This is intriguing, but is it safe?" She had the normal concerns.

My trained staff consulted with both of them. They began to grasp the numbers, and how their retirement would be dramatically enhanced. Catching wind of their plans, their family was nervous at first. Carey's father wondered what on earth he was doing, and we reassured him we weren't going to put his finances in jeopardy, but actually increase the liquidity, safety, and rate of return on their most precious financial asset. Carey realized the incredible transformation that could occur and saw that by taking this new route, cutting hair would be something he could do part-time in retirement because he wanted to, not because he had to.

Eventually they bought a beautiful new house, financing 100 percent of the purchase price by taking out a large mortgage. We helped him put into practice the concepts I had outlined in the seminars and in my books *Missed Fortune* and *Missed Fortune 101*. Carey and his wife now indeed are "set"—not in the conventional way they originally thought they would be, but in a far more sensible, although unconventional, way.

Carey, who is now fifty-six years old, will have a nest egg by the time he is sixty-five that will be considerably greater than the amount they need to pay off their house if they ever want to. That nest egg will generate enough income to not only make their after-tax mortgage payment, but also to give them a few thousand dollars left over every month. Cutting hair will be his hobby during retirement.

What I call the True Wealth Transformation™ had taken hold. When Carey realized he was going to be secure financially, he was motivated to make other positive changes in his life.

He changed his diet and lost fifty pounds—not just because the physical exam he took to qualify for the maximum tax-advantaged life insurance showed he was a borderline diabetic, but also because he now realized he wouldn't outlive his money. Carey has had to buy a whole new wardrobe. He is able to go fishing a whole lot more.

He knows that taxes and inflation won't ruin him. He is amazed at how financially savvy and confident he has become as he has dialogues with customers in his barber chair. He enjoys the amazed look on some of his friend's faces who thought his retirement resources would never amount to much. And yes, he is enjoying the enhanced relationship he has with his wife as they decorate their new home, landscape their yard, and prepare for the retirement of their dreams. Most of all, he no longer feels confused or powerless. He has greater confidence in his brighter future because he has a new direction.

REMEMBER THIS:

- Acknowledge that you may have made mistakes, as a prelude to making course corrections.
- Review your current investments; do they match long-term goals?
- Ask yourself how long you expect to live, how long you want to live, and what you can change to achieve healthy longevity.
- Write down how much money you have put away for retirement and how much more you honestly believe you need.
- Examine last year's tax returns to see what tax bracket you are in and whether you expect to be in the same bracket once you retire.
- Assess each of the ten misconceptions that Boomers have and check those that apply to you.

CHAPTER 3

Take Ownership of Your Retirement

Make Social Security the Bonus, not the Basis, for Income and Find the Right Lead Advisor to Lodge Your Money Safely

A **FRIEND OF MINE HAD SKIED** Aspen for many years. At the end of each day on the mountain, she would ski all the way down with hordes of other weary skiers along a slope called Spar Gulch. It would get crowded with so many people taking the same trail. On cold days, the bottom of the trail would be icy; in the spring, it would be slushy. In each case, it was hazardous. She knew several skiers who wound up getting hurt trying to negotiate Spar Gulch at the end of the day.

One day when it was time to head downhill for a last run, an acquaintance of hers who lived in town headed toward the gondola instead. "Spar Gulch is for tourists," he scoffed. "After all the effort I've put in on the hill the entire day, taking the gondola back down makes more sense." She thought about it for a moment. Why did she always follow the crowd? Why not take another route to the base, enjoy a great view, and get to the après-ski scene in comfort?

She decided to follow her acquaintance. From the gondola car, she looked down on the anthill of skiers carving their way down Spar Gulch, and then at the picturesque peaks around them. She realized this really was the smarter way to finish a full day of skiing.

Isn't it time for you to leave old, conventional ideas about retirement behind, and start taking the smart way to financial independence?

Now is the time to discover the best way to safely accumulate more money, even with retirement just around the corner. The sooner you empower yourself with the knowledge to attain financial independence, the greater your net worth will become.

The first things you need are a guide, a map, and a compass. I would like to be your guide. I can help you navigate through the often confusing maze of retirement options, offer you strategies (the maps and charts to wealth), and give you helpful tools (a compass) that will direct you toward systems to help you conserve your resources and put them to work.

THE MYTH OF SOCIAL SECURITY AS YOUR PRIMARY RETIREMENT INCOME

When I ask people if they have any guaranteed source of retirement, they almost always answer, "Yes, Social Security."

But is it smart to count on Social Security as your *primary* source of retirement income? Is it possible that this national trust fund could be severely depleted? Consider the facts:

- When Social Security was first enacted during the Great Depression, there were sixty workers to every one recipient of benefits. Within just a few years, that ratio was reduced to fifteen to one.
- By the 1970s, it declined to six to one. By the 1990s, there were three workers in America for every one recipient of benefits.

- Now, as the oldest Baby Boomers prepare to begin retiring (or to collect Social Security at 62, the earliest allowable age), it is estimated that before long there will be two workers in America pulling the Social Security wagon for every rider.
- To keep it solvent, the Social Security Administration has already pushed back the age at which younger persons will be allowed to collect full benefits. If you were born between 1943 and 1954, you will not be eligible for full benefits until you reach the age of 66. If you were born in 1960 or later, you will not be eligible for full benefits until you reach age 67.
- With the upcoming workforce decreasing and retirees living much longer than when Social Security was initiated, there will likely be even more Social Security reform.

Because of these factors, the reality is that Social Security benefits will likely be a small supplement to your retirement, not your primary source of income. *Even the Social Security Administration says so.*

"SOCIAL SECURITY WON'T EXPIRE IN MY LIFETIME"

Even if you don't accept the most dire predictions about how long the system will last, you need to understand what has already been disclosed by Social Security's trustees.

Every year, they issue a report on the status of the trust fund. *The 2006 Trustees Report projects that the Social Security Trust Funds will be exhausted in 2040.*[*]

"No problem," says the sixty-year-old. "I'll be dead by then."

Not necessarily. Remember the life-extender exercise? Even if at

---

*Press release, Social Security Administration, May 1, 2006.

first you only expect to live to eighty-five, you may actually live five years longer. Without reform, the Social Security coffers will be empty by then. Moreover, according to the most recent report, the projected point at which tax revenues will fall below program costs comes in 2017—not too far down the road.

Every year, the trustees urge the public and the federal government to address the future shortfalls "in a timely way to allow for gradual changes and advance notice to workers."

Meanwhile, even the administrators themselves tell us flat out that you can't count on your monthly Social Security check to cover all your expenses. They acknowledge that because Americans are living longer, they need to make provisions for those extra golden years.

Here is how the Social Security Administration frames the calculations:

Most financial advisors say you'll need about 70 percent of your pre-retirement earnings to comfortably maintain your pre-retirement standard of living. Under current law, if you have average earnings, your Social Security retirement benefits will replace only about 40 percent. The percentage is lower for people in the upper income brackets and higher for people with low incomes. You'll need to supplement your benefits with a pension, savings, or investments.[*]

In other words, the government itself tells you to find the shortfall of 30 to 60 percent of your retirement income on your own.

In a 2005 article titled "7 Social Security Myths," financial advisor Robert Brokamp stated: "Regardless of the future of Social Security, it never was—and never will be—a way to fund the retirement of your dreams (unless your dreams involve small living spaces and small portions)."

---

*Social Security Online, Retirement and Medicare, "Plan Your Retirement," p. 1.

As the earliest Boomers approach retirement, the average monthly retirement benefit is approximately $1,000—or only about $12,000 a year. Retirees should view Social Security as a *bonus* in retirement not the *basis* of their retirement.

If you don't take ownership of your retirement, believe me, the government will attempt to. But the government is not a very efficient steward of funds. You can be far more efficient in managing your retirement money than the government is. For those Boomers who don't have the financial discipline to create their own retirement fund, Social Security will probably be in existence but I predict it will end up being disbursed similar to a welfare benefit system. I have chosen to view Social Security simply as a tax to give back to society. If I get some of that tax back in the future, I'll consider it as a rebate. Then I won't be disappointed.

It's important to understand that Social Security is not a savings account. Your money is really not "on deposit." The only way the government can pay you Social Security benefits is if it takes in new money in the future to cover the obligation. I find it interesting that it can be construed as a violation of law if an individual or an entity constantly takes in new money only to cover obligations or debts owed. Could Social Security fall under that definition?

BEGIN NOW TO BE PROACTIVE ABOUT YOUR RETIREMENT INCOME

This is your wake-up call to begin living in the proactive zone. So remember, it's not just financial strategists like myself who are telling you to prepare to create the bulk of your retirement nest egg, but the Social Security Administration itself. It's important to take the reins—to maintain choice and control—rather than sit around whining.

Too many people think that the world owes them a living—that they've paid their dues. It's not the government's responsibility to take care of you in retirement. Taking ownership—accountability and responsibility—of your retirement is each individual's right and duty. We shouldn't waste energy worrying about how politicians are going to make sure Social Security is there for us. Whether or not you're upset about the issue, as with many things that happen in life, you can choose to be bitter or you can choose to be better.

So where do you begin? Think about what you must have to sleep better at night:

- You need predictable results.
- You need to be responsible and accountable for your own future.
- You need to take ownership of your retirement by using the strategies, concepts, and tax breaks explained in this book.
- You need a financial planner who understands your retirement income needs to help you.

FOUR SOURCES OF MONEY

There are basically four sources of money:

- People at work
- Money at work
- Other People's Money (OPM)
- Charity

"People at work" is the traditional way Strivers, the vast majority of Americans, have obtained money. It's a good way, but if you are laid off, sick, or incapacitated, your ability to make money becomes much more difficult.

Arrivers learn that "money at work" is much more dependable. The money in a savings account earns compound interest day after day, year after year, as we've seen. Investments can make the same money work even harder.

Thrivers have discovered that while money at work grows, using "Other People's Money" can turn affluent people into millionaires, through the power of safe, positive leverage. I'll prove how you can join the super-wealthy people of the world through leverage and the use of OPM. Once you learn these techniques, you will have no trouble contributing to charity—the fourth source of money. There's much satisfaction when you are able to increase your charitable giving and be on the giving end, rather than the receiving end.

IDENTIFY PREDICTABLE RESULTS

Social Security will give you predictable amounts of money each month once you are able to collect it. But do you really plan to live on just a small percentage of your working income? Most people expect to live on the same amount of money they bring home now. What is a predictable source of extra money you need to be comfortable?

In the last chapter I mentioned that short-term investments are not good for long-term goals, and vice versa. If you have put the bulk of your retirement money in CDs and money market funds, you will get predictable results based on interest rates at the time. But interest rates and inflation usually move up and down in tandem. Once inflation zooms ahead with interest rates, those predictable returns on fixed savings instruments will be eaten up by hikes in the cost of everyday items such as food, clothing, transportation, and gas.

On the other hand, those who have retirement money other than Social Security in stocks, bonds, or mutual funds cannot make predictions about whether those investments will serve them well or not. The stock market may go up or down. It is dangerous to rely on past results of stock and bond performances unless you are measuring them over a period of ten years or more, and only if you buy them and then hold them.

In public seminars, I hammer away at the three characteristics

your investments must have to meet the test of a prudent investment. They are:

- liquidity
- safety of principal
- rate of return

Your Social Security income is safe, at least for now, but you can
collect only so much each month once you are eligible.

Your IRAs and 401(k)s may be held in liquid investments such
as stocks, bonds, and mutual funds, but their payouts are not safe
from downturns in the market.

The biggest investment most of you have is your home. But as
I will demonstrate in Chapters 6 and 7, the equity you may have
poured into your home or accumulated there is neither a liquid
asset nor a safe one and has no real rate of return.

THE THREE LODGING PLACES FOR MONEY

The money that people set aside and accumulate for long-range
goals needs to have a lodging place where it can reside safely. There
are three categories of repositories where people store their money
for investment purposes based on their risk tolerance:

- *Low risk*—the first category is generally perceived as the
  safest and most conservative and includes money market
  accounts, certificates of deposit, bonds, annuities, and
  insurance contracts.
- *Moderate risk*—the second category is comprised of real
  estate—both residential and commercial. Most real estate
  investments pose moderate risk.
- *High risk*—the third category is comprised of stocks and
  would include investments like growth mutual funds. This
  category is generally viewed as having the greatest risk.

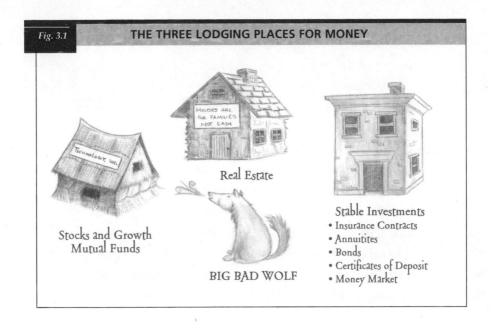

Fig. 3.1 — THE THREE LODGING PLACES FOR MONEY

Stocks and Growth Mutual Funds

Real Estate

BIG BAD WOLF

Stable Investments
• Insurance Contracts
• Annuitites
• Bonds
• Certificates of Deposit
• Money Market

Whenever people lose confidence or patience in any one of the three categories, they begin to move their money to one or both of the other two categories. For example, in the early 1980s people kept their money predominantly in bonds, money markets, CDs, annuities, and life insurance contracts. Many investors also parked their money in real estate. Most people then didn't trust the stock market, but they gradually warmed up to it.

By the 1990s, a lot of money transferred to the stock market from more conservative investments. From 1980 until 2000, America experienced the largest run-up in stock market history. In general, stocks during that twenty-year period grew to five times their 1980 value. That may sound like a significant return, but it really represents only about an 8.38 percent annual increase. To illustrate, a $10,000 investment earning 8.38 percent interest compounded annually would grow five times to $50,000 in twenty years.

The worst three years in stock market history (by percentage loss and by dollar loss) occurred during a period after spring of 2000 and into 2003. In early spring of 2000, the Dow Jones

Industrial Average hit 11,900, and the market experienced $50 billion in net inflows—people buying high. By the summer of 2002, the Dow bottomed out at 7,500, and the market experienced $50 billion in net outflows—people selling low. At that point, a lot of people were transferring their money to real estate, bonds, annuities, and life insurance contracts. This is one of the major reasons for the real estate boom during the first five years after the turn of the century.

As you can see, *money has to find a lodging place, and when it leaves one of the three repositories described above, it migrates over to one or both of the other two.*

It takes people time to regain faith in the stock market once they have taken a beating. It may even take about twenty years for demand to make the market become vibrant again. As that happens, experienced, seasoned investors will move more cautiously to preferred stocks. Tech stocks will have a hard time coming back (if they ever do) with the same vigor they once had.

With this framing, the essence of the financial strategies I am going to go over will allow you to safely take advantage of all three lodging places (repositories) while maintaining liquidity and safety of principal, and earning an attractive rate of return.

I'm going to show you how to have ownership in your home or other real estate (the middle lodging place) without much or any of your own cash tied up in it. In other words, through safe leverage you can "double-dip" by experiencing returns in real estate, without having your own money tied up in it.

Your home and other real estate may go up, then down temporarily in value, but it won't matter. There is a way that you can make money when your house goes up in value, and continue to make money (without losing what your house once gained) if it goes down in value.

Likewise, you will be able to use leverage safely to achieve great rates of return that are linked to a stock index (the third lodging place), while your money is actually not at risk *in* the stock market. Your cash can be invested safely in conservative investment vehicles (first lodging place) that will compound in a tax-advantaged environment where it is accessible and safe, employing the three marvels that I will discuss in detail in the next chapter. You will learn how you can have the best of both worlds: take advantage of the upswings in the stock market or real estate market, without your principal at risk actually *in* the market.

When I invest my serious cash that is earmarked for my retirement, I want to make sure I can get maximum results with minimal risk. As shown in Figure 3.1, if things happen in the world that I have no control over, I want the principal of my investments safe. Then if the big, bad wolf (**hurricanes, floods, tornadoes, fires, terrorist attacks, market crashes**) blows down the structures that house stocks (houses made of straw) and real estate holdings (houses made of sticks), I won't lose—because my money resides in a house of bricks. What's more, if houses of straw or sticks withstand periods of calm weather and appreciate in value, I can participate in that growth without my money actually lodged there. How can this be accomplished? Stay with me. I'll teach you. And you'll probably sleep better at night as a result.

USE LEGITIMATE TAX BREAKS

To teach you how to take control of your retirement, I will first show you where to find money you might not know exists. That's because Uncle Sam collects it, often right out of your paycheck.

Most people understand that governments require us to give back to society in the form of taxes. But too many taxpayers stick their heads in the sand, allowing the IRS to declare open season on them, and they hand over excessive money to the tax collector.

I am not suggesting that you look for loopholes or keep any money that you are not entitled to. I do suggest that by taking ownership in personal assets, you can claim legitimate tax breaks that can add up to money for your retirement.

Think for a moment why the U.S. government offers us tax

deductions. It's because when you own something, you take better care of it. Have you ever washed a rental car? If you own a house, you take better care of it than if you rent it.

Government understands this, and to help you own a house, it gives you a tax deduction on your mortgage. This leads to a higher standard of living and it means the government spends less on the costs of social ills. If you help take care of those in need, such as Hurricane Katrina victims, you get a tax deduction on your charitable giving. You help by easing the strain and the costs the government would otherwise pay to help them.

Throughout this book, I will show you how to take otherwise payable income tax and use it to support you, your family, and your retirement. For example, I have more than $10 million of life insurance (that comes along for the ride with my tax-favored retirement plan) that is paid for with otherwise payable income tax. Uncle Sam pays for my life insurance—and he can pay for yours— if it is structured properly. Like most of you, I don't object to insurance benefits, I just don't like paying the premiums. So I let Uncle Sam pay for my life insurance, as I will explain in Chapter 11.

This book will teach you how to save yourself hundreds of thousands of dollars and redirect those otherwise payable income tax dollars to regain choice and control and enhance your retirement savings by leaps and bounds. In doing this, you do nothing illegal, nor are you taking advantage of tax loopholes. When you take ownership in your retirement, the government provides and encourages certain deductions because, directly or indirectly, those tax savings stimulate the economy. This ultimately brings in more tax dollars, thus relieving the government from having to provide as much or more in Social Security and welfare benefits.

UTILIZE 100-CENT DOLLARS ON THE SEED AND THE HARVEST

As you contemplate what kind of a future you have to look forward to, let me show how to take reclaimed income tax dollars—

money misguidedly trapped in your home, and the money already sitting in your soon-to-be-taxed IRA, pension, and 401(k) plans—to develop a dramatically enhanced retirement financial plan. This kind of plan can generate 50 percent more in net spendable retirement income or can last into perpetuity, rather than running out of steam before you do.

Think of the farmer and seed analogy I used in Chapter 2 under Misconception #7. Let's say you have $1 million accumulated in a retirement fund, and it is earning 10 percent interest (to keep the math simple). How much could you withdraw each year and never deplete the principal: $100,000, right? What if you need $100,000 net, after tax, to spend, to buy prescriptions, travel to visit your grandkids, golf, and enjoy your retirement? How much more would you have to withdraw in a 33.3 percent tax bracket (which is the marginal tax bracket you would likely be in if you had $100,000 of income—see Chapter 5) to net $100,000 after tax?

The answer is 50 percent more, not 33 percent more! You would have to withdraw $150,000, pay tax of one-third ($50,000), to net $100,000 of spendable income. If you were forced to withdraw $150,000 ($12,500 per month) to net $100,000 to live, your $1 million dollar nest egg earning 10 percent return would be totally depleted in about eleven years. You would likely outlive your money by six or more years.

If you had a retirement fund that was tax-free on the back end—during the harvest years—you would be required to withdraw only $100,000 to net $100,000 for spending. So at the end of eleven years when your IRAs or 401(k)s would be depleted as described above, a $1 million retirement fund that allows tax-free harvests would still have $1 million residing in it. If you lived twenty more years—let's say from age 76 to age 96—how much would you have left in your fund even though you withdrew $100,000 every year? That's right, you would still have your $1 million nest egg. Twenty more years of tax-advantaged retirement income in the amount of $100,000 per year equals $2 million! Would you like an extra $2 million of retirement income? One that, when you finally do pass away, still leaves behind your principal of $1 million tax-free to your spouse or heirs? I will show you how to accomplish this as we proceed.

DON'T BE COUNTERPRODUCTIVE

Our family has a couple of cabins and a condo. We call them our IRAs—*Individual Retirement Abodes*. (I'll share this concept in detail with you in Chapter 10.)

One January day, we were at our mountain cabin in Utah enjoying some snowmobiling with our friends. Ten of us mounted our snowmobiles and started out for a two-hour excursion to the top of the Skyline Drive. At the head of the group, I stopped after about a mile to see if everyone's snow machines were operating correctly. One of our friends yelled that he couldn't seem to pick up much speed even though he had the gas on full throttle. His machine was squeaking with a high shrill. He was frustrated and wanted a different machine. I dismounted my snowmobile and quickly assessed the situation. The brake lever had been locked in the park position for the past mile of snowmobiling!

I often find people doing the same thing with their money. They follow accepted wisdom, setting aside money in qualified retirement accounts such as IRAs and 401(k)s, enjoying tax-deductible funding and/or tax-deferred accumulation. At the same time, they assume it's best to achieve the goal of outright home ownership and save money on mortgage interest expense by sending extra principal payments against their mortgages. *I maintain that socking away money into IRAs and 401(k)s and paying principal on your mortgage are both counterproductive*—just like my friend snowmobiling who had one hand on the gas and the other hand resting on the brake.

Later on in this book, I'll explain why I have my home equity separated from the house to increase the liquidity, safety, and rate of return. I will prove that it can dramatically enhance your net worth and your retirement resources when you learn how to manage equity successfully. In Chapter 9, I'll show how having a mortgage can also allow you to withdraw up to $60,000—maybe $70,000 a year or more from your IRAs and 401(k)s—with no tax consequence, so you can get out of the tax corner you may have painted yourself into.

There is one thing I want to make clear: I am not advocating that you go into hock up to your ears. I believe it is smart to get out of debt. But please understand that there is a difference between having liabilities and being in debt. A company can call itself debt-free even if it has liabilities, as long as it has enough liquid assets earning enough to show a positive bottom line after covering those liabilities. A bank has loads of borrowed money, but when it puts those loans to work earning interest, the resulting income becomes assets that are more than sufficient to wash away those loans.

In the same way, *I consider a house paid for even if you have a large mortgage—as long as you have sufficient liquid assets in a safe environment to wash out the liability of that mortgage.* As we go along, this book will show you the way to load up on liquid, safe investments with a predictable rate of return that will amount to far more than the liabilities you list on your balance sheet.

You do not have to do this all by yourself. My system is a little more sophisticated than the simplistic schemes you may have heard about or read in typical personal finance books. It is crucial to have trained experts prepare the documents and help you choose the best investment vehicles.

LOCATE THE RIGHT LEAD ADVISOR

You owe it to yourself and your family to choose a lead advisor—a financial quarterback or general contractor—who will help draw up your asset optimization plan, implement tax and leverage strategies, and be there for you to suggest correct ways of making sure your money is working as hard as it can for you. Ideally, this person should be someone who understands *you* more than *your money*; it should be someone who also knows what makes you tick—who and what is most important to you—someone who understands your human, intellectual, and civic assets.

Most financial planners are Jacks- and Jills-of-all-trades. They may be licensed to sell you securities and perhaps even insurance. But too many financial advisors know just enough to make them almost dangerous. It's easy for them to form biases, and they can be leery of concepts that are new to them. They usually follow the crowd and recommend tax breaks on the seed rather than the harvest.

If you ask a financial advisor about some of the strategies I present in this book, chances are 90 percent will not understand them (even though they may think they do). Some will view my ideas as a threat to what they were taught to do with money, or what they've always recommended based on their perception and experience.

(If you would like a detailed profile checklist of what you should look for in an asset optimization specialist—lead advisor—and how to select the right one, go to www.MissedFortune.com/AdvisorChecklist for a free, downloadable booklet.)

REMEMBER THIS:

- Check with the Social Security Administration to learn how much you are on track to collect at age 62, 66, or 67 in Social Security income.
- Money has to find a lodging place. It will usually reside in high-risk investments such as stocks, moderate-risk investments such as real estate, or low-risk, stable investments such as insurance contracts, annuities, and bonds.
- Learn strategies that will allow you to safely take advantage of all three lodging places for your money while maintaining liquidity and safety of principal, and earning an attractive rate of return.
- Identify legitimate tax breaks to which you are entitled that you don't avail yourself of now, such as mortgage interest.
- Create your own financial balance sheet, listing all assets (savings, investments, real estate, life insurance, and personal property) and all liabilities (credit card debt, installment loans, auto payments, taxes, mortgages, and college tuition payments).
- Obtain and review the checklist for securing a lead advisor and begin the process.

CHAPTER 4

Understand the Three Marvels of Wealth Accumulation

Let Compound Interest, Tax-Free Savings, and Safe Leverage Boost Your Net Worth

THIS MAY SEEM TO BE a bleak picture so far. But it is not too late! If you continue on this voyage with me, you will find that opportunities to become a Blazing Bloomer already exist . . . and even greater ones lie on the horizon.

The secret to optimizing your assets is not really a secret at all. The three marvels of wealth accumulation can supercharge your money, making it grow exponentially even if you are fearful that you won't be able to catch up.

The keys are:

- The magic of compound interest
- The magic of tax-favored accumulation
- The magic of safe, positive leverage

These three are not really magic acts. Like the concepts of lift, thrust, and drag in aerodynamics, these principles have always been around, but not necessarily understood. Once you grasp the power of these three marvels, you will readily see that just as lift, thrust, and drag make planes fly, these three concepts can make your retirement funds soar.

LIFT, THRUST, AND DRAG

For a bird, airplane, or any other object to fly, four forces all play a part:

- Weight
- Lift
- Thrust
- Drag

Weight is the natural force that pulls a plane toward the earth. To fly, you must overcome weight (or **gravity**) with an opposing force (lift).

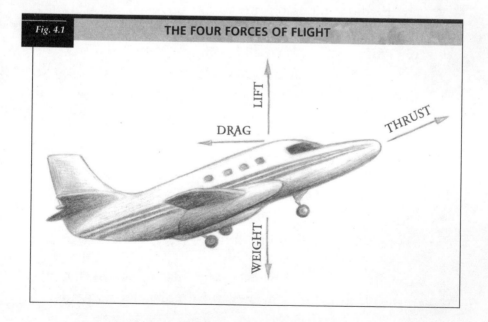

Fig. 4.1   **THE FOUR FORCES OF FLIGHT**

In finance, I compare weight, or the pull of gravity, to taxes and inflation. To become a millionaire and have money work for you (instead of *you* having to work for money), you must start out with seed money. In other words, it takes money to make more money. I'm going to show you how to come up with the money to obtain your "retirement aircraft." But be aware: Depending on the choices you make, that aircraft can sit around in a hangar, or it can take off flying. To gain altitude, you must overcome the force of taxes and inflation.

Lift is the force of air flowing over and under the wings of a plane that acts on the wings to move it upward. Most planes have wings with a curved upper surface and flatter lower surface. This causes air to move faster over the upper surface than it does on the lower surface. As explained by Bernoulli's principle, this faster air creates lower pressure on the upper surface, while the slower air underneath the wing creates higher pressure. When the forces are combined, the result is lift, which directs the plane upward. I compare lift to the power of compound interest.

Thrust is the force created by the engines and propellers that pushes the plane forward. The greater the power of the engine, the greater the thrust. In order for a plane to fly, the thrust force must be greater than or equal to the drag force. I compare thrust to the power of tax-favored accumulation. Tax-deferred accumulation is a powerful propeller engine, but *tax-free* accumulation is like a more powerful jet engine.

Drag is the force of resistance caused by the body of the plane that slows down its thrust, or forward motion. It's the most misunderstood principle, both in flight and in wealth accumulation. I compare drag to the power of safe, positive leverage—using Other People's Money (OPM), such as a loan or a mortgage from a bank.

Weight, lift, thrust, and drag all work together to make a plane fly.

These forces have always existed, but they were essentially invisible to humanity until the Wright brothers harnessed them. They were the marvels the brothers employed to propel their first plane off the ground. Engineers today use those same principles to make supersonic jets soar.

In a similar way, the super-wealthy Thrivers use fundamental forces to make their money escalate. So can you. In order for your money to take off and fly, it's important for you to grasp the marvels of:

- Compound interest (lift)
- Tax-free accumulation (thrust)
- Safe leverage employing Other People's Money (drag)

I bet you are wondering about *drag*. Why would I choose a word that sounds negative? Because just as drag helps airplanes fly, your wealth takes off when you *borrow* money for leverage and pay interest on it. You can reduce the drag by streamlining the cost of borrowing, if the interest you pay is tax-deductible.

Doesn't paying interest seem to drag you down? Quite the contrary! It allows for leverage—the use of OPM—possible. Leverage gives you a return on assets that you own but that you paid little or none of your own cash to obtain. Leverage works in conjunction with compound interest (lift) and with tax-free accumulation (thrust) to allow you to make your wealth truly soar. You will see in a moment that *drag* in this context is actually a good thing. Borrowing money is the lifeblood strategy of almost every financial institution in the world. Fortunes are made by the use of OPM. But the key is to borrow to conserve, not to consume. In other words, you use OPM to acquire assets that will appreciate—not depreciate!

LIFT: THE POWER OF COMPOUND INTEREST

Many adults think they understand interest. It's the amount that a bank or credit union pays you for the privilege of "holding" your money (which the bank then invests or puts to work). Conversely, it's the amount of money you pay the bank for using its funds, whether you get a business loan or a mortgage to pay for a house.

But there are two methods of computing interest—simple and compound. When you borrow money for your house, it is usually calculated as simple interest as you make payments on the debt.[*] When you deposit money in a bank, you earn compound interest.

A Michigan Retirement Research Center study[**] on the retirement plans of Boomers revealed that an understanding of compound interest went hand in hand with wealth and higher savings and investments.

That makes sense to me. People who understand the dynamics of money—those who realize how money socked away and left to earn interest can burgeon into wealth—are more likely to be making headway toward a livable retirement.

The difference between *simple* and *compound* interest can be the difference between paying hundreds of dollars on a simple interest, declining balance that may be tax-deductible (as in your mortgage), versus thousands of dollars climbing exponentially, in a side fund with compounding interest, which I will introduce you to later on. When you earn compound interest, you make money not only on your original deposit, but also on your accumulated gains.

The way to get rich safely is to keep putting your money away and letting it work for you by letting it compound. How much will $100 earn for you in ten years at 5 percent? If it's simple interest, that hundred bucks earns $5 every year. After ten years you have $150. But if it is compounding, that $100 becomes $163 after ten years.

Not very exciting, you say? Try adding a few zeros, and you will

---

[*]If you obtain a negative amortization loan, or if you don't pay all of your simple interest, then a small portion of the interest will accrue, which could be considered as compounding—which isn't always a bad thing. When you take out a typical amortized or interest-only mortgage and don't miss payments, the interest you are charged is simple interest.

[**]Annamaria Lusardi and Olivia S. Mitchell, "Baby Boomer Retirement Security: The Roles of Planning, Financial Literacy, and Housing Wealth," Michigan Retirement Research Center, April 2006.

be impressed by the difference compounding makes. After ten years, $100,000 grows to $163,000.

These are just examples of annual compounding. Sometimes, interest is compounded daily or monthly. And this makes your money grow to even larger sums over the long run, as Figure 4.2 shows.

Fig. 4.2	THE DIFFERENCE BETWEEN ANNUAL, QUARTERLY, MONTHLY, AND DAILY COMPOUND INTEREST			
	$100,000 12% Annual Compounding	$100,000 12% Quarterly Compounding	$100,000 12% Monthly Compounding	$100,000 12% Daily Compounding
END OF YEAR	ACCOUNT BALANCE	ACCOUNT BALANCE	ACCOUNT BALANCE	ACCOUNT BALANCE
5	$176,234.17	$180,611.12	$181,669.67	$182,193.91
10	$310,584.82	$326,203.78	$330,038.69	$331,946.22
15	$547,356.58	$589,160.31	$599,580.20	$604,785.81
20	$964,629.31	$1,064,089.06	$1,089,255.37	$1,101,882.93
25	$1,700,006.44	$1,921,863.20	$1,978,846.63	$2,007,563.63
30	$2,995,992.21	$3,471,098.71	$3,594,964.13	$3,657,658.75

To illustrate the power of compound interest over time, do this little exercise with me. Pull out a sheet of regular 8½- by 11-inch paper. (If you don't want to do it physically, at least imagine you're doing it.) Fold it in half. Now fold it in half again. Imagine you could fold this in half forty-eight more times (even though you cannot actually do that many folds) and write down how thick it would be—in some form of measurement—such as inches, centimeters, or miles. How high would the stack of paper be?

When I do this exercise in a group setting, I ask people to write their answer and reveal it. Did you guess half an inch? One inch? One foot?

That's what most people guess when I do this with a roomful of financial advisors and CPAs. A few may guess ten feet or, in rare cases, a few miles.

Fig. 4.3	THE MARVEL OF COMPOUNDING Folding a 26lb Sheet of Paper in Half 50 Times			
# of Folds	Equivalent Number of pages	Thickness		
		Inches	Feet	Miles
0	1	0.005	0.00	0.00
1	2	0.01	0.00	0.00
2	4	0.02	0.00	0.00
3	8	0.04	0.00	0.00
4	16	0.08	0.01	0.00
5	32	0.17	0.01	0.00
6	64	0.34	0.03	0.00
7	128	0.67	0.06	0.00
8	256	1.35	0.11	0.00
9	512	2.7	0.22	0.00
10	1,024	5.4	0.45	0.00
11	2,048	11	0.90	0.00
12	4,096	22	1.80	0.00
13	8,192	43	3.60	0.00
14	16,384	86	7.20	0.00
15	32,768	173	14	0.00
16	65,536	345	29	0.00
17	131,072	691	58	0.00
18	262,144	1,381	115	0.02
19	524,288	2,763	230	0.04
20	1,048,576	5,526	460	0.09
21	2,097,152	11,052	921	0.17
22	4,194,304	22,104	1,842	0.35
23	8,388,608	44,208	3,684	0.70
24	16,777,216	88,416	7,368	1.40
25	33,554,432	176,832	14,736	2.79
26	67,108,864	353,664	29,472	5.58
27	134,217,728	707,327	58,944	11
28	268,435,456	1,414,655	117,888	22
29	536,870,912	2,829,310	235,776	45
30	1,073,741,824	5,658,619	471,552	89
31	2,147,483,648	11,317,239	943,103	179
32	4,294,967,296	22,634,478	1,886,206	357
33	8,589,934,592	45,268,955	3,772,413	714
34	17,179,869,184	90,537,911	7,544,826	1,429
35	34,359,738,368	181,075,821	15,089,652	2,858
36	68,719,476,736	362,151,642	30,179,304	5,716
37	137,438,953,472	724,303,285	60,358,607	11,432
38	274,877,906,944	1,448,606,570	120,717,214	22,863
39	549,755,813,888	2,897,213,139	241,434,428	45,726
40	1,099,511,627,776	5,794,426,278	482,868,857	91,452
41	2,199,023,255,552	11,588,852,557	965,737,713	182,905
42	4,398,046,511,104	23,177,705,114	1,931,475,426	365,810
43	8,796,093,022,208	46,355,410,227	3,862,950,852	731,619
44	17,592,186,044,416	92,710,820,454	7,725,901,705	1,463,239
45	35,184,372,088,832	185,421,640,908	15,451,803,409	2,926,478
46	70,368,744,177,664	370,843,281,816	30,903,606,818	5,852,956
47	140,737,488,355,328	741,686,563,633	61,807,213,636	11,705,912
48	281,474,976,710,656	1,483,373,127,265	123,614,427,272	23,411,823
49	562,949,953,421,312	2,966,746,254,530	247,228,854,544	46,823,647
50	1,125,899,906,842,620	5,933,492,509,061	494,457,709,088	93,647,293

The correct answer is that the stack of paper will be so thick it will reach from here to the sun! That's 93 million miles! What! You don't believe me? Figure 4.3 proves that a twenty-six-pound sheet of paper folded fifty times would reach to the sun (because it doubles each time)! In other words, if you could fold the paper (doubling its thickness) one more time (fifty-one times) it would reach to the sun and back!

If you are around fifty years old, you may have just muttered: "That's nice for a piece of paper, but I still don't understand what it has to do with my money. I don't need to reach for the moon, the stars, or the sun. I just need to reach retirement and be comfortable. All you have told me is that a hundred dollars will amount to $163 in ten years at 5 percent. That will buy me a newspaper or can of soda every now and again, but that's about it. I can't afford to catch up at so slow a pace."

Thanks to the power of compound interest, you can catch up—not in an instant, but more quickly than you may think.

A moment ago I showed how $100,000 would grow. What if I told you how to get your hands on $100,000—money that you did not need right this minute? At 6 percent compound interest, ten years from now, you would have $179,085. From that point forward, at 6 percent interest, it could generate annual income of $10,745, or about $900 per month.

"That's more like it," you say. "But I'm not a magician. I can't snap my fingers, reach behind someone's ear, and find a check for $100,000 in my hands. Where will it come from?"

I'll get to that shortly. In the meantime, what if you don't need the money for fifteen years—in other words, until you hit 65 (if you are a 50-year-old). With 7 percent compound interest, that same $100,000 grows to $275,903, which could generate an annual income of $19,313—more than $1,600 per month. Starting with more money and having more time to compound, an even heftier sum awaits you.

What if, instead of 7 percent, you could put that money someplace safe where it would earn 8 percent interest compounded annually. In fifteen years, the $100,000 is $317,217. In twenty years, it is $466,096. "Pretty marvelous!" you exclaim.

If you are a 52-year-old Boomer and could come up with $300,000, at 8 percent interest, by age 68 you would have over $1 million. If you are a young Boomer and had twenty-five years until you finally retired, you would need only $150,000 growing at 8 percent compound interest to accumulate over $1 million. You may be saying to yourself, "But where do I come up with $150,000 or $300,000?" Most Boomers I work with have access to that kind of seed money—they just don't realize it.

The difference between simple and compound interest is the difference between a person pedaling a bicycle up a gentle hill and a small airplane zooming off a runway. A little bit later, I'll talk about a system for using OPM to make that $100,000, $150,000, or $300,000 (plus the interest it is earning) become money you can use for retirement.

One more thing worth mentioning in connection with the marvel of compound interest is that some people think if they have $100,000 in one account, compounding at, let's say, 10 percent interest, that money will grow to a larger sum than having $10,000 in each of ten accounts. It doesn't. More money in one pot doesn't grow any faster than the same amount divided into several pots growing at the same interest rate.

Keep this in mind for later on, when I'll discuss how to split your retirement funds and keep them in a variety of pots, rather than in just one place. I want to make sure you understand that it's the compounding that makes the growth difference, not how big each individual pot is.

DOUBLE YOUR MONEY: THE RULE OF 72

There's one more concept related to compound interest that is useful to know. The rule of 72 is used in finance to estimate how long it will take to double your money in any given investment. It depends on how much compound interest you earn on it.

To find the number of years required to double your retirement nest egg—or any money—at a given interest rate, divide the interest rate into 72. For example, the result of 72 divided by 8 shows that at 8 percent interest rate, an account worth $100,000 will become $200,000 in about nine years. At 10 percent interest, the $100,000 becomes $200,000 in about 7.2 years.

The same rule allows you to calculate how well you actually do over a period of years on a nest egg, or a home, or any investment.

For instance, let's say you bought your home for $100,000 in cash, and you sell it later for $200,000. "I doubled my money," you say triumphantly.

That doesn't impress me unless I know how long you held that property before you sold it. If you sold it after ten years, divide 72 by 10; you got only the equivalent of 7.2 percent appreciation rate on that home, compounded annually. Did you sell it after fifteen years? The same rule—72 divided by 15—shows you made less than 5 percent appreciation.

What can change these numbers significantly is the use of OPM. If you made a down payment on your house fifteen years ago of only $10,000, and took out a mortgage for the remaining $90,000, you financed most of the cost with Other People's Money. To calculate your rate of return here will be more complicated, but it will be better than only 5 percent. I'll return to this idea when I discuss leverage.

People like to brag about how much money they made not just on the sale of a house but on a stock. It's the same refrain: "I doubled my money!" But someone who tells me that, only to add that he held that stock for fifteen years, is saying he made only 5 percent interest on that investment. He possibly could have gotten the same amount with his money sitting in a CD or bank account.

HOW DOES INFLATION AFFECT YOUR NEST EGG?

You can use the rule of 72 to figure out the cost of living, since inflation grows at a compound rate. If inflation is 5 percent a year, 5 into 72 means that the cost of living will double about every fifteen years. Translated into real-world terms, that means it will take $6,000 a month fifteen years from now to buy the same gallons of gas and loaves of bread that $3,000 buys today.

Let's play with these numbers a bit more. If you are 55 years old, live another thirty years to age 85, and inflation compounds at 5 percent (a rate of inflation that has been reached periodically in recent years),[*] at age 85 it will cost $12,000 a month to buy those same gallons of gas and loaves of bread that cost $3,000 right now.

What's the takeaway lesson? It's crucial to understand both compound interest and inflation, because you need to have a nest egg that keeps up with or grows faster than inflation.

That's why I ask people how much they think they need in a nest egg to retire. "When I have enough money tucked away in a stable environment that would indefinitely produce the monthly income I'm accustomed to," is the most common reply.

Most people would rather think about what they earn *now* and project that *same amount* ten, fifteen, twenty, or even thirty years down the road. They don't take inflation into account. Then they fall victim to Misconception #4—thinking $100,000 or even $300,000 is going to serve them well when they are sipping iced tea poolside in Florida, planning their 75th birthday party.

The trouble is, by that time, inflation may have gnawed a hole in the nest egg that has been set aside for that leisurely life—unless the nest egg grows more rapidly.

All it takes is simple arithmetic, using the rule of 72. Assume you want to retire today. You get by nicely on $3,000 a month. You want to be just as comfortable in about twenty-five years. You fig-

---

[*]http://inflationdata.com/Inflation/Inflation_Rate/d DecadeInflation.asp. The average for the 1970s was 4.82 percent.

ure inflation will grow at 3 percent.[*] Divide 72 by 3. That tells you the cost of living will double in twenty-four years. This means that you would need $6,000 a month by your twenty-fifth year to be as comfortable as you are today with $3,000 a month.

I would rather be safe, and assume that we are headed for an average inflation rate of 5 percent for the next twenty-five years—and 72 divided by 5 tells me that the cost of living will double approximately every fifteen years.

I can hear you groan: "Uh-oh. The hole in my nest egg just got even wider!" You will need a nest egg of at least $900,000 if it is earning 8 percent interest to generate $72,000 a year, or $6,000 a month of income to sit comfortably by your Florida pool.

HOW COMPOUND INTEREST HELPS HOMEOWNERS

Frightened that inflation will gobble up most of your increases? Don't be scared just yet. While the cost of certain commodities has mushroomed over the years, the price of others has gone down. You pay a lower percentage out of your paycheck today for basic food items than you did in 1981, for instance.

Meanwhile, compounding appreciation has been a great boon to those who own a home, because, as you no doubt know, the *value* of houses has shot upward. If you are now 55 and bought your house thirty years ago for $30,000, you probably never dreamed your house would be worth hundreds of thousands or more today.

I know people in Morristown, New Jersey, who bought their houses for $30,000 or $50,000 thirty years ago. Today, those houses are worth $1 million. That's a compounding appreciation rate of 12 percent a year.

As I mentioned, you need to understand the marvel of com-

---

[*]http://inflationdata.com/inflation/Inflation_Rate/AnnualInflation.asp. The historical average is 3.43 percent from 1913 to 2006.

pound interest while you are saving money, since your rate of interest on savings must stay ahead of inflation.

But you should also understand that if you are a homeowner, you might have many more dollars sitting under your roof (thanks to compounding appreciation) at the same time you are paying only simple interest on your home mortgage.

Let's say you have a $100,000 mortgage and you are paying 8.5 percent interest on it. *This mortgage does not compound over the years.* It's a simple interest declining balance, if the balance is amortized over a fifteen- or thirty-year mortgage term. If it's an interest-only mortgage, you pay just $8,500 every year.

Take the same money and imagine that it is invested in an account earning about 8.5 percent interest compounded annually. In the sixth year, that $100,000 is worth just over $150,000, due to compounding.

But you are still paying simple interest on your original $100,000 mortgage. You are earning compound interest on a bigger balance than you are paying simple interest on.

THE LILY POND EXERCISE

Now let's do another exercise to make sure you really understand compounding. Picture a pond in a garden with a patch of lily pads. Each day the lily patch doubles in size. If it takes forty-eight days for the patch to cover the lily pond completely with lilies, how many days would it take to cover it halfway?

The answer is forty-seven. It's the same idea as the piece of paper reaching the sun. The first day, the pond may have only one lily pad. But if it doubles each day, the day before it is completely covered will be the forty-seventh day—and it will be only half covered on that day!

I hear so many people say, "The cost of living is going to wreck me." I say, let compounding work for you instead of against you. Why don't you put your money to work in something that compounds, instead of letting yourself get hurt by compounding inflation?

Those lilies spread by leaps and bounds because they were compounding. So can your money—and you can have that much money in retirement if you do more than just accumulate it at a great growth rate, but if you also access it tax-free during retirement. That's the power of the next marvel.

THRUST: THE MARVEL OF TAX-FREE ACCUMULATION

You can dramatically enhance the strategies that I am about to introduce if the dollars you save don't just earn compound interest, but also accumulate in a tax-deferred or, better yet, a more streamlined, tax-free environment.

With tax-deferred investments, the government giveth, but the government taketh away. As a result, the money you build up in taxable or tax-deferred investments may require you to incur greater risks in order to achieve the same net after-tax rate of return.

There are many legitimate tax deductions and tax-favorable strategies in the tax code that can really help you, especially as you approach age 59½, when you can access your retirement money without penalty. In upcoming chapters, I'll show how homeowners can utilize home equity retirement planning that may provide tax advantages (100-cent dollars) during your earning years, and more important, how you can enjoy tax-free (100-cent) dollars during your retirement years—as well as transfer any remaining funds to your heirs tax-free.

One myth I want to dispel first, however, has to do with taxes on retirement accounts. Some people embark on these forced savings plans thinking that "tax-deferred" means "tax-free." But that's not so.

With the most popular retirement accounts such as IRAs and 401(k)s, the money that you put aside is tax-deferred. Those are tax-deductible, or pre-tax, dollars (100-cent dollars) that you put in these accounts. But when you start to withdraw from those accounts, that money is taxed as ordinary income.

When some people I have spoken to realize this, their reaction is: "Let's leave that money in those accounts. I don't need it yet." That's not the best solution. You're just delaying the inevitable and increasing your tax liability.

Later on, I will show you a way to convert these retirement funds into accounts from which you can withdraw money without paying tax on it. In Chapter 9, I explain this strategy—what I call a strategic "rollout" rather than a "rollover." First, though, let's examine a classic mistake—Misconception #5. This is the mistake of thinking that when you retire, you'll be in a lower tax bracket.

Here's a classic case study . . .

I have had many teachers as clients. One spent thirty years working in the public school system. Her last best salary was $60,000 a year.

But for thirty years she knew that she would get a pension that would amount to 2 percent for every year of service that she taught—in other words, 60 percent of her last paycheck: $36,000 a year, or $3,000 a month.

To prepare for that expected shortfall, she socked away money in supplemental retirement accounts, variously called IRAs, 401(k)s, 403(b)s, and TSAs. Sure, they amounted to a major sum—$350,000. Sounds good, right?

After she retired, this woman began to receive $3,000 a month from her teachers' defined-benefit pension. But by age 70½, she was *forced* to start taking out a minimum amount from each of her other retirement funds, in addition to Social Security. The Internal Revenue Code rules required her to withdraw these minimums. By then she was receiving $16,000 in Social Security, plus minimum distributions of $28,000 a year (combined total) from her other retirement funds. This was all taxable and was added to her $36,000 a year ($3,000 times 12) pension withdrawals.

The result: Her total annual income climbed to $80,000 a year—a much higher income than she'd ever had while she was teaching.

Her house was paid off, the kids were no longer living at home, and she was no longer contributing to a retirement account. *So she had almost no tax deductions.* She found herself in a higher tax bracket than before retirement, and she was being taxed to death. She asked herself: "Whose retirement was I planning—my own or Uncle Sam's?"

YOU PAY TAX ON THE HARVEST WITH A TRADITIONAL IRA OR 401(K)

Let me rephrase a question I asked earlier—if you were a farmer, would you like to get a tax break on the price of your seed money in the spring, *and* pay taxes on the money you later get for your harvest? That's what happens with a traditional IRA or 401(k).

I'd rather have a tax-free harvest, instead of being clobbered on the back end like this teacher. We show our clients how to enjoy their harvest—those retirement accounts—tax-free. But what I *really* want is to have my cake and eat it, too. I want to get a tax break on both the seed money *and* the harvest. How much of a difference would it make?

If you got 100-cent dollars on both the front end and the back end, you could enjoy 50 percent more spendable income as a retiree. I suspect you can envision plenty of fun things you could spend that extra money on. Or your money could last into perpetuity, instead of running out before *you* run out. (In other words, it can permanently provide the same annual income that an IRA or 401(k) provides only temporarily.) I'll prove it to you as we go along.

So many times when people look at their retirement account, it seems like a big sumptuous sandwich loaded with everything on it. But after retirement, huge tax bites have consumed a large share of the sandwich.

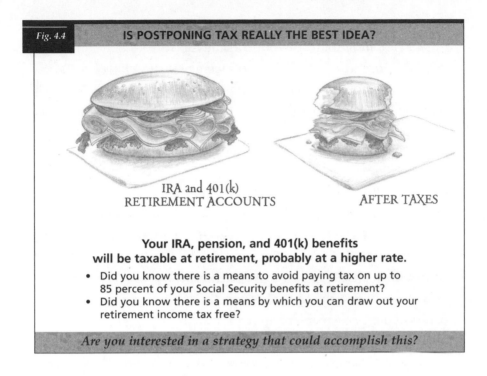

Fig. 4.4   IS POSTPONING TAX REALLY THE BEST IDEA?

IRA and 401(k)
RETIREMENT ACCOUNTS

AFTER TAXES

**Your IRA, pension, and 401(k) benefits
will be taxable at retirement, probably at a higher rate.**

- Did you know there is a means to avoid paying tax on up to
  85 percent of your Social Security benefits at retirement?
- Did you know there is a means by which you can draw out your
  retirement income tax free?

Are you interested in a strategy that could accomplish this?

Now is the best time to learn that taxes will take big bites out of your IRA, pension, and 401(k) benefits. You need to take steps now to protect yourself from that hungry federal agency with the big set of teeth.

I will teach you shortly how to avoid paying taxes on up to 85 percent of your Social Security benefits at retirement. I will show you how to possibly draw as much as $60,000 or $70,000 annually out of your retirement accounts with substantially reduced tax liability or even no tax consequence—something we have done many times for clients.

WARNING: TRADITIONAL PLANS HAVE STRINGS ATTACHED

What do we mean when we say "qualified" retirement plans? They are qualified by the IRS under the Internal Revenue Code. Whether you have a defined-benefit pension plan, profit-sharing plan, IRA, 403(b), 457, TSA, 401(k)—they're all in the same boat.

All qualified plans come with strings attached. You can deposit only a certain amount of your income, up to a certain limit each year. The limits on these numbers change every year. For instance, in 2007 the most you could contribute to a regular IRA or Roth IRA was $4,000 per person, or $5,000 if you were over 50. There are other restrictions, too. Boomers who have saved very little up to now need a method to accumulate money in retirement accounts with bigger deposits than that.

If you are 55 years old now, you don't have the luxury of putting aside only $5,000—at least, not if you want to retire comfortably in ten years. You are in a different situation than the 30- or 35-year-old who has up to three decades to steadily save money.

Another string attached to qualified plans has to do with dipping into those plans early, perhaps because of an emergency, a prolonged period of unemployment, or maybe just an investment opportunity. If you touch any of the funds in a qualified plan before you reach age 59½, you are charged a 10 percent penalty unless you borrow it out, and then you must pay it back to avoid paying tax on the distribution.

Then there is the "I'll-leave-it-until-later" string. What happens if you don't start withdrawing at least the minimum required amount from a qualified plan at age 70½? There's another penalty— a whopping 50 percent on top of the tax! So at age 70½, if you have a million bucks there and are supposed to pull out $50,000, and you don't, you have to pay a 50 percent penalty plus the tax.

Why does the IRS attach that string? Doesn't the money belong to you to use in your older age as you see fit? Not quite. The government wants to collect the taxes before you die, so they can tax it again when you die. It's the best savings bond the government ever devised for itself. The government is planning its future tax revenues.

ROTH IRAS AND ROTH 401(K)S HAVE LIMITS, TOO

Some of you probably have put money in a Roth retirement account. Named after the late Senator William V. Roth Jr., these qualified plans allow you to deposit already taxed dollars. Once you reach 59½, you can withdraw money from them tax-free, on the back end.

The trouble is that when the government has a shortfall, it broadens the Roth IRA (as it did several times after the Roth IRA was introduced in 1997), in order to get you to convert regular IRAs into Roths and generate more taxable revenue immediately.

Beginning in 2006, the Roth regulations were loosened, so you can now open or convert to a Roth 401(k). The ceiling on a Roth was lifted so that by 2010, people with adjusted gross incomes of over $100,000 can convert their regular IRAs to Roth IRAs. This is the IRS's way of regulating how much revenue it can get when it wants or needs it.

I am in favor of some of the ideas incorporated in a Roth IRA. Let's go back to the farmer, with a choice of having his seed money taxed, or the profits on his harvest taxed. *I think it is better to pay taxes on the seed money contributed to a Roth IRA or Roth 401(k) and enjoy a tax-free harvest later on.*

You cannot withdraw money from a Roth until at least five years after the first contribution is made. If you do, you pay a penalty. On the other hand, you are not required to withdraw a minimum amount from a Roth IRA at the age of 70½, as you are under traditional IRAs.

Roths are a step in the right direction, but there are too many caps on them. That's probably why they are the least popular form of IRA, owned by less than 28 percent of families that have qualified accounts. The Roth IRA "has attracted only 4 percent of assets in IRAs with an average balance of $25,920," according to the Employee Benefit Research Institute, using data from the Federal Reserve's 2004 Survey of Consumer Finances.[*]

---

*Tami Luhby, "New Tax Law Effective in Four Years Will Eliminate $100,000 Income Cap for Converting Traditional IRAs to Roths," *Newsday*, May 23, 2006.

BEWARE OF THE STRINGS ATTACHED TO MATCHING EMPLOYER PLANS

Some qualified plans do come with matching dollars from an employer. Let's say you put in a dollar, the company matches 50 cents on every dollar, up to the first 6 percent you put in. So you put in $1.00 and you have $1.50 working for you. That's not bad. It looks like a 50 percent return, although it's not. It's just a one-time 50 percent increase. *When you withdraw the $1.50 during retirement, the government taxes it, and takes back most or all of that 50 cents—plus the gain on that 50 cents.* Matching can basically mean your employer is paying your tax for you.

To summarize the *pros* of such plans, you get:

- Tax-deductible funding
- Tax-deferred growth
- Possible matching by your employer

The *cons* include:

- Limits on contributions
- Fully taxed as you use it
- Must use it up based on minimum distribution rules
- Remainder potentially taxed twice if passed to non-spousal heirs

WHAT ABOUT A TOTALLY TAX-FREE RETIREMENT PLAN?

Most people don't know where else to put their retirement dollars except in qualified plans. I'm going to show you a better place.

The plans I will show you are nonqualified alternatives. There are no strings attached. You still have to abide by IRS rules in order for your withdrawals to be tax-free. But there are no limits. If you have a banner year, you can put in as much as you want—$100,000 or $500,000, it's your choice. If you have a bad year, you don't have to put in anything.

If you are a homeowner, you can structure your retirement planning to get indirect tax deductions on the sums you contribute to these nonqualified plans. A vital feature is that these retirement funds accumulate tax-free, and you can access the money whenever you want, on a tax-free basis—including the interest or gain. You don't have to wait until you are 59½.

Another valuable difference: If you don't use up your nonqualified retirement funds before you pass away, they blossom in value, and they transfer free of income tax to your heirs.

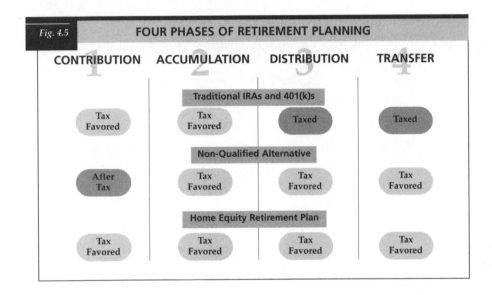

Fig. 4.5   **FOUR PHASES OF RETIREMENT PLANNING**

CONTRIBUTION	ACCUMULATION	DISTRIBUTION	TRANSFER
	Traditional IRAs and 401(k)s		
Tax Favored	Tax Favored	Taxed	Taxed
	Non-Qualified Alternative		
After Tax	Tax Favored	Tax Favored	Tax Favored
	Home Equity Retirement Plan		
Tax Favored	Tax Favored	Tax Favored	Tax Favored

Here is a sneak preview of an alternative—a strategic rollout. You strategically move the money out of your IRA or 401(k) starting as early as age 59½. Many of my clients, as I'll show you, do this over a five-, six-, or seven-year period between the ages of 59½ and 70½ with little or no tax consequence, and from that day forward their money accumulates tax-free.

You don't just get your money out, pay the tax, and then put it back into something taxable. Instead you get it out and pay the applicable taxes so they are over and done with, sometimes eliminating most or all of them. From that point forward, *I recommend you reposition the money into investments that grow tax-free, so it is never taxed again.* For the rest of your life, you can possibly enjoy $25,000, $50,000, $100,000, or $200,000 of tax-free annual income.

You know how just before a doctor vaccinates you against a disease, he holds the needle in his hand and says reassuringly, "This will hurt just a tiny bit"? A strategic rollout may be a little bit painful in the first few years. But overall it will inoculate you against future taxes.

I can save you hundreds, thousands, sometimes millions of dollars of tax by creating a nonqualified retirement plan that can last you into perpetuity. Compare this to a traditional IRA or 401(k) that will become depleted in ten to fifteen years based on the same retirement income stream.

DRAG: THE MARVEL OF SAFE LEVERAGE

As I said earlier, drag (safe, positive leverage) is a good thing. Just as you need drag in order to make an airplane fly, to make your wealth take off you need something that most people think of as a drag (in the usual definition of that word).

That something is paying interest.

"Pay interest? Like I do on my mortgage? That would drag me down!" I often get this response.

I promise you there is a smarter, counterintuitive view. *Drag* in my vocabulary is *good* and *vital* to wealth accumulation. Grasp how drag works—not to slow you down, but to make your money climb more speedily—and you will be ahead of 99 percent of your peers.

If you own a home, you have probably already experienced the power of leverage. Virtually no one hands over wads of cash to pay for a home all at once, because even if a family had that amount of money in a savings account, houses are expensive. Paying the entire amount could drain your savings, leaving no liquid cash for emergencies.

Most people put a down payment on a house and finance the

remainder of the purchase price with a mortgage. They use a small amount of cash to own or control a greater asset. That's using leverage—the same way you might use a small amount of force on a jack to raise your 2,000-pound car far enough off the ground so you can replace a tire.

To utilize the remarkable tool of leverage, you pay interest, just as banks and credit unions do when they borrow money. They pay it gladly—they are grateful for drag—because it accelerates the accumulation of more money. You, too, can do this. Like a bank or credit union, you can pay interest to earn more interest. Interest is essential to make your assets soar because it allows you to make money on a key asset—OPM. Sometimes I've heard people quip, "There are two kinds of people in the world—those that pay interest, and those that earn it." Actually, there is a third kind of person in the world—the Thrivers—who wisely pay interest in order to earn even more interest.

For a small amount of interest on the money you borrow when you buy a home, you are able to own an asset that can lift you into the skies of financial independence. How? I will soon show you how to put this asset to work in a tax-favored environment.

LEVERAGE YOUR GREATEST ASSET

Let's say you paid cash a few years ago for a $100,000 house. It then appreciated 5 percent in one year. You have earned $5,000 in that case. But what if you bought the same house using only $10,000 of your own money as a down payment and borrowed the rest?

The house value still grew the same 5 percent. That means $10,000 that you put into the house grew 50 percent instead of 5 percent. And you only tied up $10,000 to have a $100,000 asset working for you.

If you had bought the house for nothing down, rented the house to cover the mortgage payment, and someone came along and offered you more than the $100,000 you borrowed to pay for it, what would your return be? Infinite—because you didn't use one dime of your own money.

Now let's play with this principle a bit. If I have $100,000 and instead of buying just a single house, I divide it up so I can put $10,000 down on ten houses. Presto! I have a million dollars of real estate appreciating at 5 percent. By owning ten properties, my initial investment of $100,000 grows by $50,000 (10 times $5,000).

I hear you sputtering: "But, but, but . . . there's a cost associated with doing this."

That's the point. What you perceive as drag—the interest you will pay—won't slow you down. It speeds you up. How? We'll go through this step by step in Chapter 6.

If you already own a house, take 80 percent of the fair market value of your home and deduct the outstanding loans you have on your house. It will give you an idea of the leverage you might have available to you in your current home, money you can put to better use to turbocharge your retirement.

There is a broader definition of leverage, however: "The use of borrowed assets . . . to enhance the return to the owner's equity. The expectation is that the interest rate charged will be lower than the earnings made on the money."[*]

Later on, I will explain how you can separate the money borrowed against your home at simple interest at cheap rates, and invest it to reap much larger returns—compounding tax-free—to make your retirement money mushroom.

For now, hold on to these concepts:

- *Lift* is the power of compound interest, which makes your nest egg grow geometrically rather than arithmetically.
- *Thrust* is the power of tax-free accumulation, which pro-

---

*Wall Street Journal Online—http://online.wsj.com/documents/glossary.htm.

pels that money forward by allowing it to fly without fear of your aircraft going into a stall.

- *Drag* is the power of safe, positive leverage, which lets you access Other People's Money and thus lets you operate with large sums, at a small cost of simple interest.

REMEMBER THIS:

- Examine each of your savings and investments—which offer the *lift* of compound interest.
- Examine each of your retirement vehicles—which offer the *thrust* of tax-free accumulation.
- Examine all assets and liabilities to see which offer the possible *drag* of leverage for greater wealth.
- Apply the rule of 72 to calculate the return on real estate, a retirement plan, or any investment. To calculate the effective interest rate, take 72 and divide it by the number of years you have held the investment. To find how many years it will take to double your money, divide 72 by the interest rate.
- Consider if you really want to postpone taxes that you owe when deferring taxes on your seed money (contributions and accumulations of qualified retirement plans) but paying taxes on your harvest (distribution of qualified retirement income).
- Know the drawbacks of employer contributions to pensions as well as the strings attached to Roth IRAs and Roth 401(k)s.

CHAPTER 5

Liberate Yourself from IRAs and 401(k)s

Why Uncle Sam's Savings Plans Should *Not* Be Yours

FOR YEARS, you probably have been bombarded with information about how you can save for your retirement with the help of IRAs and 401(k)s. Your CPA or financial advisor may have pleaded with you to contribute pre-tax or tax-deductible dollars into these so-called qualified plans because, as they understand it, this will shelter your money as you accumulate it.

They tell you not to worry as you get ready to reach into those savings when you set a retirement date or when you hit the age of 59½. Your nest egg will be bulging, they promise.

As we have seen, there is value in having your money grow tax-free. But I've found very few advisors understand that, like the teacher I described in the previous chapter, you may get clobbered by taxes when you actually make those withdrawals. Let's examine these much touted retirement plans closely.

First, let's look at the premise of a lower tax bracket during retirement. You may be thinking, "Doug, I'm small potatoes. I'm not in a high tax bracket now, so I'm not going to worry about paying high taxes later."

Regardless of your current tax bracket, I would rather see you think about it now—and do something to ensure that you won't be hit with a tax bill you never saw coming. It's a lot easier to prevent unnecessary tax now than try to cure it down the road.

A SHORT DETOUR INTO RECENT ECONOMIC POLICY

Before going any further, let me take a short detour to talk about the economy and taxes. Do you think taxes will be lower in the future? In seminars, I ask for a show of hands on this: "Do you think they'll remain the same as they are now? Or will they be higher?"

You won't be surprised to hear that the largest show of hands is for "higher." Most people expect taxes to increase. But usually, someone will say, "Wait! In 2001 and 2003 President Bush sponsored and Congress passed the Economic Growth and Tax Relief Reconciliation Act and the Jobs and Growth Tax Relief Reconciliation Act respectively. These acts raised the tax thresholds and thus put many people in lower tax brackets. So why can't we expect new tax cuts, rather than increases?"

My reply is that those tax changes were passed merely to stimulate the economy. Why? There are two political philosophies: one is that you raise tax revenue by raising taxes, while the other is that you raise the revenue that will get taxed to generate more tax revenue. President Bush wanted to raise the revenue after an unusual period of events that impacted the economy.

Remember back before the year 2000? If you recall, with all the fears of computers' Y2K incompatibility, the Federal Reserve did not want anyone to go to their bank or credit union and be unable to access their money at the turn of the century. Through a series of interest rate reductions, the money supply was increased. Then came the bounce after Y2K, followed by a decline as the dot-com bubble burst. Interest rates were damped down. Then two planes flew into the World Trade Center towers and the markets plunged. Shortly thereafter, workers around the country lost their jobs because of the crisis. Anyone whose assets were not liquid had a terribly bumpy ride during those years.

Looking ahead, there is lots of talk about whether the estate tax, often referred to as the inheritance tax, will indeed only be repealed in 2010, or whether Congress will allow it to disappear entirely. As I write this, the estate tax applies to any estates over $2 million. While the 2001 tax cut reduces the estate tax each year and eliminates it in 2010, it is set to return in 2011 to its year 2000 schedule.

I think plans to phase it out are a big tease. The Boomer generation is on track to transfer the greatest amount of wealth in *the history of the world* to a younger generation. As a trade-off, after repeal of the estate tax, the current law providing a step-up in basis to fair market value will be repealed. (I explain this in more detail in my original work, *Missed Fortune*.) Suffice it to say that if the step-up in basis on long-term capital gains is modified, inherited appreciated assets may be subject to increased capital gains taxes when sold.

The bottom line is, you know the government will collect its tax money one way or another. With federal deficits, Social Security issues, and the war on terrorism all demanding attention, it would behoove you to assume in your retirement planning that there won't be another tax reduction act anytime soon.

Does it make sense to postpone paying taxes for an advantage you may never enjoy? No! Does it make sense to postpone paying taxes when you're convinced you'll be in a higher bracket? No! Does it make sense to let your retirement accounts grow into a big nest egg, then pull money out when your taxes have gone up? No!

The two lessons you can learn from all this are:

- It's best to be in a position of liquidity and safety so you can always act, rather than be forced to react to unanticipated events in the world.

- Rather than postpone the inevitable taxes, you need to discover a tax-advantaged way to enjoy your retirement.

Why not have it all? I don't want to pay unnecessary taxes on my retirement funds *at any point* whether it is now, on the front end, or later. I want to put my money away in a tax-favored environment and then withdraw it without paying taxes. Don't you?

WHAT'S YOUR TAX BRACKET?

You're about to learn how to deposit 100-cent dollars at the front end of your retirement savings and how to withdraw 100-cent dollars on the back end (during retirement). But first, you need a primer on how tax brackets work.

In 2007, there are six brackets for the purpose of computing federal income tax. Figure 5.1 illustrates the percentages and thresholds.

We can't be sure how tax thresholds may change in coming years. But for simplicity's sake, I'd like to use one bracket to illustrate my points. If you are a typical American taxpayer, you are probably in (or close to) a combined federal and state income marginal tax bracket of 33.3 percent right now. A couple filing a joint tax return in California earning a combined income in excess of $63,700 in 2007 would be taxed at 34.3 percent on all dollars they earn over $63,700. To illustrate these concepts, it is simple mathematically to assume that exactly one-third of your income goes for taxes. Whether your state has an income tax or your actual tax bracket is higher or lower, the concepts remain the same, so you can interpolate any illustrations in this book for your personal income tax bracket.

Bear with me—it's important to know what this all means and the dramatic impact it can have on your retirement resources.

Taxable income is calculated as adjusted gross personal income, minus personal deductions and exemptions. Deductions are allowed for expenses or investments that directly or indirectly contribute to civic assets or otherwise stimulate the economy. You are allowed exemptions for dependents, such as children living at home. If you are an entrepreneur or are self-employed, there are many legitimate business deductions that may reduce your taxable income. Itemized or standard deductions and exemptions are subtracted from the last, not the first, dollars you earn each year.

Fig. 5.1	**2007 FEDERAL TAX RATE SCHEDULES**

Schedule X — Single		
If taxable income is over—	But not over—	The tax is:
$0	$7,825	10% of the amount over $0
$7,825	$31,850	$782.50 plus 15% of the amount over 7,825
$31,850	$77,100	$4,386.25 plus 25% of the amount over 31,850
$77,100	$160,850	$15,698.75 plus 28% of the amount over 77,100
$160,850	$349,700	$39,148.75 plus 33% of the amount over 160,850
$349,700	no limit	$101,469.25 plus 35% of the amount over 349,700

Schedule Y-1 — Married Filing Jointly or Qualifying Widow(er)		
If taxable income is over—	But not over—	The tax is:
$0	$15,650	10% of the amount over $0
$15,650	$63,700	$1,565.00 plus 15% of the amount over 15,650
$63,700	$128,500	$8,772.50 plus 25% of the amount over 63,700
$128,500	$195,850	$24,972.50 plus 28% of the amount over 128,500
$195,850	$349,700	$43,830.50 plus 33% of the amount over 195,850
$349,700	no limit	$94,601.00 plus 35% of the amount over 349,700

Schedule Y-2 — Married Filing Separately		
If taxable income is over—	But not over—	The tax is:
$0	$7,825	10% of the amount over $0
$7,825	$31,850	$782.50 plus 15% of the amount over 7,825
$31,850	$64,250	$4,386.25 plus 25% of the amount over 31,850
$64,250	$97,925	$12,486.25 plus 28% of the amount over 64,250
$97,925	$174,850	$21,915.25 plus 33% of the amount over 97,925
$174,850	no limit	$47,300.50 plus 35% of the amount over 174,850

Schedule Z — Head of Household		
If taxable income is over—	But not over—	The tax is:
$0	$11,200	10% of the amount over $0
$11,200	$42,650	$1,120.00 plus 15% of the amount over 11,200
$42,650	$110,100	$5,837.50 plus 25% of the amount over 42,650
$110,100	$178,350	$22,700.00 plus 28% of the amount over 110,100
$178,350	$349,700	$41,810.00 plus 33% of the amount over 178,350
$349,700	no limit	$98,355.50 plus 35% of the amount over 349,700

A taxpayer who files an itemized federal tax return will list these deductions on Schedule A of the 1040 federal tax return. There are currently three primary categories that you typically deduct when you file this schedule (as opposed to a short form or taking the standard deduction):

- State income and sales taxes, plus local taxes such as property tax
- Cash and noncash charitable contributions
- Qualified mortgage interest expense

Under hardship circumstances, excessive medical care costs and casualty and theft losses also qualify. So do health insurance and other medical costs for self-employed taxpayers.

MARGINAL VS. EFFECTIVE TAX BRACKETS

The tax bracket that you are in as the result of the last dollars you earned is called your *marginal tax bracket*. It is different from your *effective tax bracket*. Your effective tax bracket is the tax percentage rate you pay when compared to your total income. For example: A married couple with a combined income of $100,000 might be in a marginal federal tax bracket of 25 percent and a state tax bracket of 8 percent—a combined bracket of 33 percent.

However, if you have thousands of dollars in deductions and exemptions (mortgage interest, charitable contributions, dependents at home), your taxable income is that much less. The $100,000 couple in the previous paragraph may have $20,000 in deductions and exemptions. This couple's taxable income thus drops to $80,000.

In this example, the couple might pay federal income tax of only 10 percent on the first $15,650 (which equals $1,565), 15 percent from $15,650 to $63,700 (which equals $7,208), and 25 percent on the remaining $16,300 (which equals $4,075) for a total federal tax of $12,848. Added on top of that would be the state income tax. (In the United States, forty-one out of fifty states have a state income tax with rates averaging 6.3 percent in their highest brackets—see Figure B.1 in Appendix B.) Let's assume this couple paid $5,000 in state tax on their taxable income of $80,000. The total federal and state tax paid would be about $18,000. That is only 18 percent of the couple's $100,000 gross income—the *effec-*

tive tax bracket. But the *marginal tax bracket* might still be 33 percent. (By the way, these assumptions do not include FICA—Social Security taxes—or Medicare. Those taxes are added on top of federal and state income tax in the amount of 7.65 percent, matched by the employer for another 7.65 percent.)

When you want to know the actual benefit of a new tax deduction, you should calculate it using your *marginal* tax rate rather than your effective tax rate. For example, if you deduct $15,000 of mortgage interest, it reduces your taxable income because the $15,000 comes off the last dollars you earn. In this example you might actually save 33.3 percent of $15,000, or $5,000, of otherwise payable income tax that you would not have saved without the deduction.

Here is a simple rule: If you want to calculate the true tax savings achieved from a deduction, you should always use the *marginal* tax rate, multiplied by the amount of the deduction. This is always true unless other deductions and exemptions have already taken your gross income below the next lower threshold. (In that case, you may want to use the next lower tax rate to calculate the value of a new deduction.)

Your tax preparer may tell you when you are on the verge of jumping to the next higher tax bracket—in other words, when your taxable income is about to cross the threshold from 15 to 25 percent, or from 25 to 28 percent on federal tax. Don't let this upset you. Not all your income will be taxed at the higher rate—only the dollars earned in excess of each tax threshold.

Millions of people also use software programs like Quicken, Microsoft Money, Turbo Tax (from Quicken), or TaxCut from H&R Block, as well as online calculators, which can help you determine your tax bracket and other key elements that go into a tax return. To remind yourself about marginal and effective rates, consider *marginal* to be the *more meaningful and more memorable* rate.

(For a free, complimentary current-tax-year Federal Tax Rate Schedule for single, married [filing jointly or separately], or head of household taxpayers that also contains other valuable information such as personal exemption amounts, visit www.MissedFortune .com/TaxSchedules. You may also view and download a copy of the current state individual income tax rates for all fifty states at the same Web site.)

Whether or not you use popular software to keep track of your income and expenses, sometimes it pays to invest in a good CPA to assist you. I believe a good, aggressive CPA or tax preparer is one who finds not gray areas but legitimate deductions. Often people stumble across a tax strategy that may apply to them, perhaps in a newspaper or magazine article. They pick up the phone and call their accountant: "Hey I just read about this tax change/deduction/exemption/strategy. Can I do this?"

"Yep, you sure can."

"Well, why didn't you tell me about it?"

"You never asked!" The truth is, there are plenty of parachutes that professionals are aware of, yet sometimes they become too busy to watch out for what's best for all their clients.

DO YOU LET UNCLE SAM HOLD ON TO YOUR SAVINGS?

When I review clients' tax returns, I am always struck by how many people wind up getting tax refunds of thousands of dollars, year after year. These people overpay on their withholding taxes. Are you doing the same thing?

People who do this say, "This is our forced saving account." They look forward to a refund check after April so they can splurge on a vacation or a new spring outfit. Such an "unthinking" approach drives me a little crazy.

Why? It's because you are lending Uncle Sam money for up to an entire year, without getting any interest on it. If you owed the IRS money beyond April 15, you would pay interest charges and a penalty until you fork over the money you owe. Yet if the IRS owes you money, you don't get a nickel in interest.

Doesn't it make more sense to pocket more money from each paycheck than to give Uncle Sam the use of your money in non-interest-bearing overpayments? If you received a refund last year or the year before, it is time to adjust your withholding tax so you can keep more of your earnings. I urge you to visit your employer's human resources department or accountant and ask to review your W-4. That's the Employee's Withholding Allowance Certificate. Fill out a new personal allowances worksheet that accurately reflects the number of exemptions to which you are entitled. The more exemptions you have, the less money is deducted from each paycheck.

Here's what *not* to do: Don't assume that if you have three dependents, you are limited to three exemptions plus yourself. That's just a guideline from Uncle Sam. Some people need to claim fewer exemptions so they are not hit with extra taxes come April 15, while others can claim more for withholding purposes.

If you are certain that you don't owe a certain amount in federal tax in a given year because of deductions and exemptions, by all means claim as many exemptions as necessary to pay only what you will owe. Your company's human resources department can help you make this determination.

WHAT INCOME IS SUBJECT TO TAXATION AND AT WHAT RATE?

There are three kinds of income that are taxed by the federal government:

- *Earned income*—the money you make for providing goods or services.
- *Passive income*—the money realized from passive financial activities, such as rental income from property or lease income.
- *Portfolio income*—money usually realized through interest and dividends paid on savings and investments.

Earned, passive, and portfolio income are all considered "ordinary income" and are taxed as such. Passive and portfolio income are not subject to FICA or Medicare tax, but earned income is.

Capital gains are taxed differently than ordinary income. If you sell an asset (usually stocks, bonds, mutual funds, and real estate) for more than you paid, a capital gain occurs. The difference between the original purchase price and the net sales price is considered the capital gain. It may be a short-term or a long-term capital gain.

Long-term capital gains tax rates apply only to assets held for more than twelve months. The maximum rate on long-term capital gains as of 2003 until 2010 is 15 percent (less for those whose regular income tax rate is less than 25 percent). The gain on a sale that results purely from depreciation from capital assets (real property) is "recaptured" and taxed at 25 percent.

I wish I could skip this brief survey of such yawn-inducing topics as tax brackets and taxable income, but you need to understand what you're paying taxes on before you dive in the refreshing waters of tax-free wealth accumulation. Perhaps this next chart (Figure 5.2) will be the eye-opener you need. It shows how money can grow exponentially.

The first column shows each period over twenty periods. The next column shows what happens when you start with a dollar and the result doubles every period tax-free. The third column shows how a similar dollar plods along even when the result doubles every period but is taxed as earned, assuming a 33 percent tax bracket.

TAX-FREE OR TAXED AS YOU GO ALONG?

Your eyes are not deceiving you. That solitary bill with George Washington's picture on it doubles to $2 in the second period. The sum grows to $32 after five periods, $1,024 after ten periods, $32,768 after fifteen periods, and over $1 million after period twenty. But if it were taxed, the same buck would be only $1.67 in period two, $12.86 in five periods, $165 and change in ten periods,

| Fig. 5.2 | A DOLLAR DOUBLING EVERY PERIOD FOR 20 PERIODS TAX FREE VERSUS A DOLLAR DOUBLING EVERY PERIOD FOR 20 PERIODS TAXED AS EARNED* |

Periods	Tax Free	Taxed as Earned
	$1	$1.00
1	$2.00	$1.67
2	$4.00	$2.78
3	$8.00	$4.63
4	$16.00	$7.72
5	$32.00	$12.86
6	$64.00	$21.43
7	$128.00	$35.72
8	$256.00	$59.54
9	$512.00	$99.23
10	$1,024.00	$165.38
11	$2,048.00	$275.64
12	$4,096.00	$459.39
13	$8,192.00	$765.66
14	$16,384.00	$1,276.09
15	$32,768.00	$2,126.82
16	$65,536.00	$3,544.70
17	$131,072.00	$5,907.84
18	$262,144.00	$9,846.40
19	$524,288.00	$16,410.67
20	$1,048,576.00	$27,351.11

$100,000 COMPOUNDING AT 8% FOR 30 YEARS TAX FREE
VERSUS
$100,000 COMPOUNDING AT 8% FOR 30 YEARS TAXED AS EARNED*

End of Year	Tax-Free	Taxed as Earned
0	$100,000.00	$100,000.00
5	$146,932.81	$129,666.90
10	$215,892.50	$168,135.06
15	$317,216.91	$218,015.52
20	$466,095.71	$282,693.98
25	$684,847.52	$366,560.53
30	$1,006,265.69	$475,307.69

*assuming a tax bracket of 33.3%

$2,126 and change in fifteen periods, and $27,351 after twenty periods. In other words, $1 million is achieved in a tax-free environment, but in a taxable environment at a 33.3 percent tax rate, the end result is not one-third less, it represents only about 2.7 percent of what it could have grown to.

You may say, "But, my money isn't doubling very fast, so is there going to be that much of a difference?" Please study the bottom third of Figure 5.2. This illustrates a beginning balance of $100,000 growing at 8 percent interest compounding annually, tax-free versus taxed-as-earned. Notice that over a thirty-year period, the tax-free accumulation is more than double the taxed-as-earned accumulation. A tax-free retirement resource can be 100 percent better from age 55 or 65 for a thirty-year period up until age 85 or 95.

Which column would you rather be in? That's a rhetorical question, obviously. Now, it is time to learn how to position money so *that it can grow in a tax-free environment rather than a taxed-as-earned one*—because that's the road your retirement savings are headed until you depart from the tax-heavy road of qualified plans.

CRAWL, WALK, JOG—OR SPRINT: YOUR SAVINGS OPTIONS

At what pace do you want your money to grow? Would you prefer it to crawl, walk, jog, or sprint toward your retirement goal? Metaphorically speaking, American taxpayers have these basic options for the pace of savings. How those savings are *taxed* makes a huge difference in the pace, and thus in the amount you wind up with for your golden years.

Whenever you work to earn money, it is subject to income taxation. When you put your money to work, you can structure a savings plan that is taxable, tax-deferred, or tax-free. When you borrow money, you can use tax-advantaged strategies that can make your money perform better through safe, positive leverage.

Let's start with money you have earned by working. If you put this money in traditional savings accounts and investments, each of these dollars is taxed right off the bat, so you are using 66.66-cent dollars (if you are in the 33.33 percent tax bracket). If you put this money in qualified retirement accounts, the IRS allows you to use pre-tax dollars, or you get to deduct the contribution from your gross income. This means you are using 100-cent dollars.

CRAWL TOWARD RETIREMENT

Your first option is to save or invest after-tax dollars that you earned in investments that are taxed, as interest is earned, dividends are paid, or capital gains are realized. I'm going to call this option the *crawl*.

What kinds of savings come under this option? Typically, these include passbook savings or interest-bearing checking accounts, money market accounts, and certificates of deposit. Also in this category are nonqualified mutual funds, stocks, bonds, and even some real estate investments. The dividends, interest, capital gains, or rental income you make on nonqualified investments are taxed as earned or realized.

The tax liability due on the increase is either on income categorized as portfolio income (interest and dividends) or passive income (rents and leases). Capital gains tax, remember, is calculated at a lower rate than income tax and is not payable until you realize the gain by selling the asset with a profit over the initial cost or basis.

Depending on the rate of return, it may take ten or even fifteen years before you break even with what you have to earn or allocate when using 66.6-cent after-tax dollars on the front end and paying tax on the increase as you go. That's a long wait for a Boomer.

An example of this crawl for savings is illustrated in Figure 5.3. For the sake of simplicity, in this example as in the ones that follow, I use the same numbers. I assume that you have a cumulative total of $300,000 at the very start as a one-time lump sum, that you are in a typical marginal tax bracket of 33.3 percent, and that you will earn 7.2 percent on your investments.

Fig. 5.3	$300,000 OF CUMULATIVE GROSS INCOME ALLOCATED TO LONG-TERM SAVINGS

OPTION 1:

Invest After-Tax Dollars (66.66 Cents in a 33.33% Tax Bracket) in Financial Instruments Earning 7.2% That Are Taxed as Earned

Gross: $300,000
  - [$100,000]   Less: 33.3% Tax
    $200,000   Net to Invest

Year	Gross Interest Earned [1]	Tax Liability at 33.33% [2]	Net Interest Earned [3]	Year End Balance [4]
1	$14,400.00	$4,800.00	$9,600.00	$209,600.00
2	$15,091.20	$5,030.40	$10,060.80	$219,660.80
3	$15,815.58	$5,271.86	$10,543.72	$230,204.52
4	$16,574.73	$5,524.91	$11,049.82	$241,254.34
5	$17,370.31	$5,790.10	$11,580.21	$252,834.54
6	$18,204.09	$6,068.03	$12,136.06	$264,970.60
7	$19,077.88	$6,359.29	$12,718.59	$277,689.19
8	$19,993.62	$6,664.54	$13,329.08	$291,018.27
9	$20,953.32	$6,984.44	$13,968.88	$304,987.15
10	$21,959.07	$7,319.69	$14,639.38	$319,626.53

Convert to Annual Income:

$319,626.53   10 Year Total Account Value
x   7.2%   Annual Interest Income
$23,013.11   Annual Taxable Income
[$7,671.04]   Less: Annual Tax Liability at 33.3%
$15,342.07   **Net Spendable Annual Income**

If you choose the crawl option, above, you began with a total of $300,000. Since this came from gross income you received by working, you had to pay tax on the front end of $100,000 (33.3 percent). That left you with $200,000 to save or invest. From the rule of 72, you know that if you earn 7.2 percent interest, your account will double in ten years. However, if you must pay tax on your yearly increase, you end up with a net after ten years of only $319,626.53. After ten years, you decide to begin taking out your annual interest earnings to supplement other income. If you keep earning 7.2 percent taxable interest, you have $23,013 of annual interest income. But you have to pay the 33.3 percent tax on that interest income every year, or $7,671. So you realize a net of only $15,342 in spendable annual income.

Now you know why I call this the crawl option. It's discouraging to see such a slow pace on your hard-earned money. In my opinion, this is the worst way to save and invest. Yet it is the most common method used in the United States.

WALK WITH TAX-DEFERRED SAVINGS

In the second option, you can save or invest after-tax dollars in investments that accumulate tax-deferred, but you must pay taxes on the gain when later realized. This is a bit faster, but it is still only a *walk*.

Typical investments in this category include real estate that is not leveraged and perhaps some stock or mutual fund shares for which there are no dividends, but grow only through unrealized capital gains until the asset is sold. Nonqualified deferred annuities also are in this category. An example using the same $300,000 lump sum is shown in Figure 5.4.

Once again, you start with a net after taxes of 33.3 percent of $200,000 (66.6-cent after-tax dollars). But taxes on the gain from the investment are deferred. Thus, $200,000 doubles to $400,000 at 7.2 percent over ten years. If you now realize your profit by selling—as you would if the investment were a stock with no dividends—you may owe $30,000 in capital gains tax on the extra $200,000 that you made. Assuming that the capital gains tax stays at 15 percent, you would be left with a net of $370,000.

If this were now invested in an account earning 7.2 percent taxable interest, it would generate an interest income of $26,640 each year for as long as you wish. However, with a tax liability each year on that interest in the amount of $8,880 (at 33.3 percent) you still would realize a net spendable income of only $17,760. A bit more than a crawl, but still a slow walk, indeed.

If you had put the original $200,000 into a nonqualified de-

Fig. 5.4   **$300,000 OF CUMULATIVE GROSS INCOME**
ALLOCATED TO LONG-TERM SAVINGS

OPTION 2:

**Invest After-Tax Dollars (66.66 Cents in a 33.33% Tax Bracket)
in Financial Instruments That Are Tax Deferred**

Gross: $300,000
     - [$100,000]   Less: 33.33% Tax
        $200,000   Net to Invest

$200,000 Growing at 7.2% for 10 Years = $400,000

Capital Gain Example:

$400,000	10 Year Total Account Value
[$30,000]	Less: Capital Gain Tax of 15%
$370,000	Net Balance to Re-Invest
x 7.2%	Annual Interest Income
$26,640	Annual Taxable Income
- [$8,880]	Less: Annual Tax Liability at 33.3%
$17,760	**Net Spendable Annual Income**

Non-Qualified Annuity Example:

$400,000	10 Year Total Account Value
x 7.2%	Annual Interest Income
$28,800	Annual Taxable Income
- [$9,600]	Less: Annual Tax Liability at 33.3%
$19,200	**Net Spendable Annual Income**

---

ferred annuity and it generated 7.2 percent annually in interest income, the gross annual interest would be $28,800 ($400,000 × 7.2 percent). This income would be fully taxable, because annuities receive LIFO (last in, first out) tax treatment. I'll explain this in Chapter 11. You pay a tax of $9,600 each year (at 33.3 percent), which gives you a net spendable income of $19,200. You're still on the slow track.

JOG WITH PRE-TAX SAVINGS

You can save or invest 100-cent pre-tax or tax-deductible dollars in investments that accumulate tax-deferred. But later, when you use the money, it is fully taxable, including the basis you invested. You will pick up the pace somewhat with these types of investments. In this category are traditional IRAs, 401(k)s, and other qualified plans. *This is jogging with the wind at your back at the start of a race.*

Fig. 5.5   **$300,000 OF CUMULATIVE GROSS INCOME ALLOCATED TO LONG-TERM SAVINGS**

OPTION 3:

Invest Pre-Tax or Tax-Deductible Dollars in Financial Instruments That Are Tax-Deferred and Then Later Are Fully Taxable

Gross: $300,000
            [$0]   No Tax
        $300,000   Net to Invest

$300,000 Growing at 7.2% for 10 Years = $600,000

Lump Sum Distribution Example:

$600,000   10 Year Total Account Value
- [200,000]   Less: Tax of 33.33%
$400,000   **Net After-Tax Value**

Interest Only Example:

$600,000   10 Year Total Account Value
x   7.2%   Annual Interest Income
   43,200   Annual Taxable Income
- [14,400]   Less: Annual Tax Liability at 33.33%
$28,800   **Net Spendable Annual Income**

As this option shows (Figure 5.5), you get to use 100-cent dollars. So the full $300,000 can be invested on the front end. This investment doubles to $600,000 at 7.2 percent interest over ten years. Unfortunately, if you now withdraw the money, you have to pay tax on the full $600,000. If you are still in a 33.3 percent tax bracket, you net only $400,000 ($600,000 − $200,000 = $400,000). If you decide instead to withdraw your annual interest earnings (that is, 7.2 percent each year) as income each year thereafter, your investment generates $43,200 of taxable income, leaving you a net of $28,800 after tax ($43,200 less 33.3 percent).

TAKE ANOTHER JOG WITH SAVINGS TAX-FREE ON THE BACK END

In this option (Figure 5.6), you can save or invest after-tax dollars in investments that accumulate tax-free and also use the money tax-free later, including the gain you made. You will keep up the same pace with these types of investments, which include Roth IRAs and insurance contracts that are properly structured and used.

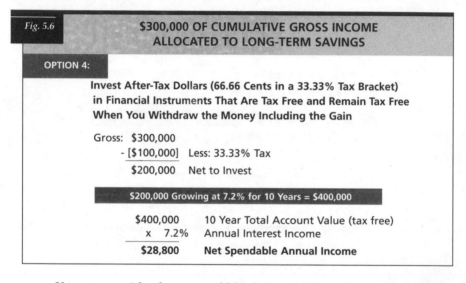

Fig. 5.6	$300,000 OF CUMULATIVE GROSS INCOME ALLOCATED TO LONG-TERM SAVINGS

OPTION 4:

Invest After-Tax Dollars (66.66 Cents in a 33.33% Tax Bracket) in Financial Instruments That Are Tax Free and Remain Tax Free When You Withdraw the Money Including the Gain

Gross: $300,000
- [$100,000] Less: 33.33% Tax
  $200,000   Net to Invest

$200,000 Growing at 7.2% for 10 Years = $400,000

$400,000   10 Year Total Account Value (tax free)
x   7.2%   Annual Interest Income
$28,800   **Net Spendable Annual Income**

You start with the same $300,000, which nets you the same $200,000 after taxes (66.6-cent dollars). You put this in an investment that is tax-free during the accumulation phase. As before, the $200,000 doubles to $400,000 at 7.2 percent interest over ten years. However, you now also get to enjoy the gain and income it can generate tax-free. Thus the $400,000 earning 7.2 percent annually gives you a tax-free net spendable income of $28,800 per year indefinitely.

In this case you are jogging with the wind at your back at the end *of the race.*

"But the two jogs wind up in a dead heat!" you say. That's right. All things being equal, there is *no* difference between trying to forge ahead with tax-free savings on the back end, or starting out with pre-tax savings on the front end. Given a choice, I would assume taxes are going to shoot higher later, especially if I accumulate a decent nest egg. Therefore I would choose to have my money tax-free during the harvest years of my life.

But you can do even better. You can sprint—with 100-cent dollars on the front *and* back ends.

SPRINT TOWARD FINANCIAL FREEDOM

In my fifth option (Figure 5.7), you can use 100-cent dollars because of indirect tax deductions that can be created using specific strategies addressed in Chapters 6, 7, and 8. You can also enjoy tax-free accumulation and tax-free use of the money using the investment vehicles explained in Chapters 11 and 12. Not only that, but you can transfer any remaining funds to your heirs tax-free, if you use properly structured insurance contracts.

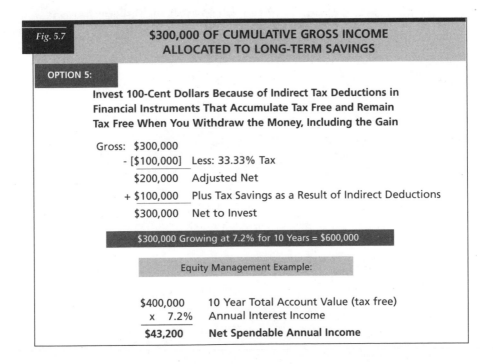

Fig. 5.7   **$300,000 OF CUMULATIVE GROSS INCOME ALLOCATED TO LONG-TERM SAVINGS**

OPTION 5:

Invest 100-Cent Dollars Because of Indirect Tax Deductions in Financial Instruments That Accumulate Tax Free and Remain Tax Free When You Withdraw the Money, Including the Gain

Gross:	$300,000	
	- [$100,000]	Less: 33.33% Tax
	$200,000	Adjusted Net
	+ $100,000	Plus Tax Savings as a Result of Indirect Deductions
	$300,000	Net to Invest

$300,000 Growing at 7.2% for 10 Years = $600,000

Equity Management Example:

$400,000	10 Year Total Account Value (tax free)
x 7.2%	Annual Interest Income
$43,200	**Net Spendable Annual Income**

As Figure 5.7 shows, you can use up to 100-cent dollars if you get indirect tax deductions due to mortgage interest offsets. If you succeed in offsetting all your contributions with this strategy, the full $300,000 would be available to save or invest on the front end. By using tax-advantaged capital accumulation vehicles, such as maximum-funded insurance contracts, you can have tax-favored treatment of all four phases—contribution, accumulation, distribution, and transfer—of your nonqualified retirement plan. The bottom line using the same initial amount, same period of time, and same interest rate results in $43,200 of net spendable income.

You might want to take a minute and look again at these five scenarios. Note that with the last one you're *sprinting* forward. You nearly *triple* the net spendable income that you might get if you chose to crawl with standard savings and investments. You more than *double* the net spendable income that you might get if you chose to walk. You get *50 percent more* net spendable retirement income than if you chose the familiar IRA or Roth IRA jog options.

Fig. 5.8

No question about it: Sprinting is a whole lot faster. It lands you in a better financial position than jogging, walking, and certainly crawling. Now, there is still the issue of matching benefits that some employers offer, which might crank up a slow jog. Remember, it is crucial to analyze each option open to you to determine whether it is wise to participate in a qualified plan.

There is no single, all-inclusive rule that dictates how you should handle various choices.

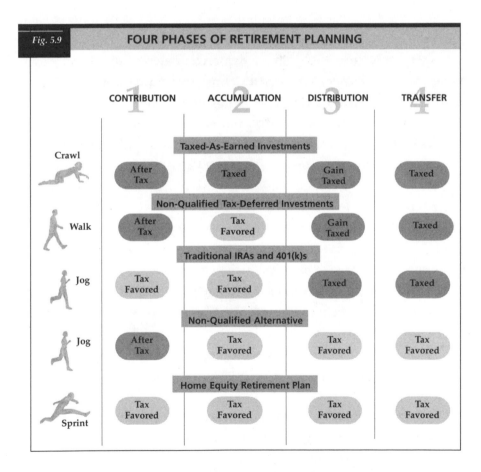

Fig. 5.9	FOUR PHASES OF RETIREMENT PLANNING			
	CONTRIBUTION	ACCUMULATION	DISTRIBUTION	TRANSFER
Crawl	**Taxed-As-Earned Investments**			
	After Tax	Taxed	Gain Taxed	Taxed
Walk	**Non-Qualified Tax-Deferred Investments**			
	After Tax	Tax Favored	Gain Taxed	Taxed
Jog	**Traditional IRAs and 401(k)s**			
	Tax Favored	Tax Favored	Taxed	Taxed
Jog	**Non-Qualified Alternative**			
	After Tax	Tax Favored	Tax Favored	Tax Favored
Sprint	**Home Equity Retirement Plan**			
	Tax Favored	Tax Favored	Tax Favored	Tax Favored

Figure 5.9 illustrates, again, the four different phases in retirement planning.

THE FOUR PHASES OF RETIREMENT PLANNING

The first phase—the first circle in each category—is when people contribute money for the future. It overlaps with the accumulation phase—the second circle—as it grows. Third is the withdrawal or distribution phase. (Some people go into "withdrawal" when they see the taxes they start to pay as they take money out during this period!) The transfer phase is when any remaining money transfers to your heirs when you die. That's where the estate tax might kick in. If you leave a substantial amount behind, your heirs could get hit with a major bill from Uncle Sam.

People have told me too many financial advisors don't focus on or simply seem to ignore the final two phases.

The third row of circles in the diagram represents the *jogging method that too many people wind up taking using traditional accounts such as IRAs and 401(k)s.* Here, you get tax-favored benefits on seed (the first two circles—contributions and accumulation). *But on the final two circles, the harvest, you get hit.* You spend years and years piling up the money on paper, but when you start to harvest it, you are forced to turn over about one-third of it to the government in income taxes.

The fourth row of circles represents those joggers *who use the Roth IRA* (even though it has strings attached) or certain nonqualified plans that invest in properly structured insurance contracts. *They pay the tax up front on their seed money, but pay no taxes on the accumulation or distribution phases.* They are also able to transfer what they leave behind to heirs in a tax-favored fashion.

The fifth row of circles represents those knowledgeable people *who can have it all.* Their retirement money zooms ahead tax-free as they contribute it, accumulate it, take distributions from it, and when it transfers to heirs.

What kind of retirement strategy would you like for your retirement money—a strategy with two, three, or all four phases receiving tax-favored treatment?

How much better is the sprint method versus the jog method to win the race? Let's say you accumulated $1,000,000 in your retirement nest egg, and it is earning 7.5 percent. You could pull out $75,000 a year and never deplete it, right? But what if you *need* a net of $75,000 a year to buy the necessities, visit the grandkids, play golf, or take an occasional cruise or trip? Remember, you might have to pull out 50 percent more in a 33.3 percent tax bracket to net the same amount as a tax-free investment. You might have to withdraw $112,500 a year out of your IRAs and 401(k)s, pay tax of $37,500 (one-third of $112,500), to net $75,000. At a withdrawal rate of $112,500 a year ($9,375 monthly), your $1,000,000 nest egg earning 7.5 percent would be totally drained (depleted) in fourteen years and eight months. You may very well outlive your money.

Under the sprint method, at the end of the race (during the harvest years), when you withdraw $75,000, you net $75,000 to spend, live, and enjoy. It doesn't affect your Social Security or Medicare benefits. If you lived another twenty years, based on a withdrawal of $75,000 a year from your $1 million nest egg, you would still have your principal of $1 million. If you lived to age 100, you might enjoy twenty more years of annual tax-free income— $75,000 a year times twenty years is an extra $1,500,000 of retirement resources that the joggers didn't get to enjoy.

To win the race toward financial independence, it is absolutely imperative that you pick up your retirement-planning pace to a sprint by optimizing all of your assets with the strategies I will further disclose. Other than that, I don't have any strong feelings on the subject!

THE INCREDIBLE SHRINKING IRA/401(K): A CASE STUDY

Louise and Stan Jones[*] are a couple from California who are both approaching the age of 60. They got married in 1976 and on the advice of the benefits administrators at the Fortune 500 companies that employed them, they began to stash pre-tax dollars into IRAs and 401(k)s.

---

[*]These fictional couples represent a combination of real-life families my associates and I have seen.

By putting away $6,000 at the end of each year for twenty years, Stan and Louise have contributed a total of $120,000 in their qualified plans by now. Over the past twenty years, their IRAs and 401(k)s have earned 7.2 percent interest. So their nest egg has grown to $250,000. To stay healthy and active, Stan and Louise will continue to work part-time until they are 70½. They will also both receive pensions that will pay a combined amount of $60,000 each year.

Let's assume they are in the 33.3 percent marginal tax bracket to keep the math simple. (In California, a married couple making between $63,700 and $128,500 a year filing a joint return are taxed at this rate based on 2007 income tax schedules.)

They look at the four phases of retirement planning diagram (Figure 5.9) and see the first two phases are tax-favored in their 401(k)s. This means they saved $2,000 a year in their 33.3 percent tax bracket—$40,000 of tax savings total on the contributions.

But tax-deferred is not as marvelous as tax-free. Why? *Because although they are both entitled to start withdrawing money from that nest egg, the minute they do so, they will get hit with income taxes that erase a large chunk of this money they plan to live on.* That third phase will see a large tax bite taken out of it.

Stan and Louise Jones would like to pull out their annual interest after ten more years. With no further contributions, their nest egg would then be worth $500,000. They would be able to draw out $36,000 each year. By paying 33.3 percent taxes on their retirement payout, how long will it take to give back the $40,000 they saved in taxes over twenty years on their contributions? In just three years and four months they will have paid back every dollar they saved during the contribution phase (33.3 percent tax on a $36,000 retirement plan distribution is $12,000 times three years and four months). All they did was postpone the pain of taxes, and their tax liability grew every year. When they withdraw their annual retirement income of $36,000, it will be added on top of any other income and will likely create an annual tax liability of $12,000, *result-ing in a net spendable income of just $24,000 a year.*

If you were in Stan and Louise's shoes, wouldn't you rather have a plan where not just the money you contribute and accumu-late is tax-favored, but so is the third phase—withdrawals? Let's continue the story taking a look at what their friends Susan and Sam Smith will do differently.

SOARING HIGH WITH SUSAN AND SAM SMITH

Sam and Susan Smith have decided *not* to follow the retirement-planning crowd like their co-workers and friends Stan and Louise Jones.

They, too, have accumulated $250,000 in their 401(k)s earning 7.2 percent and will have pensions paying them a combined amount of $60,000 a year at age 70. They live in a lovely house that they bought twenty years ago for $156,250. Their home is now worth $625,000, due to an average appreciation rate of 7.2 percent. They consult with an advisor who knows how to structure a Home Equity Retirement Plan using the strategies I favor.

The Jones and the Smith families each sell their homes and downsize to more accommodating homes worth $325,000 and second homes (vacation condos) for $300,000. In contrast to the Joneses, the Smiths do not pay cash for the homes, but instead pay a minimum down of 20 percent and finance the remainder ($500,000 between both properties) at 80 percent of the purchase price (mortgages of $260,000 and $240,000 respectively). Their mortgage interest rate is 7.2 percent. This will give the Smiths new interest-only mortgage payments of $1,560 and $1,440 per month ($36,000 per year), as well as a new tax deduction of $36,000 a year. They put their remaining $500,000 of equity from the sale of their house into a side fund earning an average of 7.2 percent.

Instead of waiting till 70½ to access money out of their 401(k)s, they decide to begin withdrawing $36,000 a year to cover their new house payments. By doing this, *the taxes they would normally have to pay on the 401(k) withdrawals are completely offset by their mortgage interest deduction*! At this rate, they will deplete their $250,000 of 401(k) funds (being credited with 7.2 percent interest in the process) over the next ten years (allowing them to withdraw a grand total of $360,000 tax-free)!

Wait a minute! Their entire 401(k) account is now gone! Well, that's actually a good thing because it doesn't end here. Remember that they put their $500,000 of home equity in a side fund earning 7.2 percent? Ten years later, that account is now worth $1,000,000. The Smiths can begin to draw the interest from that account in the amount of $72,000, pay the net after-tax mortgage payment of $24,000 a year, and end up with a net tax-free income of $48,000. (I'll show you in Chapter 12 how and why their retirement fund can be tax-free.) Compared to the Joneses' net after-tax annual income of $24,000, the Smiths have $48,000 (double) of net spendable income!

Sam and Susan are able to visit their children and grandchildren several times throughout the year, take them to their condo, and enjoy other family vacations. Occasionally they invite their friends the Jones family to join them, but most of the time the Joneses sit home wondering how the Smiths can afford twice as much.

Weren't they on the same playing field just ten years earlier?

REMEMBER THIS:

- Do you expect income taxes to increase or decrease? Understand the implications of higher taxes in your golden years.
- Will Uncle Sam take a big bite out of your retirement savings? Consider how much less you will collect when a qualified plan is reduced by taxes—and how more spendable income a nonqualified plan will give you when you pay no tax on your harvest, or distributions.
- Judge the pace you are on in saving for retirement—are you *crawling* by paying taxes on the contribution and accumulation phases of your savings that you will use in retirement?
- Are you *walking* toward retirement by having taxes deferred, or *jogging* by making contributions to qualified plans like IRAs or 401(k)s, or *sprinting* by using 100-cent tax-advantaged dollars and withdrawing retirement income tax-free?
- Investigate whether you can create savings that allow you to *sprint* toward financial independence by building a nonqualified retirement plan with tax-favored treatment on the contribution, accumulation, distribution, and even transfer of your retirement savings.

CHAPTER 6

Harness the Power of Safe, Liquid Equity

How Tax-Deductible Debt Works in Your Favor

WHETHER OR NOT YOU HAVE a pension or another retirement plan, you probably regard your home as your most valuable asset. More than three-quarters of all boomers own a home,* and many of you have seen the value of that home skyrocket in value in recent years.

But what if catastrophe strikes your home?

Imagine you lived in New Orleans when Hurricane Katrina ravaged the city. You were relocated to Baton Rouge or Houston, and you were waiting anxiously to find out when you could reenter the city and move back home. As you stared at the TV, you watched a helicopter shot of your neighborhood with floodwaters up to the roofline.

Would you prefer that your house was paid for, free and clear of a mortgage with all of your equity trapped in it—or would you rather have a mortgage with the equity removed and parked safely

---

*http://www.federalreserve.gov/pubs/bulletin/2006/financesurvey.pdf.

in an account elsewhere, which you could access with a phone call or an electronic fund transfer?

Or imagine you were the mayor of Port Arthur, Texas, when Hurricane Rita smashed through the town. In the chaos, a gas line snapped or some other event caused a fire to break out and your house burned down to the ground. This actually happened. An MSNBC reporter wondered how the mayor, having lost his house in the aftermath of the storm, was able to keep his composure. In the emotion of the moment he expressed that the sad thing was they had just paid off the entire mortgage.

Notice that he did not say: "Whew, I'm glad we just paid it off." Just the opposite! He knew his money had just gone up in flames. In another interview he explained what he would say to his wife, "Dear, we just paid it off, but we just lost it."

It doesn't have to be a calamity that makes the national news. A flood rushed through southwestern Utah in January of the same year and dozens of homes were swept downstream or damaged by the Santa Clara River. Several of those homes were paid off. Those owners lost everything except what they could physically grab and run out with. I assure you, they could not grab their home equity in that harried moment and run out with it. There was no flood insurance in force at the time on those homes. The other homes were mortgaged. Victims made statements like, "Financially, we could have sold the house the week before for about $250,000. In our dark moment of humor we said, 'Well, we didn't lose everything. We still have our mortgage.' That house was an investment as part of our retirement."

In retrospect, having a mortgage—the equity separated—was a good thing—providing accessibility to emergency funds. Not only did those people have cash that was not tied up in their house that went downstream, but it allowed them to get into a new house quicker. In all the cases I'm aware of, the mortgage company forgave the mortgage.

Were the mortgage companies required to do that? No. But

their collateral was downstream. Think about it. Who was safer, in each of these tragedies? The people who were "free and clear" with no mortgage, or those who, even though they suffered the loss of their homes, had at least some of their home equity safe, liquid and readily accessible?

Whether your house is located in Laguna Hills, California, during a mud slide or smack dab in the middle of the country during a Kansas tornado, *I believe it is better to have your equity removed and repositioned in a safe, liquid account rather than trapped in your house.* I certainly hope no one reading this has to go through a natural disaster to learn what I am about to teach: the power of safe, positive leverage to provide liquidity.

PAY INTEREST ON YOUR MORTGAGE, NOT YOUR CREDIT CARDS

In Chapter 4, I noted that leverage means using a small amount of money to own and control a much greater asset. That's what most people do when they buy a house. They use a small amount as a down payment; in return they get the use of a house that may appreciate tremendously in value.

Although as we've said leverage may sound like a drag because it involves an expense—the interest you pay to use the money you borrowed to own your house—in reality, mortgage interest, just like the drag in the laws of aeronautics, is a crucial element in making your finances fly. Paying interest does not just enable you to live in a wonderful home. It can actually catapult you into realms of greater net worth, create financial independence, and give you an exponentially greater retirement income.

Shortly, I'm going to show you exactly how this happens. However, let's start with three facts that everyone needs to fully grasp.

- Money borrowed by a taxpayer, such as a home mortgage, is *not* subject to tax.

- The interest on money borrowed against property (a house, a rental property, a second mortgage, or a home equity loan) is *usually tax-deductible*.
- Money borrowed on a personal credit card usually is *not deductible*, and the interest rate ends up being almost always higher—sometimes twice the rate or more—than what is charged on mortgage interest.

I divide interest into two categories:

- *Preferred interest* is tax-deductible interest expense. The interest that you pay on your home mortgage (or on a home equity loan or line of credit) is money that you subtract from your annual income if you itemize deductions on your taxes.
- *Nonpreferred interest* is the kind that you cannot write off on your taxes. Typically it builds up as credit card debt.

Credit cards have their place in our modern society. But every survey of consumer spending indicates that credit card debt too often gets out of hand. When you hear pundits denouncing Americans' debt-happy culture, they are often referring to spenders who max out their credit cards and then find it hard to pay down their balances. Sometimes, those wagging a finger about debt represent banks and other lenders who nevertheless love to shower you with "free" credit or debit cards (Figure 6.1).

In my strategies, I urge you to eliminate nonpreferred debt. I recommend that you pay down the balance on all your credit cards, and then only use them for conservation, not consumption. (Otherwise, take a pair of scissors and cut them up!)

But not all debt is wrong or undesirable. Preferred debt that lowers your tax bracket can be useful. You can use preferred debt—especially a home mortgage—to dramatically boost your net worth. I'll prove to you that this is not a dangerous strategy, but a smart one. In fact, you will be following the lead of some of the most successful wealth machines ever created: banks.

Fig. 6.1

Sometimes, those wagging a finger about debt represent banks and other lenders who nevertheless love to shower you with "free" credit or debit cards.

MORTGAGE INTEREST IS YOUR FRIEND, NOT YOUR FOE

Let's look at how you can make mortgage interest lighten your tax burden. If you are a married couple and you make $78,000 a year, but you pay $15,000 a year in interest on your home mortgage, your taxable income declines to $63,000. If you are in the 33.3 percent combined federal and state marginal tax bracket, you save $5,000 of the $15,000 that you otherwise would pay in tax.

Conversely, nonpreferred interest is nondeductible interest expense. If you make $78,000 a year but your home is free and clear, and you pay $4,000 in interest a year on your car loan and/or your credit card balances, *you cannot deduct this kind of interest.* Your income remains at $78,000.

However, when you borrow money that meets the test of

preferred debt, because the interest is deductible, the true cost of borrowing the money is calculated after tax. For instance, in a 33.3 percent tax bracket, borrowing money at 7.5 percent deductible interest really costs you 5 percent (one-third less).

That means 33.3 percent of your mortgage interest is what you save in tax by getting it back from the IRS (either in a refund or in owing less in tax than you otherwise would). Similarly, if you borrow at 9 percent preferred interest, your true cost is only 6 percent; 6 percent deductible interest is really only 4 percent.

Compare that with nonpreferred credit card interest, which typically is considerably higher than mortgage interest. The chart below (Figure 6.2) puts the example I just described in graphic terms:

Fig. 6.2	PREFERRED VS. NON-PREFERRED INTEREST EXPENSE		
		A	B
• Income		$78,000	$78,000
• Non-Preferred Interest		-15,000	0
		$63,000	$78,000
• Preferred Interest		0	-15,000
• Available Before Taxes		$63,000	$63,000
• Taxable Income		$78,000 ⟳	$63,000
Difference in Taxable Income $15,000			
Difference in TAX SAVINGS $5,000*			

*assuming a 33.3% marginal tax bracket

Those of you who do your own tax preparation might have deducted mortgage interest for dozens of years without realizing what a break Uncle Sam gives you. But it is there, in black and white. If a tax preparer or a CPA fills out the forms for you, those professionals may never point this out because they think you understand the concept. However, I have found that it is not always clear to homeowners.

To put this in the dry language of accountants: A homeowner can deduct mortgage interest expense on Schedule A of an itemized tax return on loans up to $100,000 over and above acquisition indebtedness on a qualified residence. (This is true unless the loan proceeds are used to increase the acquisition indebtedness by doing home improvements.)*

Your primary residence (the one you claim as your principal residence) qualifies for this special treatment under the tax code. So does one other residence you may own, as long as you declare it as a residence. It might be your vacation home or condo, but it can also be your motor home, camp trailer, or boat, if it qualifies.

The money that you borrow in acquiring, constructing, or substantially improving any qualified residence is acquisition indebtedness. The limit for deductibility on Schedule A is the interest on up to $1 million of acquisition debt. It declines if you pay down your mortgage. Even though acquisition indebtedness may begin as the amount you borrowed when you bought, built, or fixed up your house, it declines as you pay down your mortgage.**

Home equity loans and lines of credit may also qualify as tax-deductible as long as you follow IRS guidelines. Any borrowed money (other than acquisition indebtedness) that you secure with a qualified residence may be deductible according to the IRS, as long as the total amount you are claiming as debt does not exceed the fair market value of that main home minus the acquisition indebtedness. There is a ceiling here, too. The total home equity debt that would qualify for deductible interest cannot exceed $100,000 per married couple, or $50,000 per person if you file separate returns.

---

*IRS Code Section 163 defines a qualified residence, acquisition indebtedness, and home equity indebtedness.

**Here is an example. If you bought a home for $250,000 and financed 80 percent of the purchase price, your original acquisition indebtedness would be $200,000. If you paid down the mortgage to a balance of $100,000, your acquisition indebtedness would be only $100,000.

Since home refinancing becomes so popular when interest rates are low, let's look at an example. Let's say your home appreciated in value to $500,000 since its original purchase, and your original $250,000 mortgage was paid down to $200,000. If you refinance the home with a new mortgage of $400,000 and use the equity for purposes other than home improvements, you should deduct interest on only $300,000 ($100,000 above the acquisition indebtedness that you reduced to $200,000). You can reestablish new acquisition indebtedness that qualifies for deductibility if you sell your home and buy a new one and use a mortgage for most of or the entire purchase price of the home.

The IRS Code does not limit how you use home equity loans or lines.[*] Unfortunately, some people interpret this as a license to borrow and spend, which I think is the wrong interpretation. In the summertime, I see a lot of home equity lines of credit flitting around Utah lakes—boats, Jet Skis, and so on. Again, I would urge you to borrow to conserve, not to consume. Either way, since tax law changes frequently, it is imperative that you understand these matters when you begin to act on the strategies I suggest. You should always check with your tax advisor to confirm what kind and how much interest you are permitted to claim.

My goal is to illustrate that there are many borrowing avenues you can take to reduce the amount of your income subject to taxation. It is advantageous to use an interest-only mortgage and accumulate the excess—the amount that would have gone to reducing the principal of the loan—in a separate, liquid side fund. With an interest-only mortgage, your payment is a smaller amount than you would pay on a conventional mortgage. The same would be true when using an Option ARM (an adjustable-rate mortgage, which will be explained in detail in Chapter 8), where you can choose to pay less than the interest accrued each month. This is often called a negative amortization loan, but I

---

[*]IRS Code Section 163(h)(3), Temporary Regulation 1.163-8T(m)(3).

prefer to call it a deferred-interest loan. But you must establish a disciplined system to set aside the savings in payments. By conserving rather than consuming the difference, you will actually accumulate enough money in a conservative side fund to be able to pay off or offset an increasing mortgage balance sooner than using an amortized loan.

Sometimes tax advisors caution borrowers against taking out interest-only or option ARM loans, saying they are riskier than conventional loans. They argue that while you may initially pay a lower monthly amount for the first few years, you may be faced with much higher payments later on. I will prove that interest-only and even deferred-interest loans can pave the way toward "paying off" your home on your balance sheet sooner by having enough cash to cover your mortgage debt. Also, they are flexible—they can be converted or refinanced to a traditional amortized mortgage at any time.

Personally, I usually just refinance every few years. Every time I refinance my home with a newer, larger mortgage, I actually get on schedule to pay off the newer, higher mortgage faster than I was going to have the money accumulated to pay off the older, lower mortgage. But I never, ever physically pay off my house, because I consider it already paid for on my balance sheet. I'll explain a bit later. The point is, *I am a great advocate for establishing the highest amount of acquisition indebtedness possible,* by paying little or no cash down when you sell a home and buy a new one. My strategy maximizes your deductible interest. It also lets you manage your equity for dramatic results. You'll see why soon. (For more detailed information about equity management, please refer to my previous books, *Missed Fortune* and *Missed Fortune 101.*)

The bottom line on deductibility is that with very little cash out of your own pocket, you can leverage safely to achieve substantial rates of return, making up for lost time and maximizing the time you have left to prepare for retirement.

WHAT ABOUT CASH FLOW?

Here's a common complaint that I hear:

"I own my house free and clear. If I take out a mortgage, that means I suddenly have to find $3,000 a month to pay for it. I'm already saving for my kids' college education and for a new car, and I need money for food, clothing, the movies, the dry cleaners, and day-to-day living expenses. Where does that money come from?"

I hear this from members of the "Sandwich Generation," those Boomers who may still have older children in high school or college, but who also need to help aging parents cope with unexpected health-related expenses. (According to AARP, 35 percent of Boomers "have been or are responsible for the care of their elderly parents.[*]) This is the cash flow quandary. Let me ease your concerns right away.

If you have a qualified residence without any mortgage, you can get a mortgage that is structured so that you obtain enough cash to cover your payments. Since it is tax-deductible, a $3,000-per-month interest-only loan payment is not really $3,000—just subtract the tax savings and it is only $2,000 a month. Likewise a $1,200-per-month loan payment is really only $800 per month in a 33.3 percent marginal tax bracket.

If you already have a mortgage, you can switch from a fifteen- or thirty-year amortized loan to an interest-only or deferred-interest loan. Once you do this, you can possibly pull out $100,000, $200,000, or more of equity without increasing your net after-tax monthly payments. For example, a $300,000 fifteen-year amortized mortgage at 7.5 percent on a home valued at $500,000 would have a monthly payment of $2,781, but you get only about $625 of that paid by Uncle Sam in the form of tax savings. So the net out-of-pocket payment is about $2,156. If you sold that home and purchased a new one to reestablish acquisition indebtedness and took out a $500,000 mortgage (separating $200,000 more home equity)

---

*AARP, "Boomers Envision Retirement II," 2005.

with an interest-only mortgage at 7.5 percent, you would have a monthly payment of $3,125—but you would get about $1,042 of that paid by Uncle Sam in the form of tax savings. So the net out-of-pocket payment is only about $2,083—less than the payment on the $300,000 loan.

I will show that if you took the $200,000 of harvested equity and invested it in a conservative, liquid side fund, it could compound and grow to a sizable nest egg that could pay off (or make the full payments on) your new home's $500,000 mortgage faster than you would have paid off your old home's $300,000 mortgage.

"But I have to wait until next April, when I prepare my tax return, to realize the tax savings," you protest. "Where do I get the money now?"

You don't have to wait for next April. As I explained in Chapter 5, there is no reason to send your taxes early to Uncle Sam. To make sure you don't overpay the government, you can go to your payroll department and change your exemptions on your withholding form immediately (or you can pay less in quarterly estimated tax) because you will have a higher mortgage deduction. Remember, Uncle Sam pays no interest on the extra money you turn over. Once you change your withholding amount or your estimated payments, you get that money right away, in a weekly or monthly paycheck that is bigger because your exemptions are higher. In one action, you have freed up money to use in a smarter way.

"But I still have day-to-day living expenses. Where do I find the extra money?"

The answer is that my system involves not just taking out a more productive tax-deductible mortgage, but also immediately finding a place to put that money to work. Even if you don't, you can carve out a portion of the loan proceeds, park it in your checking account, and make your house payments from there for a few months while you get the rest of your financial ducks in a row. That's not always the smartest way to go about this, but for those of you who are concerned about coming up with a monthly payment, this is one way.

In most cases when I reposition clients' assets, people have other monthly loan payments that are not tax-deductible. If you are paying off an auto loan, or credit card debt, you can use the monthly payments you have just freed up to afford a higher mortgage payment immediately. *The key is to not run up the credit cards again. You want interest to work for you—not against you.*

In even a worst-case scenario, if necessary you can make the mortgage payments from a portion of the interest you earn on the equity you pulled out of your house. I will explain in detail how you can do all of this a little later.

HOW TO GET A TAX BREAK EVERY TWO YEARS

Many Boomers are beginning to think about downsizing from a large house to a smaller one once their children have left the nest. Others want to move closer to their adult children. America has experienced a nationwide surge in the appreciation of home values over the past two decades, so the sale of your current house could produce a very sizable cash bonus. In many cases, you can do this without worrying about triggering a major taxable event. You can make a handsome profit and pay no tax (or very little) on your capital gain.

In 1997, the government eliminated the rule requiring you to roll over any gain you made on the sale of your old home into a new home. You may not realize it (especially if you have lived in the same house for many years), but the new rules about selling your house offer you a great exemption.

Today, married couples are entitled to a $500,000 exemption ($250,000 for single taxpayers) on the gain that you make selling a principal residence. If you must sell because of a change in employment, health, or other unforeseen circumstances, you may be eligible even before two years have passed.

Those who have been keeping records of rollover gains on their old house can finally toss them out. Bear in mind that you need to know the *basis* in your current home. That's the purchase price, plus home improvement costs, minus any depreciation taken on the house. Your capital gain is calculated as the difference between the basis and the net sales price. From this sum you deduct your $500,000.

Some people think that to avoid capital gains tax, you must pour as much as possible of the cash you received from the sale of a previous residence into your new home. This is a myth. You do not need to put a dollar of equity from a former residence into your next home. I have never taken any equity from the sale of my former homes and invested it into a newer home—not even for a cash down payment.

NO MONEY DOWN

The phrase "no money down" sounds like a shady gimmick to some people. What I mean is that money may be required as a down payment, but it doesn't have to come out of your own pocket. It is the opposite. It's a good way to leverage your dollars using OPM, and build up the highest amount of acquisition indebtedness you can, so you have as big a tax deduction as possible.

Let me give you an example. My wife and I have bought and lived in several different homes in our thirty-three years of marriage. Never once did I put my own cash down on a house. Naturally, there was a cost (for the closing or title work) to buy a house without a cash down payment, but it was nominal. There are a variety of equity management strategies available to minimize your cash outlay when you purchase property. Rather than tie up equity unnecessarily, it makes sense to keep such equity in a liquid side fund that will maintain safety of principal and can earn a rate of return greater than the cost of using OPM. After all, how much interest does the mortgage company pay you on any down payment? Nothing! So why pay anything down out of your pocket?

There are various strategies you can use to buy property with little or no money down:

- If you can qualify for an FHA or VA loan, you might be able to pay a very low down payment or no down payment.
- If you have good credit and income to qualify, you can use an 80/20 loan arrangement, where you take out an 80 percent loan-to-value first mortgage, and simultaneously or shortly thereafter take out a 20 percent home equity loan.
- You might be able to purchase property by assuming the mortgage held by the seller.
- In a soft market, a seller with a lot of equity in a home might be amenable to self-finance your purchase or carry a contract.
- Another alternative is to lease a property with an option to buy. In such a case the seller collects "rent" monthly and possibly a bonus amount that goes toward the sales price.

As you will see in the next chapter, such strategies can work well for the seller, not just for you, the buyer. (Many books, videos, and audio programs are available that explain the details of buying property with no money down. For more information on buying a home without using any of your own cash, please refer to my first book, *Missed Fortune*, Chapter 13.)

LIQUIDITY, SAFETY, RATE OF RETURN

You are probably familiar with the precision of laser beams. When I speak at conferences in large assembly halls throughout the country, I often walk to the back of a room of 2,000 people and refer to a diagram on the screen at the front of the room using a laser pointer. The small laser dot is very precise, powerful, and recognizable. Likewise I have a precise, powerful, and recognizable test to determine if an investment is prudent. Its initials—LSRR (also pronounced "LASER")—represent:

- **L**iquidity
- **S**afety
- **R**ate of **R**eturn

Think of it as a powerful beam that precisely points you toward investments that are prudent as well as productive. I've found that LSRR also leads you down a "Lower Stress Retirement Road."

"Liquidity, safety, and rate of return" is a phrase I use over and over. These are the three tenets that a wise investor seeks at any stage of life. When you look at any investment, it makes good sense to apply the test of *liquidity, safety, rate of return*. Ask yourself these questions:

- Can I get my money back quickly and easily, even in tough times—is it liquid?
- How safe is my money—is it guaranteed or insured?
- Will my money grow and multiply substantially over time—is it earning a rate of return?

An investment that meets these criteria is a good investment. If it is also tax-advantaged, it becomes a great one. We all want the highest return at the lowest risk.

HOW WELL DOES YOUR BIGGEST INVESTMENT MEET THE "LASER" TEST?

Take a look at the features of the following investment, and tell me if, as a potential customer, you would be interested in putting a great deal of your savings into it:

- You can determine the amount of your monthly contribution and the length of time that contributions will continue.
- You can pay more than the minimum monthly contribution, but not less.
- If you try to pay less, the financial institution handling the investment keeps all of the previous contributions.
- The money invested is not liquid; it could take many months to put your hands on it in an emergency.
- The money invested is not safe from loss of principal.
- Each contribution made to the account results in less safety of the principal.
- The contributions that are deposited earn zero percent rate of return.
- Your income tax liability increases with each new contribution.
- When the investment is fully funded, there is no income paid to you.

The investment I just described deserves a thumbs-down from smart investors. I don't think you would put serious cash into it. Yet many of you already do! The investment I just described is a house with a traditional amortized mortgage.

A house with a traditional mortgage contains equity that is certainly not liquid. In a buyer's market, it might take you months, even years, to find a buyer offering you your asking price on your house. Is it safe? Ask the mayor of Port Arthur, or the people whose houses were washed away by Katrina. Anyone who had paid down their mortgage on those houses watched their savings float downstream. As for the rate of return, does your lender thank you for paying down the principal by paying you interest? Sorry—if you think the lender will give you anything for doing that, you're simply dreaming. If you think you sleep better at night with your house paid off, just be patient until I finish establishing my case through the next chapter. You probably won't sleep soundly until your equity is separated in a position of liquidity, safety, and earning a good rate of return. Remember—the rate of return on your equity trapped in your house is zero.

This usually prompts lots of shouts at seminars.

"Whoa! I'm from Encinitas, California, and we've been in a real estate sellers' market for years now! My $250,000 ranch house is now worth $1 million. Of course, I only get to collect that money when I sell, but I can have two buyers lined up tomorrow."

"Doug, the same is true for me—prices of houses in the Boston area just go in one direction, and that's up!"

"Hey, Boston is small potatoes compared to how real estate has shot up where I live in northern New Jersey."

My reply is: You may think you are safe. But so was your neighbor who kept funneling contributions into S&P 500 stocks for a decade starting in 1991. The luxury liner *Irrational Exuberance* started sinking a year before the 9/11 tragedy occurred and has been buffeted by stormy seas ever since. If there is a real estate bubble that might burst just around the corner, do you really want to have most of your money trapped in your house? If your home is worth $1 million, but the market softens to the point where you can get only $800,000 for it, I guarantee you will lose $200,000. Wouldn't you rather separate your equity when the house is worth $1 million in a liquid fund someplace else? I assure you that if your house value goes down, you won't lose that money if it is repositioned into an account that passes the LSRR test.

While you are thinking about that, consider this choice: You can keep storing your equity in your house and hope for the real estate bubble to continue, or you can remove it and invest it more wisely. You can keep putting yourself to work, or you can put your money to work. You can follow the crowd of real estate and stock market speculators, or you can do what banks and credit unions do to make a profit in good times and bad: borrow money at a lower rate and put it to work at a slightly higher rate.

(To learn more about the concepts in this chapter and those that will follow, I implore you to read and study my previous work, *Missed Fortune 101*. If you would like to listen to a free audio recording that summarizes what you will learn in my *Missed Fortune* books please go to www.MissedFortune.com/MF101Summary.)

REMEMBER THIS:

- The idea of paying extra principal on a mortgage is counterproductive; you are poised for greater gains and safety from unexpected setbacks when your equity is *separated* from your house.
- Mortgage interest is your friend, not your foe; do the math to figure how much you can adjust your reported income downward on your tax return by adding tax-deductible interest.
- Get rid of costly nonpreferred debt by paying off your credit cards and expand tax-deductible debt as often as every two years via a new home mortgage.
- Safe, positive leverage allows you to avoid the dangerous swings of a housing bubble and its aftermath, a burst bubble.
- The key to great retirement investing is to beam a "Laser" on your investments by finding those with the most liquidity, greatest safety, and highest rate of return.

CHAPTER 7

Learn How to Become Your Own Banker

Put Other People's Money to Work on Your Behalf

PICTURE YOURSELF AS THE PRESIDENT of a regional or national bank. At the annual meeting, you report to your stockholders that customers have kept an average of $100 billion deposited in your bank in the form of savings, money market accounts, and CDs for the last five years. You announce that this year you paid these depositors $5 billion in interest—but you *made* $12 billion this year because you have been investing the money at more favorable interest rates during the last five years, and the profits have compounded. The result this year is $7 billion of profit, and next year is projected to be even better!

Your stockholders are thrilled. They look at you as if you are the Warren Buffett of banks. Well, you don't need to have billions to become your own banker, or to be the Warren Buffett of your family.

There are four things people can do with their money:

- Spend it
- Lend it

- Own with it
- Give it away

If you borrow and lend rather than spend, you'll be ahead of the game, just like a bank is. A banker borrows at one rate and lends or invests to earn a higher rate. You can do the same thing.

Why does a bank or credit union pay you interest (and sometimes lure you into opening a new account with a toaster) when you hand over a deposit to them? Because while they are borrowing money from you, they know they can put that borrowed money to work earning an even greater rate of return.

Individuals who are not sophisticated in the ways of money think there are only two kinds of people in the world: those who earn interest, and those who pay interest. Actually, there is a third kind of person: Those who pay interest at one rate but earn interest at a higher rate.

These people do exactly what banks and credit unions do—they borrow money at a lower interest rate and then invest the money they borrow to earn a higher interest rate on it. Even though the spread between one and the other is small, you can become wealthy with a minimal spread. Once you understand this message, you are one step ahead of the crowd, and you will understand why becoming your own banker is a wonderful idea.

Bear in mind that bankers are not like some stockbrokers or hedge fund managers. They don't take major risks. They don't bet all their assets on dangerous or wildly fluctuating investments. They are conservative, and you should be, too, especially as you grow older.

The technique of buying and selling investments to take advantage of small differences in price is called *arbitrage*. This fundamental practice is one of the conservative risks that bankers take. They borrow money at a discount from a Federal Reserve Bank, or they borrow from the general public by offering certificates of deposit. Let's peg the interest rate they pay when borrowing in this example at 4.5 percent. When they turn around and lend money, they may charge as much as 7 or 9 percent interest (Figure 7.1).

Arbitrage at Work

After they subtract their costs and overhead, they may net only 5.5 to 7 percent interest. That leaves them a spread of 1 to 2.5 percent. It doesn't sound like much, does it? Yet even with such a small spread, financial institutions (not just banks, but also institutions such as insurance companies) achieve remarkably profitable results.

As an individual, you can achieve great results by practicing your own arbitrage, especially since your overhead undoubtedly is much lower than that of a bank.

BORROW ONLY TO CONSERVE, NOT TO CONSUME

I realize the word *debt* strikes fear into the hearts of some of you. "Doug, the very last thing I want to do as I approach my retirement is load myself down in debt," you might be saying to yourself. "Isn't it a virtue to be debt-free, so I can sleep at night instead of worrying that I owe some institution money?"

Fear of losing a home by missing a mortgage payment can prevent Boomers from taking steps to free the lazy, idle dollars trapped in their houses. The fear originated with the Great Depression. Many of you have heard that anxiety voiced by your own parents who lived through the Depression. When people began to make runs on the banks during that period, a common clause in loan agreements gave banks the right to demand full repayment of the loan at any time. You might not have missed even a single payment—but if they wanted to, lenders could call that mortgage due.

Depression-era homeowners became frightened. "My heavens, I've got to get this house paid off immediately so the bank doesn't get it." The value of homes back then dropped as much as 80 percent. People's homes were foreclosed on when they weren't even behind on their payments. That mentality—pay off your mortgage, get out of debt at all costs—was passed along to us, the next generation. But in actuality, since the Depression, many people have lost their homes in foreclosure *because* they were trying to "get out of debt" by sending extra principal payments to the mortgage company, and they gave up their liquidity. I'll explain how I define "being out of debt" in a bit.

The laws are different today compared with what they were in the 1930s. You can't be foreclosed on unless you miss three consecutive months of payments, and the truth is, I know families who have missed payments and continued to live in their houses *for two years* without the bank coming to foreclose. But the misconception lives on that banks are looming over people, ready to take their houses away. The same fears apply to those who know about reverse mortgages—which I will describe shortly.

Ask most mortgage companies which homes they foreclose on the soonest and they will tell you that the homes they foreclose on most quickly are those with the greatest equity in them. They foreclose most slowly on those with the biggest loan balance remaining.

Remember that a home with a large mortgage balance is easiest to sell in a soft market. Why? When you have liquidity, you can arrange self-financing, a lease with an option to buy, creative contracts, or other ways to make your home far more attractive financially to potential buyers than homes with mortgages paid in full. In both of my previous books, *Missed Fortune* and *Missed Fortune 101*, I explain this concept in detail—how to get a higher price for your home and sell it more quickly in a soft market by removing as much equity as you can. (I myself have picked up bargains in soft markets when the sellers of properties didn't understand this concept.)

Let me emphasize again that I am *not* suggesting that you bury yourself in debt. My rule is that you borrow only to *conserve*, not to *consume*.

If you load up your credit card by spending money on electronics, jewelry, and all the other great consumer goods offered to you, and you don't pay off the total each month—you are borrowing to consume. The credit card company may charge you 18 percent interest month after month. You are piling up nonpreferred debt.

But if you borrow money for a mortgage at 7.5 percent, you are taking on preferred debt. The same is true of a home equity loan or line of credit. You save in two ways: 1) the interest on a mortgage or home equity loan is 7.5 percent, so you are saving 10.5 percent compared to a credit card, and 2) the interest is preferred, so it is tax-deductible, with the after-tax cost only 5 percent (7.5 less 33.33 percent tax savings). Thus the savings of 10.5 percent over a credit card is really 13 percent (18 percent credit card interest minus the 5 percent after-tax cost of mortgage interest) because of the tax savings.

BORROW LIKE A BANK DOES

Think about this: What is a bank's greatest asset? Money—that they borrow! *A bank's greatest asset is its liabilities*—the loans they obtain from us when we deposit our money there. If a bank had no money borrowed from you it would have no means to make money. Its greatest asset is the money you deposit in CDs, money market accounts, and checking accounts, which it then puts to work to make more money.

A bank's debt shows up on the debit side of its balance sheet. But it has much greater revenue (or assets), which appear on the credit side. On your own personal ledger, debt does not exist in a vacuum. You, too, have both liabilities and assets. When you have more than enough assets in a liquid, safe environment to wash out liabilities, your net result is positive.

Imagine you have a wad of cash in your right-hand pocket and a pile of bills due each month in your left-hand pocket. The cash in your right-hand pocket is liquid; you can earmark it to pay bills in the left pocket. If you hold more than enough cash in the right-hand pocket to cover those bills in the left-hand pocket, you have more assets than liabilities. Your assets are *out* of debt, in other words, over and above it.

There are many major Fortune 1000 companies and even religious institutions that admonish people to try to become debt-free, and yet they themselves are sitting there with millions of dollars in liabilities. Are they hypocritical? No. Their assets outweigh their liabilities.

Where does the money these companies hold come from? They borrow it. It's OPM—Other People's Money. The road to wealth is paved with OPM. Most self-made millionaires, from Cornelius Vanderbilt and John D. Rockefeller to Warren Buffett and Bill Gates, have achieved their lofty financial status with the help of OPM.

Do you have a mortgage on your house? Congratulations; you are already employing OPM. Why not use your mortgage to earn more money than it costs you?

HOW TO WASTE OPM

Conventional wisdom teaches you that as you get older, you should pay down your mortgage as quickly as you can. At first, that sounds reasonable. A thirty-year mortgage amortization schedule can be intimidating because fifteen years into the mortgage, you may still owe 75 percent of the original amount. How come? Interest. A tremendous amount of interest is due in the first fifteen years. Depending on the interest rate, you will pay back a good deal more than you initially borrowed. So there is a temptation to make it go away. Who wants to have that kind of loan hanging over them?

So as you approach the age of 50 or 60, you decide to send extra money to your mortgage lender. The problem is that if you do so, you are killing your partner, Uncle Sam, in the process. Every time you hand over an extra $100 to your mortgage lender or bank, you are saying, "Take this money. Don't pay me interest on it. If I need it back, I'll borrow it—on your terms—and I will prove that I need it."

No wonder banks are so profitable!

It is true that if you do this consistently you will pay off your mortgage earlier. But the more you reduce your mortgage, the lesser the amount of interest you have to claim as a tax deduction. I repeat, you are killing your partner, Uncle Sam.

Let me ask you a couple of questions: If you paid a down payment for your house, how much interest is the mortgage company paying you on that down payment? And what would be the largest down payment you could ever make when acquiring a new piece of property? My point is, you earn nothing, zip, nada, zero on any down payment that you make.

THE BEST WAY TO PAY OFF YOUR MORTGAGE

For years I have shown clients who want to make extra mortgage payments how to pay off their homes more quickly and shrewdly, making use of their money and Uncle Sam's. If you deposit those extra payments in a separate, liquid, safe side fund, you earn interest on it and thus accumulate for yourself enough money to pay off the mortgage more quickly than if you apply those extra payments toward the principal balance of the loan. Meanwhile, you continue to enjoy the tax break you get from paying mortgage interest.

This is illustrated in Figure 7.2.

Fig. 7.2	ACCUMULATING THE NET DIFFERENCE BETWEEN A 30-YEAR MORTGAGE PAYMENT AND A 15-YEAR MORTGAGE PAYMENT IN A SIDE FUND EARNING 8% INTEREST**				
END OF YEAR	[1] 30-YEAR MORTGAGE LOAN BALANCE	[2] 15-YEAR MORTGAGE NET PAYMENT AFTER TAX	[3] 30-YEAR MORTGAGE NET PAYMENT AFTER TAX	[4] DIFFERENCE BETWEEN NET PAYMENT AFTER TAX	[5] DIFFERENCE EARNING 8% COMPOUNDING
1	297,494	26,534	18,446	8,088	8,735
2	294,780	26,833	18,516	8,317	18,416
3	291,841	27,156	18,591	8,565	29,140
4	288,657	27,507	18,672	8,834	41,012
5	285,210	27,886	18,760	9,126	54,149
6	281,476	28,297	18,856	9,441	68,677
7	277,433	28,741	18,959	9,783	84,736
8	273,054	29,223	19,071	10,152	102,480
9	268,311	29,745	19,192	10,553	122,076
10	263,175	30,310	19,323	10,987	143,708
11	257,612	30,922	19,465	11,457	167,577
12	251,588	31,585	19,619	11,966	193,907
13	245,064	32,303	19,786	12,517	222,937
14	237,998	33,080	19,966	13,114	254,935 *
15	230,346	33,920	20,162	13,759	290,189 ◄

$59,843.32

EXCESS CASH BEYOND MORTGAGE BALANCE

* Notice that you would have enough money in your liquid side fund to pay off the mortgage sometime between the 13th and 14th year.
** Both the 30-year mortgage and the 15-year mortgage are amortized assuming 8 percent interest.

Let's assume you have a new conventional thirty-year fixed mortgage at 8 percent interest, but you want to pay it off in fifteen years. Column 1 shows your loan balance after each year. Column 2 shows what your payment would be yearly after tax if you had a fifteen-year mortgage, while the larger amounts in column 3 show what your payments on that thirty-year mortgage after tax actually are. What if you were able to save the difference each year—shown in column 4? And what if you could put that amount into a safe side fund that *earns* 8 percent a year? The result is shown in column 5.

You would most likely accumulate enough money in that side fund in between your thirteenth and fourteenth year to pay off your thirty-year mortgage in full. Your unsung partner is Uncle Sam, who in essence is paying part of your mortgage by letting you deduct the interest from your taxes. Hidden from view is the *lift*— the wonder of compound interest that allows your side fund to flourish.

HOW LIQUID IS YOUR HOME EQUITY?

If you are still convinced that paying off your mortgage early will give you peace of mind, you are still stumbling over Misconception #3.

There are even more serious problems involved in paying off your mortgage. Imagine you are holding a tin can in one hand and a $100 bill in the other. Now put the greenback in the tin can, and imagine burying it in your backyard. Is the $100 bill liquid? Sure it is (provided you remember where you buried it!). What about the thousands of dollars you tie up when you pay off your house? Is that money liquid? Sorry, but the answer is no. The money in the tin can has more liquidity than the money tied up in your equity.

Once your house is paid off, the equity you have invested in it is anything but liquid. If the economy stalls, or if you have a financial setback and you must dip into your savings, all the money you poured into your house stays there, trapped inside—just as it did with houses washed away by a flood.

A safe side fund would be handy indeed. Perhaps you learned during the dot-com bust of 2000 that to ride out a two-year market downturn you had to sell some of your investments at a loss.

On the other hand, investors with ready cash do not have to

sell stocks, bonds, or mutual funds at an inopportune time. They ride out the market cycle until it recovers.

WHAT'S THE RATE OF RETURN ON YOUR HOME EQUITY?

No one can assure you that the value of your home will continue in an upward, unbroken line. Home equity is defined as the fair market value of your home minus all outstanding loans against it. So, if you have a home valued at $300,000 with a first mortgage of $175,000 and a home equity line of credit with a balance of $25,000, the remaining $100,000 is your bottom-line equity.

But once your house is paid off, then the fair market value represents your entire equity. Where does that leave you when the housing bubble bursts or deflates? The market for your home softens; there are more sellers than there are buyers. Your home value goes down. If your job requires you to move, or if you are looking ahead a few years and decide the time has come to move to a warmer climate, or if this is the moment you have decided to downsize, you can sell your home only at whatever its value is in the current market cycle. You may have paid $50,000 outright or paid down a $1 million mortgage: Once you have spent the money, it is trapped between the finished basement and the attic. Is it safe? No! It is *not* out of harm's way if you cannot get all the trapped dollars out when you put the FOR SALE sign on your front lawn.

Not every geographic area goes through the housing cycle at the same time. During the mid-1990s, the housing market for Utah was going great guns but California was in a soft market period. Las Vegas went through a recent period when new houses were snatched up the moment they were offered. At the same time, some home sellers in Texas were watching prices plummet.

Do varying market conditions make it difficult to calculate the rate of return on home equity? Not a bit. Do you have to factor in the geographic area? Absolutely not. It does not matter whether your home (or second home) is in Las Vegas, Nevada, or Las Vegas, New Mexico.

The rate of return on home equity is always the same: zero!

When your home equity grows, you may think that it has a rate of return, but it doesn't. Equity grows as a function of your home appreciating in value or the debt being reduced, but equity itself has no rate of return.

I suspect that at this point, you have a frown on your face and skepticism in your mind, so let me explain this in more detail.

Let's go back to the tin can that you buried in your backyard. You already know that the $100 bill inside it is more liquid than the house fronting the backyard. The same $100 bill is safer than the money poured into your home in difficult times. Is the $100 bill earning a rate of return? No, obviously it is not. In fact, it might be losing value (or purchasing power) because the cost of living, otherwise known as inflation, is going up.

What is the difference between the rate of return on the $100 bill in the tin can and the dollars you have tied up in your house? Nothing.

THE PITCHER OF WATER VERSUS THE EMPTY GLASS

When I give seminars, this is the moment that I introduce the most memorable visual aids I have ever used. Picture yourself holding an empty drinking glass in one hand and a pitcher containing water in the other (Figure 7.3). The glass represents your house. For simplicity's sake, let's say it is worth $100,000. It's an asset. Let's say you have $100,000 of cash in the bank (the pitcher)—that's liquid wealth. The glass is empty because you have not put a penny into your house, but on paper, on a balance sheet, you would still list it as a $100,000 asset. Meanwhile the pitcher of water represents another asset—$100,000 in cash.

ASSETS = $200,000

Fig. 7.3	BALANCE SHEET

ASSETS
Home $100,000
Cash   <u>$100,000</u>
Total Assets $200,000

LIABILITIES
Home Mortgage ($100,000)

NET WORTH
Assets - Liabilities = **$100,000**

$100,000 Home

$100,000 Cash

What's the total amount of your assets? $200,000. What happens if you pour the water into the glass (Figure 7.4)? You have reduced your assets by $100,000. You've combined $100,000 in cash to a glass already listed as an asset worth $100,000, and all you have to show for it is $100,000. You have cut your assets in half!

Fig. 7.4

$0 Cash

$100,000 Home

What happens when we pour all of our cash into our property?

We cut our assets in half...
$100,000 IN ASSETS

On the other hand, when you separate the liquid cash from the glass-sized house that is free and clear, you double your assets (Figure 7.5). That's what happens when you separate equity from your house and put it in a liquid investment. But you're not finished. Assume the empty glass-house appreciates at an average of 5 percent a year. After one year, what's the value of the empty glass? $105,000. If you pay off the mortgage on the glass (pour the water—or money—back into the house) what is it worth? The same $105,000—whether it is mortgaged or it is free and clear—because equity has no rate of return when it is trapped in a house.

Fig. 7.5

What happens when we separate equity from our property?

$100,000 Home $100,000 Cash

We double our assets...
$200,000 IN ASSETS

Next, pour the water from the glass back into the big pitcher. You've just removed $100,000 from your house and put it into an investment earning—let's say—10 percent. At the end of the year, how much money will you have in that pitcher? Look at that! It's grown to $110,000! In your other hand is your house, worth $105,000 at the end of the same year, thanks to appreciation (Figure 7.6).

Leave the water in the pitcher.

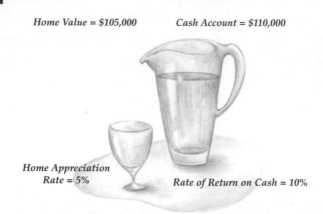

Fig. 7.6

END OF YEAR ONE

Home Value = $105,000   *Cash Account = $110,000*

Home Appreciation Rate = 5%   *Rate of Return on Cash = 10%*

Increase in Assets when separated = $15,000.

How much have you earned by separating your equity from your house in the course of just a single year? $15,000. How much would you have earned if you had left the water in the glass? Only $5,000—one-third as much.

"But, but, but—the mortgage wasn't free! I had to pay some interest." That's right, you did. Let's say the mortgage was at 7.5 percent. That's $7,500 subtracted from $15,000 for a net gain of $7,500, instead of just $5,000. You are still 50 percent ahead than if you had not removed the equity from your house. If the mortgage interest is deductible, then the net cost of the mortgage is really not $7,500, but $5,000 in a 33.3 percent marginal tax bracket. So the net profit is $10,000 ($15,000 minus a net, after-tax mortgage expense of $5,000)—or twice as much as you made if the house was paid off!

Here's another quick analogy: Would you rather have one horse working for you or two? Can two horses work for you, even if you owe money on one of the horses?

The object of this demonstration is that no matter what else you do, *when you separate your equity from your house, you increase your assets.* Even though there is a charge for doing that—the simple interest you pay on a mortgage—it makes a whole lot of sense to take out a mortgage and use it to make your assets grow.

Do you recall the president of the bank I mentioned at the start of this chapter? What you've just done—taken out a mortgage and used the money to make more money—is what he did. You didn't make billions, but you made a profit in the same exact manner. By separating equity from your house, you give it the ability to earn a rate of return. Employ this strategy each year, and the profits will compound.

HOW TO FREE UP THOSE LAZY, IDLE DOLLARS

If you separate equity from your house, you free up thousands of dollars that are sitting inside, lazy and idle. When you take those dollars and put them into an investment that earns interest tax-free, you exploit what may seem like a small difference to manufacture real wealth. That's arbitrage. It may sound like an esoteric strategy, but it is a trade that everyone who has a savings or checking account participates in. The very lifeblood of financial institutions is borrowing money at one rate to earn money at a higher rate of interest and profiting on the spread.

You may still be skeptical of this strategy because you are not accustomed to thinking of mortgage interest as your friend. Perhaps you don't like the cost of doing business this way. I urge you to see the interest you pay on a mortgage as the *employment* cost. If you are a business owner, you gladly pay a great employee a bigger salary than your competitor does because the employee makes more money for you than you otherwise would earn. Think of mortgage interest as the employment cost for money that works harder for you.

What you may not realize at the outset is that the lazy, idle dollars you leave trapped inside your home will incur *the same cost*— we refer to this as the *opportunity cost*. You have no choice—you're going to incur one cost or the other. You are not playing it safe by leaving your equity in your house—it's costing you! If you've got hundreds of thousands of dollars of equity, and you don't remove it in order to put it to work for you, you give up the opportunity to earn serious cash. So if you choose to leave behind $100,000 that you could pull out of your house and earn 8 percent interest, you have given up an opportunity cost of $8,000 a year. If you put that $100,000 to work by separating it and getting a mortgage at 7.5 percent, you pay an employment cost of $7,500.

But guess what? The employment cost is actually lower than that.

The key here is that in dealing with the cost of a mortgage, you are paying an employment cost that is usually tax-deductible. The opportunity cost of letting the money sleep in your master bedroom is not deductible. Doesn't it make sense to shake that sleepy head and send it off to work using a mortgage? Then, if you are in the 33.3 percent tax bracket, 7.5 percent interest is really costing you only $5,000. All your equity has to do now is to earn 5 percent or better to make a profit. Can you do that? Sure. As I will prove, the magic begins to happen as you pay tax-deductible, *simple* interest on OPM, and you employ that money in a *compounding* liquid and safe investment that is tax-advantaged.

Let's go back to the pitcher and the glass. Take the $100,000 that you poured out of the house, and imagine you obtained it by using a mortgage at 7.5 percent deductible interest on an interest-only loan. At 7.5 percent interest rate, your annual interest cost will be $7,500. Your monthly payment would amount to $625. Assuming you are in a 33.3 tax bracket, you get approximately a third of that money—$2,500—back in the form of a tax refund. However, I don't think you need to wait until April 15. As I explained in Chapters 5 and 6, you can change your exemptions to adjust your withholding tax on your paycheck, and get a fatter paycheck right now. By receiving the extra $2,500 now, spread out over twelve months, you increase your monthly take-home income by about $208. Your true cost will be only $5,000 a year, or $417 per month.

Now look at what happens when, instead of spending the

money (the $100,000 in equity you just separated from your house), you invest it in a conservative side fund that earns the same interest (7.5 percent) that you are paying on your mortgage. By the end of the first year, you have $107,500 in the pitcher. By finding an investment that passes the liquidity, safety, and rate of return tests, you can do this. However, if you can also find an investment with *thrust*—where your money accumulates tax-free—your net profit will soar dramatically higher.

Here's a little simple math: If you earn $7,500 and your cost is $5,000, you have a 50 percent increase. But if you earn that $7,500 in a taxable situation, you net only $5,000 after tax, and you haven't made any headway. So if you earn only the same rate you are borrowing at, it is critical to invest under tax-favorable circumstances. I'll go into this in detail in Chapters 11 and 12. Let's assume you invest and realize a 1 percent higher earning rate than the borrowing rate (which is very attainable, as you will see later). So, let's use an interest-only mortgage at 7.5 percent and put the loan proceeds to work earning 8.5 percent. The first year, your $100,000 of separated home equity grows to $108,500. During the second year, you earn the same 8.5 percent on the new balance. Thanks to the *lift*—the compounding interest—your total interest in the second year is $9,223.

So far, so good, right? Let's look ahead to the fifth year. At the end of five years, the original $100,000 of equity accumulating at 8.5 percent interest, tax-deferred, would have grown to over $150,000. You have made $50,000. Your employment cost, the interest, was a net of $5,000 a year for five years, for a total of $25,000. Voilà! Your profit becomes $25,000 on the lazy, idle dollars that used to be snoozing in your house, earning a zero rate of return.

Now you are entering your sixth year. You would earn 8.5 percent interest on your growing $150,000 of separated equity. At the end of the sixth year, that equals $12,750. Thus, in your sixth year you earn $12,750 with an employment cost of only $5,000 (since you are still paying a net after-tax interest cost of only 5 percent on the original loan balance). After six years, putting the equity to work cost $5,000, yet earned $12,750—a 155 percent increase that year! Your net profit is $7,750 on lazy dollars that used to earn a zero rate of return. Congratulations! You have become just like the profitable banker described at the beginning of this chapter.

IT'S NOT TOO LATE!

Remember, even if you are a Boomer who didn't get the wake-up call until now, even if you are starting late in the game, you still can accumulate wealth this way. By acting as your own banker, you can climb aboard this jet-fueled system and watch lift, thrust, and drag propel you into new realms of money over time.

Would you like to peek at what your balances would look like after ten years? In ten years, the same lazy, idle dollars would grow from the original $100,000 to $226,098 at 8.5 percent. That's an increase of $126,098 that you attained with an investment cost of $50,000 ($5,000 × 10). As an investor, you would have to earn nearly 16.35 percent compounded annually on an annual investment of the same $5,000 to arrive at $126,098 in ten years!

Let's dream a little. What if instead of 8.5 percent interest on $200,000 of separated equity, you could earn 9.6 percent. Your side fund would sprint to over $500,000 in ten years, or an increase of $300,000 over the mortgage balance owed. An investor would have to earn 19.36 percent interest compounded annually on a net, after-tax annual investment of $10,000 (the net interest-only mortgage payment on $200,000) to match your $300,000 profit! If you have more time, you can earn exponentially more money, thanks to the lift compound interest provides.

What if you separated $300,000 of home equity at age 55 and achieved an average annual return of 9.6 percent? It would grow to nearly $1 million by age 68. If you separated $400,000 of home equity at age 55 and earned an average of 9.6 percent, it would grow to over $1 million by age 65. You can see that if you borrow more equity right from the start (or every few years as your house appreciates in value), your nest egg gets larger, sooner.

WHO UNDERSTANDS ARBITRAGE BETTER THAN THE FEDERAL RESERVE BANK?

In August 2006, the Federal Reserve Bank of Chicago released a very interesting analysis in their working papers titled, "The Tradeoff Between Mortgage Prepayments and Tax-Deferred Retirement Savings." The study was assembled by Gene Amromin, Jennifer Huang, and Clemens Sialm. In the abstract at the beginning it states:

> We show that a significant number of households can perform a tax arbitrage by cutting back on their additional mortgage payments and increasing their contributions to tax-deferred accounts. Using data from the Survey of Consumer Finances, we show that about 38% of U.S. households that are accelerating their mortgage payments instead of saving in tax-deferred accounts are making the wrong choice. For these households, reallocating their savings can yield a mean benefit of 11 to 17 cents per dollar, depending on the choice of investment assets in the tax-deferred accounts. In the aggregate, these misallocated savings are costing U.S. households as much as 1.5 billion dollars per year.

I will reveal more details about this lengthy thirty-seven-page study with my own commentary in Chapter 13. At this point, suffice it to say that even the Federal Reserve Bank is conducting detailed studies that will help consumers become educated about the asset optimization, equity management, and wealth empowerment strategies contained in this book. Who better to learn from on how to become your own banker than from the Federal Reserve Bank?

HOUSE-RICH BUT CASH-POOR? TRY A REVERSE MORTGAGE

Take a moment to sit in your den and pretend you're a banker by collecting monthly checks from someone. You can do this by taking out a reverse mortgage. However, this investment is open to you only after you reach the age of 62. But it's good to know that the opportunity exists, especially if you own your house free and clear or close to that point.

A reverse mortgage is just what it sounds like—the opposite of a traditional mortgage. Instead of borrowing from a lender and paying the money back each month with interest, a bank or other lender gives you cash based on your age or, in the case of a couple, the combined average age plus the value of the house. You can take the money either in a lump sum, a monthly payment, or a line of credit that you use when you need cash. There are no out-of-pocket closing costs, and the money is tax-free. You are annuitizing the equity in your home by converting it to a lifetime, tax-free income.

What makes this a useful alternative for seniors is that you never have to make a payment on this loan, even though you retain full ownership of the property and can stay in it as long as you wish. The house or condominium must be your principal residence. There are no medical or income requirements. The loan comes due only when you decide to move from that home permanently, when you sell the home, or when you die. At this point, the loan is paid back by the sale of the house.

What about interest? There is interest accruing on the money you get from the lender. That's why the amount of the loan can never exceed the value of your house. Federally insured or government-sponsored reverse mortgages have caps. But private loans are available with virtually no limit on the amount of the loan based on your home's value. The older you are, in general, the more money you can obtain, and the lower the built-in interest rate will be.

Reverse mortgages appeal to elderly people who want a simple way to tap the lazy, idle dollars in their houses without having to make payments, and who, having been in their home for a long time, have seen the appreciation skyrocket. One drawback is that you are slowly spending down your equity, which may affect the amount left behind to your heirs. Heirs would likely need to sell the house to satisfy the reverse mortgage. One alternative is to use part of the cash you receive with a reverse mortgage to buy an inexpensive "second-to-die" life insurance policy so there will be tax-free money to pay off the loan balance when both you and your spouse pass away. (I discuss this option in my first book, *Missed Fortune*, where I dedicate an entire chapter, Chapter 14, to the subject.)

MANAGE YOUR EQUITY TO TURBOCHARGE YOUR WEALTH

I hope you are thinking at this point that paying off your house may not be the best strategy in your "last-chance" efforts to capture true wealth. Burning the mortgage may have been a great idea back in the 1930s, but today it is just as outdated as black-and-white movies. You're entitled to your prime-time years in full color, on a giant plasma screen.

In the next few chapters, I'm going to explain exactly how you can manage those lazy idle dollars in your home to turbocharge your wealth. Managing equity successfully is like installing a turbine at the base of a dam. It takes your liquid cash and puts it to work to add light and life to your assets. Ready to become a Blazing Boomer? Follow me!

(To hear and see these concepts explained in more detail as I teach them in public educational seminars, you can view a ninety-minute DVD containing highlights of my three-and-a-half-hour public seminar titled "Missed Fortune True Wealth Transformation." Please go to www.MissedFortune.com/SeminarHighlights).

REMEMBER THIS:

- Banks and credit unions use arbitrage—borrowing at one interest rate and lending at a higher rate—to make money; learn how you can do that, too.
- No matter how much your property has appreciated, the rate of return on lazy, idle dollars trapped in your home is always *zero*.
- Use Other People's Money by obtaining a mortgage that frees up as much of your home equity for repositioning as you can.
- When you pay simple interest on a mortgage, you can use arbitrage to put that money to work earning compound interest.
- If you are cash-poor but house-rich, investigate the income possibilities of a reverse mortgage.

CHAPTER 8

Locate the Key to Your Retirement: It's Sitting Under Your Own Roof

How to Find the Home Mortgage That Works Hardest for You

HOW MANY OF YOU THINK your home has been a great in-vestment?" From Seattle to San Diego, from Minneapolis to Miami, whenever I ask this question, hundreds of hands in my seminar audiences shoot up. Americans coast to coast have watched appreciation in the value of their homes gallop at a pace that would have made Seabiscuit proud. While every market has its ups and downs, the net increase in housing appreciation over the past thirty years has been stupendous.

How stupendous? We've got $19 trillion worth of homes in the United States. No, that is not a typographical error. Not billions—trillions. What amazes me is that $10 trillion of it is *not* mortgaged. That's more than enough in dollar bills to stretch from here to the moon and back. The amazing reality is that $10 trillion is sitting out there earning nothing! Zip! Nada!

Home equity, as I proved earlier, has no rate of return. Doesn't it behoove you to protect your future and safeguard your cash by capturing those lazy, idle dollars and putting them to work for you?

Sometimes when people get the shorthand introduction to my strategy of wealth optimization, they are outraged. "Borrow against my house to manage the equity in order to increase my net worth? You've got to be kidding!" My answer is: You're shortchanging yourself when you don't take advantage of the retirement money that is sitting under your own roof. You simply don't know what you don't know.

BE PROACTIVE, NOT REACTIVE

Your *home* is sacred, not your house. *Homes were designed to house your family, not to store cash.* Certain investments are designed to store cash—safely. The core of my system is managing the lazy, idle dollars sleeping in your house to create a retirement plan that won't run out of steam before you do.

Even though the run-up in housing prices has been mind-boggling in some locations, housing prices do not necessarily jump every year in every location. The housing market is as cyclical as any other market. Just ask the folks who owned property in Houston in 1980, or the Gulf Coast residents who sold their ruined houses for a fraction of their former worth after Hurricanes Katrina and Rita in 2005.

Economic changes are just one kind of disaster lurking when you keep your cash locked up and illiquid in your house. When you lose your job and thus your ability to make your house payment, you put yourself in jeopardy. There can be a variety of reasons: Your employer might have financial difficulties and start layoffs; you might be the victim of outsourcing; or you might suffer a health crisis. One of the biggest causes of home foreclosure is physical disability. Don't expect your lender to comfort you in times of distress. But banks really don't want your house; they are not collateral lenders. They loan you extra money based mainly on your ability to repay it.

No matter how much extra you have forked over to your bank in order to pay off your house, your lender still expects to get a regular payment from you every thirty days. I've learned of people that had sent their mortgage company several thousand dollars to apply against the principal of their loan, only to lose it all later because they lacked liquidity and couldn't make continual payments when needed.

Let's say you bought a house for $400,000, and your original mortgage was $300,000. A few years later, you have paid down your mortgage to $200,000, and the house has appreciated in value to $600,000. The bank now has great safety in its investment—a $200,000 loan secured by an asset worth three times that. So, who is proportionately *less* safe as you paid down your mortgage? You!

Another danger, despite all those trillions of dollars, is the deflation of the housing bubble. Desirable locations attract more and more builders eager to jump into the housing pool. Sooner or later, some of those markets will have more homes than buyers, or the high prices will start to deter newcomers and send them searching the real estate listings in other areas that are cheaper. Then, as surely as night follows day, the value of your property will decline.

Remember the three lodging places for money that I introduced in Chapter 3? I would rather have my money tucked safely in a stable investment earning moderate, predictable, tax-favored rates, and still have participation and ownership in real estate or even stocks (without having my own money at risk) in the event the big bad wolves show up out of nowhere.

Now pretend for a moment once again that you are the president of a bank. You need to be responsible to your stockholders. To re-emphasize a point introduced in Chapter 7, pretend once again that you've got several mortgage loans that are delinquent (people are behind on their mortgage payments). Which houses will you start foreclosure proceedings on first: the houses that have a lot of equity (low mortgage balances) or the houses that have very little equity (high mortgage balances)?

Let's say two houses sit side by side: Both were once worth $300,000, but the market has gone soft and now they are worth only $200,000. One homeowner owes you $100,000, while the next-door homeowner still owes $250,000. Chances are you'll go after the house that has the most equity, not the one where the loan is now more than you can get for it once you turn it over to a foreclosure sales specialist.

"WHETHER-PROOF" YOUR HOUSE

Once again, let me make myself clear: I don't advocate going into debt for consumption. I *do* believe in a personal balance sheet that shows assets worth more than liabilities. And I strongly advocate that you separate your equity from your house, because only by doing so will you make it safer, create liquidity, and allow it to earn a good rate of return. My plan is designed to keep your pitcher full. Then you can weather any kind of natural disaster or personal setback as you approach your golden years.

Separating the equity from your house and investing it in a safe, tax-favored investment is the key to optimizing your wealth:

- Whether or not you are planning to retire in five years or in twenty-five years.
- Whether or not you are the entrepreneurial type and, like so many Boomers, you expect to begin a later-in-life career once you leave your current job.
- Whether or not you need more cash to support children still dependent on you or to help out your aging parents.
- Whether interest rates rise or fall.

I said earlier in this book that the first misconception that Boomers have is to use short-term investment vehicles for long-range goals. While you are still working, you have more flexibility than you may have later in life. Removing equity now from your house allows you to invest it for the longer term, where your money can take root and grow in the fertile fields of tax-free accumulation. You should now understand that it costs the same to live in your house whether you own it free and clear (opportunity cost) or borrow from it by taking out a mortgage (employment cost). But with your equity invested in a savings instrument that gets a lift from compound interest, your money grows and grows.

"BUT MORTGAGE RATES KEEP GOING UP!"

Because interest rates are relative, you don't need to fret as they climb. Please recall that my strategy exploits the spread between simple interest rates that you pay for the employment cost of money (the interest you pay on a mortgage), and the compound interest rate that you earn in a liquid, tax-favored investment. When interest rates for borrowing money head north, so do the interest rates credited on savings and investments.

"WHY SHOULDN'T I JUST HURRY AND PAY OFF MY HOUSE?"

Let's say you have $1,000 a month in discretionary money from your paycheck or other sources. You were contemplating sending it to your lender as extra principal payments on your mortgage. The following example illustrates how much better it will do in a separate, liquid, safe side fund.

In the first scenario, suppose you have just taken out a $200,000 fifteen-year amortized mortgage at 8 percent interest, as shown in Figure 8.1. Each month, you pay part of that as principal (column 2) and part as deductible interest (column 4). Thus your monthly mortgage payment is $1,911.30, or $22,935 per year for fifteen years. But you want to hurry and get your house paid off in half the time, so you send your $1,000 of discretionary money to the mortgage company each month. So the total you send monthly is $2,911.30, or $34,936 a year (column 5). Let's assume you are in a 33.3 percent marginal tax bracket, so you can deduct the interest on your taxes on Schedule A of the IRS long form. Thus your partner, Uncle Sam, helps you save $5,096 in the first year (column 6). Your net mortgage payment the first year is $29,839 (column 7.)

At that pace, you would have your mortgage paid off in seven years and seven months—wow, what a great feeling! Now, if you stay disciplined, you can sock away that $2,911.30 a month for the remaining seven years and five months (to your retirement age) in an investment (hopefully tax-deferred), and it grows to $294,247 (top half of Figure 8.3). At 8 percent you could take interest withdrawals of $23,540 annually, but you would pay tax on that income of $7,846, and net only $15,694 to spend. This is what most people do to prepare for retirement.

Fig. 8.1	AN ACCELERATED 15-YEAR AMORTIZED MORTGAGE WITH AN ADDITIONAL PRINCIPLE PAYMENT OF $1,000 PER MONTH						

ORIGINAL PRINCIPAL	$200,000			LOAN TYPE	Amortized		
LOAN BALANCE	$200,000			PAYMENT MODE	Monthly		
PAYMENT (P&I)	$1,911.30			TERM (years)	15		
EXTRA PAYMENT	$1,000						
INTEREST RATE	8.00%			TAX BRACKET	33.33%		

	(1)	(2)	(3)	(4)	(5)	(6)	(7)
End of Year	Loan Balance	Principal Payment	Extra Payment	Interest Payment	Total Payment	Tax Savings	Net Payment After Tax
1	$180,354	$7,646	$12,000	$15,290	$34,936	$5,096	$29,839
2	$159,078	$9,276	$12,000	$13,659	$34,936	$4,553	$30,383
3	$136,036	$11,042	$12,000	$11,894	$34,936	$3,964	$30,971
4	$111,082	$12,955	$12,000	$9,981	$34,936	$3,327	$31,609
5	$84,056	$15,026	$12,000	$7,910	$34,936	$2,636	$32,299
6	$54,787	$17,269	$12,000	$5,667	$34,936	$1,889	$33,047
7	$23,089	$19,698	$12,000	$3,237	$34,936	$1,079	$33,857
8	$0	$11,089	$12,000	$3,113	$26,202	$1,038	$25,164
TOTAL		$104,000	$96,000	$70,751	$270,751	$23,581	$247,170

Notes:
a. Tax Savings assumes a state and federal marginal tax bracket of 33.33% multiplied by the Interest Payment.
b. Mortgage interest is generally tax deductible; however, certain limitations are applicable. Please review with your tax advisor.
c. Net Payment After Tax equals Total Payment less Tax Savings.

Now compare the fifteen-year mortgage with an interest-only mortgage for the same amount (Figure 8.2). See the totals that I've shaded? No doubt about it, an interest-only mortgage costs you more each year in interest, which is why your Depression-era father advised you to take out a fifteen-year mortgage.

Fig. 8.2	A PROPOSED INTEREST-ONLY MORTGAGE ANALYSIS TO ALLOW SAVING THE DIFFERENCE IN PAYMENTS AND THE ADDITIONAL $1,000 PER MONTH					
ORIGINAL PRINCIPAL	$200,000			PAYMENT MODE		Monthly
LOAN BALANCE	$200,000			TERM (years)		15
PAYMENT	$1,333.33					
INTEREST RATE	8.00%					
LOAN TYPE	Interest Only			TAX BRACKET		33.33%
	(1)	(2)	(3)	(4)	(5)	(6)
End of Year	Loan Balance	Principal Payment	Interest Payment	Total Payment	Tax Savings	Net Payment After Tax
1	$200,000	$0	$16,000	$16,000	$5,333	$10,667
2	$200,000	$0	$16,000	$16,000	$5,333	$10,667
3	$200,000	$0	$16,000	$16,000	$5,333	$10,667
4	$200,000	$0	$16,000	$16,000	$5,333	$10,667
5	$200,000	$0	$16,000	$16,000	$5,333	$10,667
6	$200,000	$0	$16,000	$16,000	$5,333	$10,667
7	$200,000	$0	$16,000	$16,000	$5,333	$10,667
8	$200,000	$0	$16,000	$16,000	$5,333	$10,667
9	$200,000	$0	$16,000	$16,000	$5,333	$10,667
10	$200,000	$0	$16,000	$16,000	$5,333	$10,667
11	$200,000	$0	$16,000	$16,000	$5,333	$10,667
12	$200,000	$0	$16,000	$16,000	$5,333	$10,667
13	$200,000	$0	$16,000	$16,000	$5,333	$10,667
14	$200,000	$0	$16,000	$16,000	$5,333	$10,667
15	$200,000	$0	$16,000	$16,000	$5,333	$10,667
TOTAL		$0	$240,000	$240,000	$80,000	$160,000

Notes:
a. Tax Savings assumes a state and federal marginal tax bracket of 33.33% multiplied by the Interest Payment.
b. Mortgage interest is generally tax deductible; however, certain limitations are applicable.
   Please review with your tax advisor.
c. Net Payment After Tax equals Total Payment less Tax Savings.

But at the same time, the interest-only mortgage offers you a much greater amount of tax savings. *So over the longer period, your actual net mortgage payment is substantially lower on the interest-only mortgage.*

Fig. 8.3	UTILIZING A 15-YEAR MORTGAGE PLUS AN ADDITIONAL $1,000 PER MONTH TO PAY OFF THE MORTGAGE (Fig. 8.1) AND THEREAFTER INVESTING THE SAVINGS			
INVESTMENT RATE 8.000%	**AGE**	**END OF YEAR**	**INVESTED SAVINGS**	**ACCOUNT VALUE**
	50	1	$0	$0
	51	2	$0	$0
	52	3	$0	$0
	53	4	$0	$0
	54	5	$0	$0
	55	6	$0	$0
	56	7	$0	$0
	57	8	$26,202	$27,365
	58	9	$34,936	$57,002
	59	10	$34,936	$89,098
	60	11	$34,936	$123,859
	61	12	$34,936	$161,504
	62	13	$34,936	$202,275
	63	14	$34,936	$246,429
	64	15	$34,936	**$294,247**

THE DIFFERENCE IN UTILIZING AN INTEREST-ONLY MORTGAGE VERSUS A 15-YEAR MORTGAGE PLUS AN EXTRA $1,000 PER MONTH				
INVESTMENT RATE 8.000%	**AGE**	**END OF YEAR**	**INVESTED SAVINGS**	**ACCOUNT VALUE**
	50	1	$19,172	$20,706
	51	2	$19,716	$43,656
	52	3	$20,304	$69,077
	53	4	$20,942	$97,220
	54	5	$21,632	$128,360
	55	6	$22,380	$162,799
	56	7	$23,189	**$200,868**
	57	8	$23,231	$241,802
	58	9	$24,269	$286,134
	59	10	$24,269	$334,145
	60	11	$24,269	$386,141
	61	12	$24,269	$442,453
	62	13	$24,269	$503,438
	63	14	$24,269	$569,486
	64	15	$24,269	**$641,015**

What if you took the difference between the two mortgages after taxes and invested that money in a tax-favored, interest-bearing side fund that pays the same 8 percent (bottom half of Figure 8.3)?

In the second scenario, during the same fifteen years, you pay interest-only annualized payments of $16,000 on your $200,000 mortgage at 8 percent. That leaves you with a huge difference that you could immediately begin socking away in your equity management retirement plan. The first year, the difference (including the tax savings) allows you to set aside $19,172—that's the difference in the net payment after tax on the amortized mortgage and the interest-only mortgage. Each year through year seven, the difference that you can set aside becomes greater, as shown in the invested savings column, Figure 8.3, because in the first scenario, you are killing your partner, Uncle Sam, by paying down your mortgage so fast. After seven years, you would have enough ($200,868) to pay off the mortgage if you want to (seven months earlier than the first scenario, by the way), but that would not be wise. You *want* to keep a mortgage. So you keep socking away $34,936 a year, less the after-tax mortgage payment of $10,667, for a net annual investment during the last seven years of $24,269.

Look how much more you accumulate in the second scenario— $641,015! Later, I will show you how to not only accumulate this money tax-free, but also generate tax-free income from your equity management retirement fund. If you withdrew annual interest earnings of 8 percent from $641,015, it would generate a $51,281 income stream into perpetuity.

"But I would still have a $200,000 mortgage on my house!" Sure you would. But you could withdraw $200,000 anytime you wanted, pay off the mortgage, and end up with $441,015, which would generate $35,281 a year of income (more than twice the net income as the first scenario). But why would you do that? I would rather keep managing my equity by keeping my tax deduction and paying the net house payment ($10,667 a year) from the $51,281 income stream. That way I would end up ahead with $40,614 of net income, which is over 250 percent more net spendable income than the first scenario. Hmm, I just might refinance my home two or three times during the next fifteen years as it appreciates and really sprint toward my retirement.

The greater your mortgage and home equity, the greater the difference is. On a $400,000 mortgage (doubling everything in the example), you could realize over $100,000 of tax-free retirement income (assuming the same 8 percent interest paid on the mortgage and 8 percent interest earned in the side fund). On a $600,000 mortgage (tripling everything in the example), you could realize over $150,000 of tax-free retirement income on an equity management retirement nest egg of $1,923,045—nearly $2 million.

There's a catch, of course: You might have to eventually pay 33.3 percent[*] tax on the money you are earning in the equity management retirement fund (unless you use the investments I describe later). Despite this, as long as the side fund grows tax-deferred and you are taxed only on the back end, you wind up ahead. You can see how much more you would have if that fund were tax-free (50 percent greater in a 33.3 percent tax bracket), as are some of the investments I will describe in Chapters 11 and 12.

Furthermore, even if you *never* paid off the interest-only mortgage, I would argue that keeping a mortgage with discretionary money in a side fund is a better investment than a fifteen-year mortgage to achieve a "clear and free home" on your balance sheet. You have safe, liquid money that you can tap in an emergency in the side fund, plus the added value of a real rate of return and tax benefits. You have money in your right-hand pocket that you can use to wash away the debt in your left-hand pocket.

---

*Throughout this chapter, as in the previous ones, I assume for the sake of simplicity that you are in the 33.3 percent marginal tax bracket.

FIND THE MORTGAGE THAT'S RIGHT FOR YOU:
WHAT'S YOUR CREDIT SCORE?

I'm about to prove to you that my contrarian advice about mortgages can help you boost your retirement savings while safeguarding your home. If you already own your home without a mortgage or have already sunk a bundle of equity into your home, it's still not too late to become wealthy. Consider taking out a new mortgage, an interest-only mortgage, a home equity loan, or a home equity line of credit.

Mortgages today come in a variety of "flavors"—there are different lengths, payment options, amortization schedules, and so on. Lenders include your neighborhood bank or perhaps your credit union, but there are additional choices. You can obtain a mortgage from:

- A *mortgage banker*—an individual or financial institution dedicated solely to property loans. Mortgage bankers (primary lenders) typically sell their loans to secondary lenders such as Fannie Mae (the Federal National Mortgage Association—FNMA—a publicly held company chartered by Congress) or other companies in the secondary market that purchase mortgages from primary lenders such as Freddie Mac and Ginny Mae. Freddie Mac is a nickname for Federal Home Loan Mortgage Corporation (FHLMC), an organization that was created to purchase mortgages, primarily from savings and loans. Ginnie Mae is a nickname for Government National Mortgage Association (GNMA).
- A *mortgage broker*—a kind of wholesaler who represents more than one lender and thus may offer very competitive rates. Mortgage brokers are paid a fee for their services.
- A *private lender*—this might be a friend or member of your family.

- A *private pension plan or an employer*—a person or institution available for what are called nonconforming loans that provide additional flexibility.

It is to your advantage to be familiar with your choices so you can work with a lender to obtain the best arrangement for your situation.

You should be aware of mortgage insurance as well. Mortgage insurance protects the lender against loss in the event the borrower defaults and foreclosure becomes necessary. Lenders will usually require private mortgage insurance (PMI) when a conventional mortgage is made with a loan-to-value ratio greater than 80 percent—that is, when you borrow an amount that is higher than 80 percent of the fair market value of your house. Loans from the Federal Housing Authority (FHA) require mortgage insurance premiums on all loans. The Veterans Administration (VA) charges a funding fee on all its loans rather than mortgage insurance. In general you purchase mortgage insurance at the closing on your loan. You may be required to pay the premium at closing, over a scheduled time period, or as part of the loan amount.

A *first mortgage* or *senior mortgage* gives the lender first priority over any other liens on your property. The liens held by *junior mortgages* are subordinate (of lesser priority) to those that have been filed ahead of them. Because the lender's risk is directly related to the priority of the mortgage, lenders demand a higher interest rate for greater risks.

Fixed-rate mortgages are the "plain vanilla" of mortgages. In the past, fifteen-year and thirty-year fixed-rate mortgages were the most common. But according to former Federal Reserve Chairman Alan Greenspan in February 2004, "Americans' preference for long-term, fixed-rate mortgages means many are paying more than necessary for their homes." He went on to say that a Fed study suggested many homeowners could have saved tens of thousands of dollars in the last decade if they had ARMs—adjustable-rate mortgages.

With long-term fixed-rate mortgages, not only are interest rates fixed, but also the payments. They are usually amortized (paid off through regular payments that reduce both the principal amount of the loan and the interest on it). These payments do not change unless late-payment interest and/or penalties are incurred. You may come across the term PITI, which stands for principal, interest, taxes, and insurance. To make sure taxes and home insurance are always current, a lender may require regular payment for those and have them held "in escrow," that is, by a third party. The tax and insurance portion of the monthly fixed-rate mortgage may vary each year depending on those rates, but the sum of the principal and interest is constant.

Adjustable-rate mortgages, defined on the previous, page, are loans on which the interest rate may vary over the life of the loan. A lender may accept a lower qualifying income on an ARM because of initially lower interest rates. This makes housing more afford-able, but in exchange, there may be a provision for interest rates to escalate in the future. To determine the amount of such adjust-ments, interest rates in ARMs are tied to one of many indexes that represent the general movement of interest rates, such as the prime rate (the rate banks charge their most creditworthy commercial cus-tomers). Lenders may also add percentage points, referred to as the margin, to the index to determine the adjustable rate.

ARMs are available for periods ranging from ten years to forty years. Typically, there is an interest rate cap that limits how high the interest rate can go. The periodic rate cap limits the adjustments dur-ing a stated time period. Changes in the monthly payment amount are limited by the payment cap. Even though the interest rate can go up, the increase in the monthly payment amount may be limited by the loan's payment cap. You may be offered a conversion option, which allows an ARM to be converted to a fixed-rate mortgage with-out the normal expenses of refinancing. A flat fee or a certain number of percentage points is usually charged to exercise this option, and it must be exercised during a specific time period.

The *interest-only mortgage,* usually offered as an ARM, has burgeoned in popularity in recent years. As of 2006, they accounted for about one-quarter of all home loans.[*] In general, I'm a believer in the interest-only mortgage or Option ARM that allows you to pay interest only or deferred interest, so you have smaller monthly payments. At the same time, you can usually deduct the interest paid each year to reduce your taxable income.

Sometimes people will ask me, "Is a negative amortization loan good or bad?" I respond with, "It depends on what you know." I would rather allocate future dollars (which are cheaper) to cover my mortgage, than use today's (more expensive) dollars. In other words, I would rather trade some of my future cash flow to not have negative cash flow (by applying money to the principal, which earns nothing) at the beginning.

Critics try to scare borrowers by warning that interest-only and Option ARM loans lure people into buying a more expensive house than they can realistically afford and subject them to higher monthly payments once they reach the point where they must pay off the principal. I recommend you should buy only a house that you could afford assuming you were required to make a thirty-year or fifteen-year amortized mortgage payment. But instead, you take out an interest-only or deferred-interest loan and then set aside the difference between the two payments in a compounding side fund.

I usually refinance fairly often to harvest lazy, idle dollars that accumulate in the house due to appreciation. So I don't ever worry about a loan converting to an amortized loan, because, chances are, I've already refinanced before that happens. I don't ever want to pay down principal, thereby lowering my acquisition indebtedness and losing the tax benefits. I urge you to shop around to find an interest-only loan or Option ARM that comfortably fits your financial situation.

Here's a warning: You must be extremely disciplined and have a system of accountability to use deferred-interest (negative amortization)

---

[*]http://money.cnn.com/2006/03/28/real_estate/mortgage_danger_years/index.htm.

mortgage loans, or you may end up consuming your equity. It is imperative that you set aside the money you are saving (by not paying even the interest accruing each month) to make more money. Otherwise, I would suggest that an interest-only mortgage is the most aggressive approach that you should undertake. If you have a system, a thirty-year amortized mortgage works *good,* an interest-only mortgage can perform *better,* and an Option ARM with deferred-interest can perform *best.*

CHECK YOUR CREDIT SCORE

Before you look for a new mortgage or apply for refinancing, you should put the wheels in motion to learn what your credit score is and then take the necessary steps to improve it, if necessary. The higher your credit score is, the lower the interest rate you will get on any kind of important loan, not just a mortgage.

Your credit score is determined by a company called Fair Isaac Corporation (FICO). The highest possible score is 850; the top range is 760 or better.[*] Your score is based on such things as your bill-paying history, the number and type of accounts you have, late payments, collection actions, outstanding debt, and the age of your accounts.[**]

Three credit reporting companies, Equifax, Experian, and TransUnion, each compile a credit score for you. They are not necessarily identical. These agencies look at more than your credit cards; also taken into account are such things as retail store accounts, installment loans, regular payments such as your phone bill and the like, as well as such details as how long your credit history is, new credit applied for, and any delinquent payments.

The difference between getting the best interest rate on any kind of a mortgage and getting stuck with a higher rate can amount to thousands of dollars over the life of a mortgage, so it is crucial to

---

[*]http://www.myfico.comCreditEducation/.
[**]http://www.ftc.gov/bcp/edu/pubs/consumer/credit/cre24.htm (Federal Trade Commission).

investigate your scores on your own and to *correct any errors* before you approach a mortgage lender. Under federal law, you are entitled to one free report from each reporting company every twelve months, if you request it.

To order your free annual report from one or all national consumer reporting companies, visit www.annualcreditreport.com. The law says that you may dispute what you consider incorrect information and reporting companies are obliged to correct any errors, but bear in mind that this is not something that can be done overnight. It pays to keep yourself up-to-date on what credit reports say about you.

For more general information on your credit reports, I suggest that you visit the Federal Trade Commission site at www.ftc.gov/credit/.

Philip Tirone, a friend and one of my TEAM members,[*] wrote a great book titled *7 Steps to 720*. In it he teaches people how to win the credit game. You can learn how to turn even poor credit into great credit and into an opportunity to save hundreds of dollars a month. He states that a borrower could save $589 a month on a $300,000 home loan if they had a 720 credit score instead of a lower score. That adds up to $212,000 over thirty years. He also teaches that with a 720 credit score, lenders will compete for your business, giving you lower interest rates, insurance premiums, and more—helping you save tons of money. That money can be used for enhancing your retirement fund even more.

I would recommend *7 Steps to 720* as a must read for those who have a FICO credit score less than 720 or who want to maintain their credit score as high as possible. I have arranged with Philip to have a special edition of his book available at a substantial discount

---

[*]TEAM is an acronym for The Equity Alliance Matrix: a national network comprised of several thousand professional mortgage planners, financial planners, CPAs, attorneys, and Realtors who have been properly trained and know how to design plans that help people responsibly achieve their goals with asset optimization and equity management strategies.

off the normal retail price to readers of *The Last Chance Millionaire.* You can also receive a free forty-page booklet titled "I'll Bet You Didn't Know This About Credit." It contains thirty-eight important facts about credit that you can't afford not knowing. Go to www.MissedFortune.com/7stepsto720 to download the free booklet or to order Philip's book.

Even if your credit score is under 720, don't put off the implementation of the equity management strategies contained in *The Last Chance Millionaire.* I would recommend that you begin an asset optimization plan with a mortgage rate as attractive as you can get to establish liquidity and safety of principal. You can then enhance your rate of return by improving your credit score for the time you next refinance, even if you refinance as soon as six months to a year down the road.

SHOP FOR YOUR MORTGAGE AND COMPARE OFFERS FOR THE BEST DEAL

So many innovative mortgage products have been introduced in recent years that the discussion above merely scratches the surface. Each type of loan has its pluses and minuses. Start by keeping in mind the mantra: *Borrow only to conserve, not to consume.* Know what your credit score is and what you may be paying on your current mortgage, if you have one.

Then, go shopping for money. Don't simply go to the bank where you have a checking account and accept the first mortgage package offered to you. That might be the way your parents got their mortgage, but there's a whole smorgasbord of mortgages out there. Compare rates and terms. Seek a mortgage that matches your ability to make monthly payments. Consider how long you expect to stay in your current home; if it is just a few years, an ARM with a low initial rate might work best for you. Ask a savvy financial services professional or mortgage specialist to show you a selection of mortgages that fit your needs.

If this book was given or recommended to you by a financial professional, you may choose to seek his or her services, as well as advice from your personal tax advisor. If you are not acquainted with a professional trained in the strategies contained in this book, don't despair. You may visit www.MissedFortune.com/TEAMprofessionals for help in locating a properly trained TEAM member from among a national network of several thousand financial experts.

OTHER MORTGAGES WORTH YOUR CONSIDERATION

In recent years, many homeowners jumped at the chance to refinance their mortgage at a lower rate than they had been paying. If you are one of these people, you may do better with a *home equity line of credit*, often referred to as a HELOC, which allows you to preserve the low rate on your first mortgage and borrow additional funds with few, if any, closing costs.

What if you missed out on low-interest refinancing? It's still not too late. It pays to develop a trusting relationship with a professional mortgage planner who will shop for you and keep your best interest at heart based on your goals. A fixed-rate mortgage might have been the easiest, most uncomplicated choice for you when you first bought your house. But now might be a good time to maximize tax-deductible interest. You might even consider using some of the money from your refinance to pay off credit card balances (since their interest rates are high and not tax-deductible).

Option ARMs give you four different, basic ways to pay every month:

- A fifteen-year amortized payment amount
- A thirty-year amortized amount
- The interest-only amount
- A minimum payment based on a deferred-interest formula

In actuality, you can pay whatever you want above the minimum payment. Consult a good mortgage professional who can offer you a comparison of different products with a system to save and accumulate the difference when choosing an interest-only or deferred-interest loan. The system should not send the savings to be applied against the principal of the mortgage, like biweekly payment plans or Canadian amortizations do. Those systems tout that you can accelerate the payoff of your mortgage, but you will be killing your tax deduction and actually lengthening the time to accrue enough money to cover your mortgage.

Just to recap . . .

"So, Doug, should I always keep a mortgage on my house?" Yes, I would recommend it because:

- It doesn't lower the value of the house.
- Mortgages become cheaper over time.
- You should harvest idle equity anytime you can.
- It's the cheapest money (OPM) you can buy.

THREE COUSINS: NORM, RICH, AND MAX

To illustrate how you might manage your equity, let's look at three cousins: Norman, Richard, and Maxine. They go by the nicknames Norm, Rich, and Max.

Norm is 45; Rich is 50; Max is 55. They all have families and own their own home. But Norm is the one who always complains that he can barely scrape by on his household's income. Norm's children are attending a local college and live at home. In contrast, both Rich and Max seem to live the good life. Rich and Max send their offspring to colleges away from home despite the rising cost of education. Norm spends his vacation visiting Rich, who has a lovely vacation condo in the mountains, a few hours' drive from the metropolitan area where they live. Max devotes leisure hours to golf at the club where she owns a second home near the eighteenth hole and takes a Mediterranean cruise every year with her husband.

Let's Start with Norm . . .

Norm and his wife are both management executives who make a good salary. Rich and his wife are in marketing. Max and her husband are high school teachers. The difference in their lifestyles obviously has much more to do with the way they manage their finances than what kind of paychecks they collect.

Norm was bequeathed his parents' home when he was 35—a house in Atlanta that was purchased thirty years ago. Believe it or not, it originally cost only $31,250, and it appreciated nicely at an average rate of 7.2 percent (meaning it doubled three times over three decades). It's now worth $250,000. He and his wife wanted to move to a more contemporary house in a different neighborhood. They recently picked out a handsome three-bedroom model in a spanking-new subdivision. It cost them $250,000—slightly higher than the median price of a new home in the United States.[*]

Norm feels good because he avoided having to pay a capital gains tax on the sale of his old home. Because Norm is an average homebuyer, he believes that if he pours his former home's equity into a new home, he will sleep more soundly at night. So he plans to pay cash for his new home and avoid a mortgage altogether. Norm trusts conventional wisdom that says no mortgage means there are no costs.

Norm makes a very good income, but is it any surprise that the family budget is tight? Norm is trying to sock away $15,000 a year ($1,250 a month) into their 401(k)s and IRAs to make up for the first twenty years of their marriage when he and his wife were consuming so much. However, he loves to spend, and it seems as if he

---

[*]http://www.realtor.org/PublicAffairsWeb.nsf/Pages/JuneForecast06?OpenDocument.

is getting taxed to death. He has $250,000 lazy, idle dollars tied up in his new home earning nothing, just as he did in his old one.

Here's Rich's Approach . . .

Rich, who is five years older than Norm, is less inclined to accept conventional wisdom as gospel. He recently sold his house because he got a new job in Seattle. He, too, made a nice profit, but he has also accumulated a nice side fund from successfully managing the equity in his former home. While he now has $375,000 of liquid cash, he has decided to pay only 20 percent down on a new $375,000 house so he can keep the remainder of his equity management fund liquid. He will put just $75,000 down on his new house and take out an interest-only mortgage at 7.5 percent for the remaining $300,000.

Rich has wisely leveraged the equity in his new house. He has taken out a bigger mortgage than Norm did, but he has invested the balance of the profits from his former home ($300,000) in a safe side fund that earns him 7.5 percent interest. Meanwhile, he has monthly mortgage payments that Norm doesn't have, but he gets a tax deduction every year. So with his wife, Rich has allocated about $22,500 a year for retirement planning. Rather than pay $22,500 a year into 401(k)s and IRAs like Norm, Rich considers his $300,000 of home equity that he kept separated as his nonqualified retirement fund.

His annual mortgage payment on a $300,000 mortgage at 7.5 percent is $22,500; his mortgage payment becomes his retirement contribution, because it has the same tax advantages that a retirement contribution would receive. (In other words, it doesn't matter if he contributes $22,500 to a tax-favored qualified plan or makes interest-only mortgage payments of the same amount—both can be deductible with the same net outlay of $15,000 as a taxpayer. It just appears in a different place on his tax return.) So Rich starts out with 50 percent more than Norm ($375,000 compared to $250,000) and allocates 50 percent more toward retirement planning than Norm ($22,500 a year compared to $15,000 a year). We'll see shortly if Rich is just 50 percent better off down the road.

And now, for Max . . .

Max, a math teacher, has made it a priority to learn about successful wealth optimization. She's 55 years old and is already on the fast track to retire comfortably at age 65 if she chooses. She sold her house in Boston not long ago because she wanted more space. Wise in the ways of equity management, Max has put nothing down on her spacious new suburban home. She plans to keep the entire $625,000 she has already accumulated (by successfully managing the equity in all of her previous homes) in a safe, conservative liquid side fund. She takes out an interest-only mortgage for the entire $500,000 price of their new home.

Max, with her husband, has allocated $37,500 a year to set aside in their nonqualified equity retirement plan. Her annual interest-only mortgage payment at 7.5 percent on a $500,000 mortgage just happens to be $37,500, which is fully deductible. Her after-tax net outlay is only $25,000 a year. Like Rich, she, too, considers her house payment as her retirement contribution, because she has $625,000 in her equity management fund (that is earmarked to provide future retirement income) growing at 7.5 percent. So, Max starts out with 150 percent more than Norm ($375,000 in addition to $250,000) and allocates 150 percent more toward retirement planning than Norm ($37,500 a year compared to $15,000 a year for a total of 2.5 times as much). We'll see if Max's retirement fund is just 2.5 times better.

Let's fast-forward ten years and see what a difference these choices can make. As disclaimers always caution—while past performance is no guarantee of future returns—I'm going to assume that each of the new homes appreciates at 7.2 percent a year (doubling the value of the homes in ten years) and that the side funds all earn 7.5 percent per year. Take a look at Figure 8.4.

Yes, Norm, Rich, and Max all benefit from the appreciation in the fair market value of their homes. Their homes are all worth double ten years later. But let's see who is better off after ten years.

Norm's 401(k)s and IRAs have accumulated $223,803, which represents an after-tax value of about $150,000. His home is now

Fig. 8.4	THE TALE OF THREE COUSINS—Norm, Rich and Max

COUSIN NORM

Year	Home Value $250,000	401(k) $15,000	After Tax $10,000
1	$268,000	$15,624	$10,416
2	$287,296	$32,460	$21,641
3	$307,981	$50,604	$33,737
4	$330,156	$70,156	$46,773
5	$353,927	$91,225	$60,820
6	$379,410	$113,931	$75,958
7	$406,727	$138,399	$92,271
8	$436,012	$164,767	$109,850
9	$467,405	$193,182	$128,795
10	$500,000	$223,803	$149,209

Net Worth	$649,209
Gross Annual Income	$16,785
Net Annual Income After Tax	$11,191

COUSIN RICH

Year	Home Value $375,000	Equity Management $300,000
1	$402,000	$322,500
2	$430,944	$346,688
3	$461,972	$372,689
4	$495,234	$400,641
5	$530,891	$430,689
6	$569,115	$462,990
7	$610,091	$497,715
8	$654,018	$535,043
9	$701,107	$575,172
10	$750,000	$618,309

Net Worth	$1,068,309
Gross Annual Income	$46,373
Net Annual Income After House Payment	$31,373

COUSIN MAX

Year	Home Value $500,000	Equity Management $625,000
1	$536,000	$671,875
2	$574,592	$722,266
3	$615,963	$776,436
4	$660,312	$834,668
5	$707,854	$897,268
6	$758,820	$964,563
7	$813,455	$1,036,906
8	$872,024	$1,114,674
9	$934,809	$1,198,274
10	$1,000,000	$1,288,145

Net Worth	$1,788,145
Gross Annual Income	$96,611
Net Annual Income After House Payment	$71,611

* Assuming a 33.3% tax rate

worth $500,000. He has the equivalent of about $650,000 in net assets—mostly derived from home equity appreciation. But most of Norm's assets are tied up in his house. If he were retiring today, his retirement account worth $223,803 would generate an annual interest income of $16,785. After tax, he might net only about $11,191 a year. That's not going to cut it, so it's a good thing Norm is only 55 years old and can keep jogging toward retirement.

Rich's house is now worth $750,000, and his equity management retirement fund has grown to $618,309. Because he manages his home equity in investments that enjoy tax-free harvests, he will not have to pay tax on the gain in his side fund. Rich has a total of $1,368,309 between the value of his house and his side fund. If he subtracts the mortgage balance of $300,000, he has accumulated a net of $1,068,309 that he can continue to harvest and manage. Rich could retire if he wanted to and withdraw the annual interest earnings of $46,373 from his $618,309 equity management fund tax-free. He would still have a net after-tax mortgage payment of $15,000 a year, so he would net $31,373 in annual income, or almost triple what Norm would receive—even though he set aside only 50 percent more.

Max's house is now worth $1 million, and her equity retirement fund has grown to $1,288,145 for a total asset value of $2,288,145. Because she also manages her home equity in investments that enjoy tax-free harvests, she will not have to pay tax on the gain in her side fund. After subtracting the mortgage balance of $500,000, Max has a net of $1,788,145 that she can continue to harvest and manage. Max could also retire if she wanted and withdraw the annual interest earning of $96,611 from her $1,288,145 equity management fund tax-free. She would still have a net after-tax mortgage payment of $25,000 a year, so she would net $71,611 in annual income, or over six times as much as Norm would receive—even though she set aside only 2.5 times as much.

Of course, in reality, knowing what they know, Rich and Max would have probably harvested the equity in their homes at least a

couple of times during that ten-year period and enhanced their retirement even more. In fact, in the next chapter I will show you
that by keeping their mortgages high, they will maximize their tax
deductions and be able to offset taxable income throughout their
retirement.

Rich and Max both get a *lift* from the compound interest
earned in their liquid side funds, but since Max put more money in
those investments, she gets a far greater lift in the course of ten
years. Both Rich and Max feel the *drag* of leverage on their homes.
But notice how that mortgage drag allows Rich to realize a greater
net increase on the money he has put to work. And observe how
even greater leverage allows Max to earn a *much greater* amount.

Poor Norm. He's still struggling. But if he gets hold of this book,
it's not too late. He still has time left to turn things around during
his last ten to fifteen working years.

LOCATION, LOCATION, LOCATION

What else have Rich and Max done to make their financial lives
easier? Both Rich and Max have liquid side funds. If they choose,
they can use the money to add another bathroom to their homes,
modernize their kitchens, or make other home improvements that
would increase the value of their houses. They have "whether-
proofed" their homes against a soft real estate market and stored up
money they might need in an emergency.

Finally, as they approach their leisure years, both Rich and Max
have created an opportunity for *thrust*—tax-free accumulation.
Both can convert their side funds along with their home equity
into nonqualified retirement plans, which will earn them tax-free
dollars that they can harvest whenever they wish. They are poised
to grow their net spendable retirement income by as much as 50
percent over however much money IRAs and 401(k)s may hold.

In the real estate market, the phrase you always hear is "location, location, location." Rich and Max have discovered that the

best location for their home equity is not buried within the walls of their house, but put to work *outside* it.

TAKE ADVANTAGE OF YOUR MORTGAGE TO BECOME A THRIVER

In Chapter 1, I talked about people with different financial attention spans. Strivers want to handle their money more wisely but all too often they seem to have the financial version of Attention Deficit Disorder—they can't focus their attention for long on any one plan. Arrivers are able to climb higher on the wealth ladder simply by understanding the three marvels of compound interest, tax-free accumulation, and leverage. Thrivers use this knowledge to climb even higher by repeating the magic steps.

Let's examine how people who are about to buy their next home can improve their financial situation by paying just a little more attention. In every case, the person is 50 years old and has bought a house worth $250,000. Each can afford to make a net, after-tax mortgage payment of about $1,000 a month and has $200,000 of equity from the sale of a former home. (Although these scenarios are hypothetical, the home value is close to the median existing-home sales price in their area.)

• Arthur Amble lives in Albuquerque, New Mexico. He puts $200,000 down on his newly purchased house and takes out a $50,000 fifteen-year fixed amortized mortgage at 7.5 percent interest. This means his monthly mortgage payment is only $463. Arthur has heard the Strivers' siren song of "pay off your house as quickly as you can," so he sends his lender an extra $637 a month for a total payment of $1,100. He doesn't understand that the rate of return on his extra principal is zero. His mortgage interest comes to about $3,600 the first year, so he tallies a tax savings of approximately $1,200, or about $100 a month. Subtract his monthly tax savings from his regular monthly payment, and his net after-tax payment is approximately $1,000. But he's killing his best partner, Uncle Sam, by throwing away his tax advantage. Arthur is a Striver.

•   Charlotte Chugalong lives in Charleston, South Carolina. Having heard about liquidity and rate of return, she puts less down—just 20 percent, or $50,000—on her new home and takes out a $200,000 thirty-year amortized mortgage at 7.5 percent interest. Her monthly mortgage payments come to just under $1,400, giving her a monthly tax savings of about $400. That means her net payment is about $1,000. The difference is that Charlotte has kept $150,000 of her former home's equity apart from her new house. She can earn $1,000 a month in interest on it in a safe side fund earning 8 percent. So if push comes to shove, she could make her entire after-tax mortgage payment from the equity she kept out of her house. I'd label Charlotte an Arriver.

•   David Dasher lives in Dover, Delaware. Knowing that equity has no rate of return, he seeks safety and liquidity. He puts nothing down on his new house and takes out what often is referred to as an 80/20 mortgage for the full purchase price of $250,000. That means he gets an interest-only loan for 80 percent of the purchase price and an equity line for the additional 20 percent, both at an interest rate of 7.5 percent. His monthly tax savings, courtesy of Uncle Sam, is $521, so he pays a net of only $1,042—slightly higher than Arthur and Charlotte. But David has a booming $200,000 of liquid equity that he has kept separated from his house. Having found a safe liquid side fund averaging 8 percent, he earns $16,000 in interest the first year ($1,333 a month) on his equity. David is well on his way to becoming a Thriver.

What can you learn from the stories of the Amble, Chugalong, and Dasher families? First of all, by trying to be thrifty like Arthur and taking out a small fifteen-year amortized mortgage, you may wind up actually costing yourself (in lost opportunity) far more than someone else who does not put a nickel down on a house. Arthur is paying approximately the same net after-tax mortgage payment as Charlotte and David, yet he is not taking strides to build his net worth sooner. David is not taking much more of a risk than Charlotte or Arthur, but by managing his home equity wisely, he's in the fast lane, en route to greater net worth.

Can you see that withdrawing equity from your home and investing it safely might be a sensible strategy as you approach your golden years? I hope so. Actually, by adding *thrust* (tax-free accumulation) to the power of *lift* (compound interest on investments) and *drag* (the leverage inherent in a mortgage), *you can create wealth even when you borrow and invest at exactly the same rate of interest.*

DON'T LET RISING INTEREST RATES GET YOU DOWN

Back in the 1980s, I was borrowing money at 12 percent deductible interest—which was like paying 8 percent. Guess what I was earning on my investments? It was 13.75 percent. When interest rates are high for borrowing—mortgages, for example—they are also high for earning. I could have made enough money with mortgage interest rates of up to18 percent because the after-tax rate in a 33.3 percent bracket is 12 percent. Still, I kept hearing, "Enjoy yourself now, Doug, because when interest rates go lower, it's all over." I just smiled. As time went by, interest rates did sink lower and lower until they cratered around 5 to 6 percent. In the past few years, I've borrowed at net costs of 3, 4, and 5 percent and invested the loan proceeds in investments crediting 6, 7, 8, and 9 percent. Now people say, "Enjoy this low-interest-rate environment, Doug, because when rates go up, it's curtains for you." And I smile again.

Interest rates are relative.

You can create tremendous wealth managing your equity by borrowing money for mortgages at *any* interest rate and investing it at the *same* interest rate—or even less—provided your money management passes two tests: the interest paid on borrowed funds is tax-deductible, and the investment you put that money into earns compound interest.

If the investment earns compound interest in a tax-favored environment, you can reap even more bountiful harvests. I'll explain in Chapter 11 how to find such investments, especially in an often neglected corner of the financial world—tax-favored insurance contracts.

Boomers such as Arthur, Charlotte, or David could probably have thirty years or more to profit from the three marvels (the lift of compound interest, the thrust of tax-free accumulation, and the drag of leverage) all working together. In the first ten years, $200,000 of equity invested at 7.5 percent grows to $412,206 when it compounds tax-free. If each of these folks earned 8.5 percent on the same $200,000, their equity management fund would grow to over $1 million in twenty years. If they invested $200,000 of equity at 8 percent interest compounded and nontaxed, thirty years down the road, their nest egg would be over $2 million.

For the sake of simplicity, if you wanted to know what only $100,000 of equity would grow to in the above examples, simply cut the end results in half, because you are investing only half as much. Likewise, if you are managing twice as much equity ($400,000), simply double the end results. If you are managing $1 million of equity from the beginning, the end results would be five times as much, because you started with five times more.

The secret is that as time goes by, over the life of a mortgage, whether interest rates are low, average, or high, you earn interest on a higher and higher balance than you are paying interest on. This works best with an interest-only mortgage. The potential for growth is tremendous when you borrow in a tax-deductible environment and invest the proceeds in a nontaxed environment. You can do very nicely earning at just a slightly higher rate than the net cost you are borrowing at; but you do very well if you can borrow at a net interest rate that is 2 or 3 percent *lower* than the rate you earn. However, you do not need pie-in-the-sky returns to make lots of money over time using this concept. Safe, conservative rates of return are best to invest serious cash.

First, let's consider a very conservative example. Let's assume a homeowner separates $100,000 of home equity one time with an interest-only mortgage at 7.5 percent. His net after-tax annualized mortgage payment would be $5,000. Let's also assume that he earns only 6 percent interest, tax-free, on his $100,000 of separated equity. What? Borrow at 7.5 percent and invest the proceeds at only 6 percent? How can this homeowner get ahead doing that?

Because of the marvel of lift, $100,000 compounding at 6 percent grows to nearly $240,000 in fifteen years, while the net after cost of the mortgage was only $75,000 (15 × $5,000).

THREE WAYS TO STACK UP A MILLION DOLLARS OR MORE

"Hold on. I thought this book was going to teach me how to make a million dollars or more. So, how about more optimistic projections?"

What if a homeowner earns a rate 2 percentage points higher than the borrowing rate? Please refer to Figure 8.5. The first example illustrates a homeowner borrowing $100,000 at 6.5 percent tax-deductible interest and investing the loan proceeds at 8.5 percent interest compounding free of tax. In ten years, the side fund has grown to $226,098, which results in a net profit of $126,098 after deducting the mortgage balance of $100,000. In year twenty, the net profit is $411,205, and in year thirty, the net profit is $1,055,825. If the annual employment cost of $4,333 were invested in an alternative investment earning 8.5 percent, it would grow to only $583,971 by year thirty. To match the profit of $1,055,825, the $4,333 annual investment would have to earn a nontaxable interest rate of 11.53 percent or a taxable rate of 17.3 percent.

What if a homeowner has $175,000 of available equity? The second illustration employs $175,000 of home equity by separating it at 7 percent and investing the loan proceeds at 8 percent for thirty years. The liquid equity management account balance (after deducting the mortgage balance) would be $1,023,483 in twenty-five years, and $1,585,965 in thirty years.

You may say, "But I don't have thirty years until I retire." I say, "I'm not necessarily talking about how much time you have until

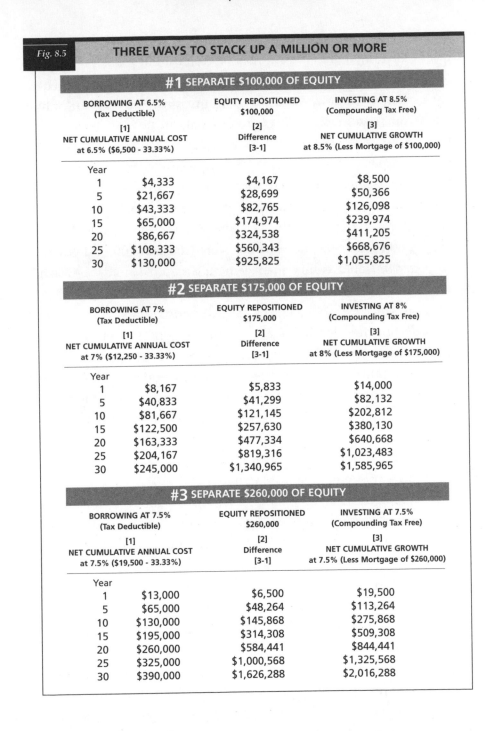

Fig. 8.5

THREE WAYS TO STACK UP A MILLION OR MORE

#1 SEPARATE $100,000 OF EQUITY

BORROWING AT 6.5% (Tax Deductible) [1] NET CUMULATIVE ANNUAL COST at 6.5% ($6,500 - 33.33%)	EQUITY REPOSITIONED $100,000 [2] Difference [3-1]	INVESTING AT 8.5% (Compounding Tax Free) [3] NET CUMULATIVE GROWTH at 8.5% (Less Mortgage of $100,000)
Year		
1 $4,333	$4,167	$8,500
5 $21,667	$28,699	$50,366
10 $43,333	$82,765	$126,098
15 $65,000	$174,974	$239,974
20 $86,667	$324,538	$411,205
25 $108,333	$560,343	$668,676
30 $130,000	$925,825	$1,055,825

#2 SEPARATE $175,000 OF EQUITY

BORROWING AT 7% (Tax Deductible) [1] NET CUMULATIVE ANNUAL COST at 7% ($12,250 - 33.33%)	EQUITY REPOSITIONED $175,000 [2] Difference [3-1]	INVESTING AT 8% (Compounding Tax Free) [3] NET CUMULATIVE GROWTH at 8% (Less Mortgage of $175,000)
Year		
1 $8,167	$5,833	$14,000
5 $40,833	$41,299	$82,132
10 $81,667	$121,145	$202,812
15 $122,500	$257,630	$380,130
20 $163,333	$477,334	$640,668
25 $204,167	$819,316	$1,023,483
30 $245,000	$1,340,965	$1,585,965

#3 SEPARATE $260,000 OF EQUITY

BORROWING AT 7.5% (Tax Deductible) [1] NET CUMULATIVE ANNUAL COST at 7.5% ($19,500 - 33.33%)	EQUITY REPOSITIONED $260,000 [2] Difference [3-1]	INVESTING AT 7.5% (Compounding Tax Free) [3] NET CUMULATIVE GROWTH at 7.5% (Less Mortgage of $260,000)
Year		
1 $13,000	$6,500	$19,500
5 $65,000	$48,264	$113,264
10 $130,000	$145,868	$275,868
15 $195,000	$314,308	$509,308
20 $260,000	$584,441	$844,441
25 $325,000	$1,000,568	$1,325,568
30 $390,000	$1,626,288	$2,016,288

you retire. I'm more interested in a strategy and resource that will last as long as you do—which may be thirty more years."

What if a homeowner has $260,000 of available equity? The third example employs $260,000 of home equity by separating it at 7.5 percent and investing the loan proceeds at the same rate of 7.5 percent for thirty years. The liquid equity management account balance would be $769,308 ($509,308 after deducting the $260,000 mortgage balance) in fifteen years, which could generate about $57,700 a year of tax-free income, depending on the investments selected. After deducting the net, after-tax mortgage annual payment of $13,000, the net income would be $44,700. If left untapped, the liquid equity management account would be worth $1,325,568 in twenty-five years (after deducting the mortgage balance). It would be worth $2,016,288 after thirty years.

Let's imagine that Maxine, the woman from Boston I referred to a few pages ago, did what Figure 8.5 shows in the third example. Keeping $500,000 of her cash out of her new home, she borrowed the full 100 percent to pay for her new house. In other words, she kept her equity separated in a tax-free investment. After the first year, Max would be already ahead of the game—she's earned $37,500, but since the mortgage cost her only $25,000 (net after tax) that year, she has made a tax-free profit of $12,500.

Hmm. That's already enough for Max to build a terrific home theater with a state-of-the-art large plasma screen. But Max wants to conserve, not consume. If she has used my strategy, Max's tax-free investment is her nonqualified retirement plan. So with a tax-free plan, she's taken the first giant step toward worry-free retirement. After ten years with 7.5 percent interest earnings in her side fund, her $500,000 of home equity she has kept separated from her house has grown to more than $1 million.

"Wait a minute! What if Max can't get those kinds of interest rates!" you retort. Perhaps she borrows the same amount at 8 percent but receives only 6 percent tax-free. After ten years, Max still has accumulated nearly $895,424 toward her retirement years.

REPEAT AFTER ME—REFINANCE, REFINANCE, REFINANCE

A lot of people would be thrilled to reposition the equity in their homes to build the kind of tax-free retirement nest egg that Max has. But she, and you, can do even better. You'll recall that Thrivers not only grasp the three marvels of wealth accumulation, but also they know how to *repeat* them.

Since separating equity from your home starts you on the path to great wealth, why not take that path more often? What if you repeated the process every five years? Let's use our friend David Dasher in Dover as an example. Let's assume that his new $250,000 home appreciates every year by 7.2 percent. His house will double in value every ten years. Rather than wait ten years to refinance, five years down the road he will be able to borrow an additional $103,927 of appreciated equity. As he continues to remove 100 percent of appreciated equity, either by refinancing or by selling his present house and buying a new one, he can invest that money in either a liquid side fund or a nontaxed investment.

Fig. 8.6 **TURBO CHARGE YOUR WEALTH GROWTH RATE**

Example of separating $200,000 of equity initially and continuing to separate 100 percent of the equity every five years thereafter, on a home with a beginning fair market value of $250,000 appreciating at 7.2 percent annually for twenty-five years, borrowing at 7.5 percent tax deductible and investing the loan proceeds at 8 percent compounding with no tax.

YEAR	HOME VALUE AT 7.2% [1]	EMPLOYED EQUITY [2]	FUTURE VALUE IN 15 YRS AT 8% [3]	FUTURE VALUE IN 25 YRS AT 8% [4]
0	$ 250,000.00	$200,000.00	$634,433.82	$1,369,695.04
5	$ 353,972.20	$103,927.20	$224,371.02	$ 484,400.21
10	$ 501,057.84	$147,130.64	$216,183.19	$ 466,723.29
15	$ 709,351.99	$208,294.15	$208,294.15	$ 449,691.44
20	$1,004,235.84	$294,883.85		$ 433,281.12
25	$1,421,705.50	$417,469.66		$ 417,469.66
TOTALS:				
15	$ 709,352.00	$659,352.00	$1,283,282.18	
25	$ 1,421,705.50	$1,371,705.50		$ 3,621,260.75

Columns 3 and 4 are the ending values of the separated equity (Column 2) at the end of 15 and 25 years.

As you see from Figure 8.6, David can sprint from being an Arriver to a Thriver by tapping the marvels of compound interest, tax-free accumulation, and leverage whenever interest rates and home appreciation in Dover make it feasible. In fifteen years when he may decide to retire, he's turbocharged his money: That tax-free investment is now worth $1,283,282. After twenty-five years, when David is a spry 75-year-old, his nest egg is $3,621,261!

You can do for yourself and your family what *thrivers* do. Step one is to move the lazy, idle dollars in your house. You must be disciplined; hold off buying that big TV for just a little while. Put those dollars to work for you in a tax-free investment. Then repeat the process over and over again, and with Uncle Sam himself as your partner, you can amass enough money to put a 52-inch plasma screen TV in every room of your house, take a luxury cruise every year, and become an important donor to the annual fund drive of your favorite charity. You don't have to start out with much money, because it doesn't matter which on-ramp you take to enter the expressway to wealth. The only thing that matters is where you finish.

REMEMBER THIS:

- *Your home is sacred, not your house.* Separating your equity from your house is the key to optimizing retirement income.
- Before seeking a mortgage, learn your credit score and improve it by eliminating errors and negative items that lower your credit rating.
- Be proactive in shopping for a mortgage that can give you an indirect tax deduction for your nonqualified retirement contributions with the same possible effect as tax-deductible IRA and 401(k) plans.
- All mortgages are not created equal. Shop for innovative mortgage products such as Option ARMs and interest-only mortgages, and use strategies to obtain 100 percent financing.
- Once you obtain a mortgage, be alert for opportune times when your property appreciates and turbocharge your wealth by refinancing.

Sprint to Retirement Wealth via Tax-Smart Alternatives

Prepare a Strategic Rollout of IRAs/401(k)s to Save Taxes

NOT LONG AGO, a provocative report looked at the financial future of Boomers and asked, "Is the future really so dark?" The report went on to state: "Data on defined benefit plans, defined contribution plans, and wealth accumulation suggest that many baby boomers may not have adequate resources for a comfortable retirement. . . . Even those who appear financially well prepared for retirement face risks related to inflation, longevity, and health care costs."[*]

This dire warning came not from a newspaper or magazine columnist but straight from the Federal Deposit Insurance Corporation (FDIC), the agency that supervises U.S. banks. However, the report held out this hope: "The financial situation for many baby boomers is not as dire as it may seem. Changing preferences may lead baby boomers to seek a different type of retirement than their parents."

---

[*]http://www.fdic.gov/bank/analytical/regional/ro20061q/na/2006_spring01.html.

My financial freedom plan offers a different type of retirement strategy—an alternative to escape the trap of qualified retirement plans.

You'll recall that Misconception #7 is believing that IRAs and 401(k)s are the best way to save for retirement. By now, I expect you have questioned that belief. As I have shown, your tax bracket upon retirement may be as high or higher than the one you are in now, because you may have fewer deductions to lower your taxable income. And I have also illustrated that the typical pension, IRA, 401(k), or similar qualified plan takes such a big tax bite out of your retirement pie, it can look like a pizza after the delivery guy has helped himself to a few wedges. (Roths are the exception on this point, but they have, too, many other limitations.)

Don't despair; there's still hope! Even if you have already funneled a great deal of your hard-earned cash for one or more of the traditional plans, you still have time to convert them into a nonqualified plan that lets your retirement bloom in a tax-free environment.

MAXIMIZE YOUR DEFINED BENEFIT PENSION

There are two types of pensions. Depending on which companies, government offices, or institutions you have worked for, you may be enrolled in one or more. The more traditional is the *defined-benefit* retirement plan. There are not nearly as many of these around as there once were. The other is the *defined-contribution* plan, with the 401(k) probably the best known.

A defined-benefit plan promises you a specific monthly benefit once you retire. It might be an exact dollar amount, or it might be calculated via a formula based on your years of service and your salary. The calculated version is the most common. As an example, it could be 2 percent of average salary for the last five years of employment for every year of service with an employer.[*]

---

[*]http://www.dol.gov/dol/topic/retirement/typesofplans.htm.

In a defined-benefit plan, the employer typically gives you choices on how you can receive your benefit when you reach the required age. If you know you are entitled to such a pension, I would urge you to *maximize* it. Otherwise it could be the most expensive life insurance policy you have ever purchased.

The three most popular choices among the distribution plans are:

1. *Single life only*—You receive a set amount each month for the remainder of your life, but if you die, your spouse gets nothing. There is no provision for benefits to be paid to a survivor.

2. *Joint and survivor annuity*—You receive a reduced set amount each month (usually about 17 percent less than the single life only option). When you die, your spouse receives the same monthly payment.[*] However, if your spouse predeceases you, and you remarry, your second spouse doesn't receive anything.

3. *50 percent survivor option*—You receive a reduced set amount each month (usually about 9 percent less than the single life only option). When you die, your spouse receives 50 percent of that amount. However, if your spouse predeceases you and you remarry, your second spouse does not receive anything.

Under some plans, you are entitled to receive a lump-sum payment or partial lump-sum payment when you retire. To maximize your defined-benefit plan, the best idea may be to accept this lump sum, but there is no blanket rule. Whatever the specifics of your plan, you maximize it by choosing the no-survivor option. If you don't, it is as if you bought from your employer an incredibly costly life insurance plan, since by agreeing to a reduced amount you are

---

*http://www.bls.gov/opub/cwc/cm20030409ar01p1.htm.

voluntarily giving up what could be hundreds of thousands of dollars in benefits.

Let's say Tom is a retiring male age 65 with a life expectancy of twenty more years, to age 85. His wife, Mary, is also age 65 and has a life expectancy of twenty-seven more years. Tom's single life only monthly retirement benefit is $3,000. In order to provide $3,000 a month, which is $36,000 per year in income, it would require an asset of $450,000 earning 8 percent interest to generate that income into perpetuity.

If the income is projected to be needed for only twenty years (Tom's life expectancy), then it would require an asset of only $360,000 earning 8 percent to generate a monthly income of $3,000. The benefits counselor asks Tom, "Don't you want to share that $450,000 asset with Mary?" "Sure I do," Tom replies. "Well then, if you will take a reduced amount of $2,500 per month ($500 less) we will guarantee that when you die, Mary will continue to receive $2,500 per month as long as she lives." Sounds good, doesn't it?

When Tom thinks about it, it sounds good only if he dies early. If he lives twenty more years as expected, he and Mary will be giving up $500 per month, or $6,000 a year (which totals $120,000). The "time value" of that money at 8 percent is nearly $300,000! If Tom passes away at age 85 and Mary lives seven more years to age 92, she would receive $2,500 a month ($30,000 a year) for seven more years, for a total of $210,000—but they gave up the equivalent of $300,000 to ensure that.

In the remainder of this book, I'm going to show how someone like Tom could end up having $450,000 or more of life insurance that comes along for the ride, and that is paid for with otherwise payable income tax. Then if Tom passes away, anytime, he would leave behind $450,000 tax-free that could generate an annual income of $36,000 tax-free, into perpetuity (rather than the pension taxable income of $30,000). He can also change the beneficiary if Mary passes away first. This would enable them to enjoy $500 more per month of retirement income as long as Tom lives. This strategy is referred to as pension maximization.

I urge most clients to choose the no-survivor plan and then arrange for Uncle Sam to cover your spouse, using properly structured life insurance contracts with otherwise payable income tax, as I explain them in Chapters 11 and 12. The key, as always, is *liquidity*, *safety*, and *rate of return*. You can prepare for a no-survivor defined-benefit plan even before you retire, and you will be doing the right thing for your survivors. Although a defined-benefit option that pays out in a monthly retirement income does not allow for access to lump sums thereafter, they generally are safe (some are insured by the federal government) and offer a rate of return based on how well they are managed. A trained retirement specialist can help you determine whether you should take the lump-sum option (if available) and invest it in a conservative portfolio.

ANALYZE YOUR EMPLOYER'S "MATCHING BENEFITS" PROGRAM

Since 1982 when the 401(k) plan was introduced, it has become a widespread financial method through which people who work in salaried jobs save for their retirement. (It was named for the section of the federal tax code that gave these programs tax-advantaged status.) It allows you to contribute a portion of your salary before it is taxed to a fund where your money (plus any gains it accrues) grows without being taxed. In some instances, but not all, employers match your contributions either partially or 100 percent. Often you have to wait a year or more before you are eligible to participate in such plans and even longer before you are "vested." The idea is to help you save for retirement—but also to lock you in "golden handcuffs" designed to keep you at the same company.

Matching benefits may be useful to you, but you need to analyze them carefully, since they have some restrictions. There is no single formula that every company must follow in matching benefits. In addition to vesting, your employer may have other limits. In some cases employees contribute the maximum amount allowed under law on such plans, while the employer kicks in less than 100 cents on the dollar. Some employers have a "100 percent matching" program but it applies only to the first 4, 5, or 6 percent of your income. In other instances, an employer will contribute a percentage of your income to a company-sponsored plan regardless of whether you are contributing anything.

True matching occurs when an employer agrees to match dollar for dollar on a percentage of an employee's contribution. To get the most out of matching, it is typically in your best interest as an employee to contribute at least the amount or percentage required to qualify for full matching benefit. After all, the matching dollars are "free." However, note that the money is tax-deferred, not tax-free. If you draw on your 401(k) before you reach age 59½ you must pay the taxes, plus a 10 percent penalty. After age 59½, you still pay taxes on any withdrawals.

There are safeguards built into 401(k) programs that are not attached to old-fashioned pensions. The assets in these programs are held in trust for you, in a separate account, so in case your employer goes bankrupt or gets entangled in corporate swindles, the company cannot touch your 401(k) holdings. Also, the accounts are portable. You are permitted to take the assets with you when you leave that particular job. However, a portion of your company's contributions may be in the form of company stock, and that can be a terrible investment, as former employees of companies such as Enron or WorldCom can attest.

Many employees contribute additional funds on top of the amount required to receive a full matching benefit, but is that a good idea? It depends first on where the contributions are invested and what the performance of that investment is. If you can get the same yield in a nonqualified personal retirement account that is tax-free during the harvest, I generally advise an employee to contribute only up to the amount matched by your employer. The best deal is at least a 50 percent matching benefit.

You should also know that the IRS has a cap on how much you can contribute each year to a 401(k) account. That ceiling has been increased in recent years, and there are catch-up provisions for Boomers who start late. In 2006, those 50 years old or older could save an additional $5,000 on top of the limit of $15,000, and the catch-up amount was scheduled to rise by $500 a year thereafter. But I urge you to pay close attention to the provisions of a 401(k) before you channel pre-tax earnings into it.

Here's why: When you contribute a dollar and it is matched 50 cents on that dollar by your employer, your 401(k) has $1.50 earning interest. The illusion is that you are getting a 50 percent return on your money. While it is true that the principal has risen 50 percent, the interest rate from that point forward is whatever the portfolio earns. The 50 percent increase is only on the seed money deposited into your account. If you could withdraw your money without incurring a 10 percent penalty immediately after you contributed it—and the matching was immediately vested in a 33.3 percent tax bracket—you would pay in taxes the 50 cents that your employer contributed. In other words, your employer in this instance is more or less paying the portion you end up paying in tax. If the plan grows, the tax liability grows.

Employer matching can function as a good extra layer that supplements your retirement money to cover future tax liabilities. However, all other things being equal, I generally recommend that you should not contribute any funds to a qualified plan beyond the amount required to receive matching contributions by your employer. Be aware that your distributions will be taxed on the back end—your harvest years. All qualified plans have strings attached, and that is just one of them.

At present, employers usually will contribute matching funds only to qualified plans, not to nonqualified plans such as the ones I suggest. I look forward to the day when the market is more educated, and employers are willing to match retirement savings whether the employee contributes to a qualified or a nonqualified plan.

CONVERT DURING THE YEARS YOUR TAXABLE INCOME DIPS

One strategy for escaping the confines of a qualified plan is to convert money from your IRA or 401(k) to a nonqualified alternative during your tax-advantaged years. Even before you reach 59½ (the age at which you can withdraw money from a qualified plan without penalty), you may find a year here or there when you have less taxable income than before. Perhaps you made a job change, took a nonpaying sabbatical, or were laid off. Or perhaps you had unusually high expenses for such deductible items as caring for an ill parent or sending a son or daughter to college.

If this is the case, *take advantage of your lower tax bracket to shift a portion of the funds in your qualified plan to a nonqualified account.* You must pay the taxes, but you would be taxed on that same money eventually anyway. And if you, like the majority of people I speak to, expect taxes to go up in the coming years, you are smarter to pay those taxes now, not later. Remember, the key is to reposition these after-tax dollars to an investment that is tax-free from that point forward and that transfers to heirs tax-free at death. I describe which investment vehicles are best to accomplish this in Chapter 11.

Another opportunity to shift retirement accounts arises if, in any given year, you have room to maneuver between two tax brackets. Too many people avoid a step up to the next tax bracket, not realizing that they can lose a lot more than the 3 percent between the 25 percent bracket and the 28 percent bracket if they delay a strategic withdrawal.

To get an estimate of the amount of income you could realize through a withdrawal from a qualified plan without crossing the next tax threshold, feel free to use our online calculator at www.MissedFortune.com/Calculator/TaxThresholds. When using this calculator, it will be necessary for you to have an estimate of what your taxable income will be. Otherwise, you will need to know your projected annual income and the approximate amount of any adjustments, deductions, and exemptions that would apply.

If you are not yet 59½ when you move funds from your qualified plan, you will be required to pay a 10 percent penalty. But the difference may be a wash: If you are temporarily in the 15 percent bracket, your total tax (even with the penalty) comes to 25 percent—the same bracket you might have been in during a good year. You may never have another opportunity, so why postpone the inevitable?

PREPARE A STRATEGIC ROLL*OUT*, NOT A ROLL*OVER*

I advise a strategic roll*out*, not a roll*over*. Perhaps, in the past, a financial planner has counseled you on how to withdraw funds from a pension or 401(k) and switch them into a different qualified plan investment (such as an IRA) without triggering a taxable event. That's a roll*over*. You often do this by filling out forms that transfer funds in one plan to another without your receiving any of the money. It is common for a financial services company to offer this service. You can also achieve a rollover by collecting the money yourself and depositing it in another qualified plan within sixty days. However, if you miss the cutoff date, you get slapped with taxes and penalties.

I recommend instead doing what I call a roll*out*. This means taking funds out of a qualified plan and repositioning them in a nonqualified plan. Are there tax consequences? There can be. Are there ways to minimize or mitigate the tax consequences? Yes. But even with tax consequences, I will show that you are often still better off with the rollout.

When it comes to timing the rollout, who should switch to a nonqualified plan immediately, and who can wait? There are a lot of variables to consider before making this decision. In general, some of you who are under 55 might be better off switching immediately, despite the penalty, depending on the yield on the tax-free investment you choose for your nonqualified plan and the tax bracket you are in. On the other hand, older Boomers age 55 and up can often afford to wait a few years and save themselves the 10 percent penalty that Uncle Sam levies when removing money from a qualified plan early.

Under Section 72(t) of the Internal Revenue Code, there are certain circumstances under which a taxpayer can take distributions from a qualified retirement plan prematurely. The rules are somewhat complicated, but in general, there are provisions by which a taxpayer can avoid the 10 percent penalty on distributions that are (as worded in the Code):

- Made on or after the date on which the employee attains age 59½.
- Made to a beneficiary (or to the estate of the employee) on or after the death of the employee.
- Attributable to the employee's being disabled within the meaning of subsection (m)(7).
- *Part of a series of substantially equal periodic payments (not less frequently than annually) made for the life (or life expectancy) of the employee or the joint lives (or joint life expectancies) of such employee and his designated beneficiary.*
- Made to an employee after separation from service after attainment of age 55.
- Dividends paid with respect to stock of a corporation, which are described in section 404(k).
- Made on account of a levy under section 6331 on the qualified retirement plan.

Other technical provisions allow for distributions under special circumstances such as:

- Medical expenses (within limitations).
- Payments to alternate payees pursuant to qualified domestic relations orders.

- Distributions to unemployed individuals for health insurance premiums.
- Distributions from individual retirement plans for higher education expenses.
- Distributions from certain plans for first home purchases.

If you are under age 59½, and would like to explore the possibility of transferring some of your money out of a qualified plan under the provisions in Section 72(t), it would behoove you to seek the advice of a professional tax advisor.

As explained in the Code, the 10 percent penalty tax does not apply to distributions that are part of a series of substantially equal periodic payments made at least annually for the life or life expectancy of the individual or the joint lives or joint life expectancies of the individual and his or her designated beneficiary. Therefore, 72(t) annual distributions under this provision will represent a relatively small percentage of your overall account balance.

IRS Notice 89-25 describes three basic methods in which payments are considered to be substantially equal periodic payments:

- *Life expectancy method*—calculated under the minimum distribution rules.
- *Amortization method*—the account balance amortized using life expectancies and a reasonable interest rate.
- *Annuitization method*—the account balance divided by an annuity factor using both a reasonable mortality table and interest rate.

The IRS has specified that "period payments" means at least one payment per year. Once the distributions begin, the account owner must take payments for the equivalent of five years, or until age 59½, whichever period is longer. Once the longer period is over, the owner is free to change the payment amount or stop withdrawing money altogether until age 70½.

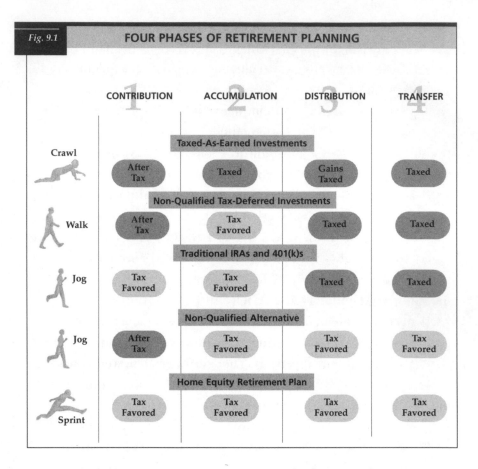

Fig. 9.1 — FOUR PHASES OF RETIREMENT PLANNING

It can become even more complicated when you have money in an employer's qualified plan and you leave your job. If you want to make the rollout yourself, your former employer is required to withhold 20 percent to pay expected taxes. Still another option, if you have more than $5,000 and you switch employers, is to let your money stay parked where it is, in your former employer's plan. Fortunately, the laws that govern 401(k) plans shield your money from raids by a financially troubled or bankrupt company. (On the other hand, anyone who has allowed contributions to pile up in company pension plans might be setting themselves up for an Enron or General Motors–style nightmare.)[*]

*http://www.kiplinger.com/personalfinance/columns/ask/archive/2005/q0815.htm.

UNCLE SAM SAYS "PAY ME NOW OR PAY ME LATER"

The only certainty is that Uncle Sam will have his hand out demanding his share whether you let your money sit in a qualified plan for several years or prepare a rollover. That is why I recommend rolling your qualified plan money *out*, getting the taxes over with (or offset), and repositioning the remainder into a tax-free investment.

Remember the visual guide to the four phases of retirement planning from Chapter 5 (Figure 9.1)?

The main point is to avoid the *crawl* by repositioning your retirement assets in a nonqualified tax-free plan in a timely fashion so your harvest is tax-free.

THE PRICE OF PROCRASTINATION

I have heard poignant stories about hardworking people who were so concerned about saving taxes that they waited too long to roll out their retirement savings. Then some of them were forced to make the move at an inopportune time, such as during the 2001–2003 downturn in the market.

Because so many financial institutions and planners put the emphasis on the intake phases—contribution and accumulation— while neglecting the withdrawal and transfer phases of retirement planning, some people who reach age 59½ simply don't realize the risk they are taking by letting their savings sleep in qualified plans for the next eleven years. At 70½, you must start withdrawing a minimum based on all your qualified accounts (the "required minimum distribution," in financial parlance), whether you need the money or not. Those who fail to start their withdrawals at 70½ get hammered by Uncle Sam, as the government collects a 50 percent penalty in addition to the tax (Figure 9.2).

At first, the amount you are required to pull out each year seems like a very gentle distribution, and taxes may not seem significant. But as you continue your minimum distributions, you end up paying extensive taxes when all the years are totaled together.

Fig. 9.2

There is a complicated formula for calculating the minimum amount that must be withdrawn starting at age 70½. The best Web site I have found to help you make the calculations is provided by TIAA/CREF, the giant financial services company that caters primarily to those in academic, medical, cultural, and research fields. Go to https://www3.tiaa-cref.org/mdo/index.jsp and fill in the birth dates for you and your beneficiaries, the value of your accounts, and the growth rate you feel you'll earn during your retirement years.

In my experience, retired couples sometimes pay more than twice the amount of taxes on their retirement plans when they string them out using the government's minimum distribution formula. On the other hand, you may pay 60 percent *less* in taxes if you simply bite the bullet and pay the tax according to a systematic withdrawal plan or strategic transfer over five to seven years. This is true provided you reposition your after-tax distributions into a tax-free environment from that point on.

TRANSFERRING QUALIFIED RETIREMENT PLANS TO HEIRS

Upon the death of the first spouse, the surviving spouse may inherit or be the beneficiary of qualified funds. At that point, there are rules that allow a beneficiary under the age of 59½ to receive those funds without being subject to a 10 percent penalty. The funds could also be converted to an IRA under the beneficiary's name, but the distribution and subsequent tax would then be postponed. Survivors or beneficiaries may be tempted to "stretch" the IRA by using this option when inheriting a qualified account. However, in many instances, it may be better for them to take out the money, pay the tax at today's rate, and put the tax liability behind them. They could then reposition those after-tax funds into nonqualified accounts, possibly accumulating tax-free from that point forward, using the information in Chapter 12.

For a retired couple, if there are still funds remaining in a qualified retirement plan upon the death of the second spouse, the value of the account is included in the estate of the deceased and must be added as part of the total value of the estate assets. The tax on a large estate can get very steep indeed, depending on whether the government decides to change current tax law.

But that's not the end of a beneficiary's obligation to the government. Income tax will still have to be paid on those qualified funds at the tax rate of the beneficiary if the funds are not rolled over to another IRA. Such a transfer will generally boost the beneficiary into a higher federal tax bracket. Estate tax may be owed to the IRS on top of any income tax.

I am spelling out the tax impact on qualified plans during the distribution and transfer phases because few people realize how heavy the tax burden can become. Sometimes, between the estate tax and income tax, surviving heirs actually keep only about 22 to 28 cents on the dollar out of their deceased parents' IRAs! What at first may seem like an adequate amount to sustain heirs beyond the death of the account holders soon gets shredded by Uncle

Sam. In case you haven't noticed, "THE IRS" combined together spells THEIRS.

REDUCE YOUR INCOME TAX WITHOUT LOSING A CENT

As I explained in Chapter 8, tax-deductible mortgage interest is the key to offsetting the tax you will owe Uncle Sam once you start withdrawing money from an IRA or 401(k), whether you remove that money with a penalty before age 59½, between age 59½ and 70½, or after 70½ when you are forced to remove at least a minimum.

Do you have a copy of your most recent federal tax return? I know this may not be fun, but please, suppress the groan and do this anyway: Take it out and examine it.

On the front of your 1040, notice lines 15 and 16. This is where you declare any distributions you take from a qualified retirement plan, pension, or annuity. It immediately boosts your taxable income; you can't hide it. On the reverse side, about line 42 or 43 (depending on the changes the IRS makes from year to year), you will see the total of that taxable income after adjustments, deductions, and exemptions.

Now turn to 1040 Schedule A. This is the best place to offset gross income, because here you list deductions that you subtract from that gross income. You create a new deduction by listing mortgage interest. Do you see the section for entering "interest you paid"? This is why leverage, translated as mortgage interest, is the *drag* that makes your money soar.

Every dollar you generate in a new interest deduction that you did not have before can offset a dollar you have withdrawn that year from your IRA. Therefore, in effect, you can pull money out of your IRA "tax-free." If you generate $10,000 in mortgage interest, you can potentially offset 100 percent of $10,000 that you removed from an IRA for repositioning. If you withdrew $20,000 from an IRA and you have $10,000 in mortgage interest deduction, you have cut your tax liability in half. I've had numerous clients for whom I have totally offset tax using this strategy.

My rollout strategy has two steps:

1. The first step is to withdraw money from your qualified retirement plans and pay the tax immediately so it is over and done with. (I will soon show you how to reposition the money into a nonqualified retirement plan that is tax-free as you go forward.)
2. The second step is to offset the tax you must pay by creating a new mortgage interest deduction based on my equity management strategy.

They work independently of each other, but if you combine them, it's like melody and harmony—the music created is particularly sweet. You see, if you have a $1 million mortgage, and you are paying 6 percent interest, that could be possibly generating $60,000 a year in a mortgage interest tax deduction. As explained in Chapter 8, you already know you can make back more than the cost of that. The other benefit is that while you are managing equity in your home, you can get this new $60,000 deduction you didn't have before. That allows you to possibly withdraw $60,000 a year out of an IRA or 401(k) with no tax consequence. If you can accomplish that for ten years, you could have withdrawn $600,000 from your IRA/401(k) tax-free, because you might have washed away the tax with mortgage interest offsets. *The withdrawals that you declare on the front of your tax return and the mortgage interest that you deduct on Schedule A can cancel each other out.*

I have a simple formula illustrated by the examples I am about to show you: If you have twice as much home equity (that you can separate and qualify as deductible mortgage interest) as you have trapped in an IRA or 401(k), you can potentially withdraw all of your IRA or 401(k) money over a ten-year period with no tax. What if you could cut your taxes only 10 percent? Would you be interested? Some people would give their eyeteeth to cut taxes by 10 or 25 percent! I'm about to show how you can cut them 25, 50, or 100 percent.

START YOUR STRATEGIC CONVERSION EARLY

Doesn't it make sense to analyze *now* what kind of savings you might pocket in your long-term retirement years if you convert your nest egg from a qualified plan to nonqualified plan—even if there are taxes to pay in the short term? Regardless of whether you have accumulated as little as $36,000 in an IRA or 401(k), $100,000 or $1 million, these illustrations should help part the curtain that often blocks the view of what's in store. Even if you have no plans to retire in the foreseeable future (well before you reach the ceiling of 70½), you can ensure significant accumulation years without concern for the changing (and sometimes fickle) revisions imposed by government revenue collectors.

Let's look at four Boomer couples, each with a different timetable:

- Clark and Carrie Centsible, 50 years old, plan to retire at 65
- Frank and Felicia Faralong, 50 years old, plan to retire at 70
- Ed and Elizabeth Eager, 55 years old, plan to retire at 65
- George and Gail Gainsworthy, 60 years old, plan to retire at 70

In these illustrations, for simplicity's sake, I make the following assumptions:

- Each individual has a spouse.
- Each couple is in the 33.3 percent tax bracket.

- The couples earn between $70,000 and $115,000 a year and have various tax deductions (mortgage interest, charitable contributions, state and local taxes, and exemptions).
- Each couple annually files a joint tax return assuming the 2006 tax brackets.
- Each couple has qualified plans worth varying amounts.

As you will see, by the time each of these couples reaches their retirement, they will have rolled out their IRA and 401(k) or other qualified retirement plan money and repositioned it in a nonqualified plan to sprint ahead tax-free. Let's see how this is accomplished for each family.

The Centsibles Look Toward a Bright Future

Clark and Carrie, both of whom work for large corporations, are expecting pensions as well as Social Security in the future. They could continue down the same seemingly sensible route until their planned retirement date fifteen years from now and possibly postpone any substantial withdrawals from their IRAs and 401(k)s until age 70½. But at that point, they would probably be in the same predicament as the schoolteacher I mentioned in Chapter 4 who got hit with heavy taxes because her retirement income came to $80,000, and she had fewer deductions than she did while working.

Instead, the Centsibles decide that when they turn 60, they will withdraw money (gradually, over a five-year period) from their qualified plans and invest in a tax-free environment, which I'll describe in detail in Chapters 11 and 12. Although at the urging of a financial planner they had recently paid off the mortgage on the house they bought years ago, now Clark and Carrie heed the equity management advice in Chapter 8. They sell their $300,000 home and purchase a new one with the same market value, obtaining an interest-only mortgage in the amount of $240,000 at 7.5 percent interest. They use $60,000 of their former home's equity for a down payment on their new home. Let's assume they decide they will re-finance their home ten years from now (when they turn 60), to a new mortgage balance of $340,000, because their home will have gone up in value. This will allow them to offset more taxes when they start to roll out the qualified plans—not to mention they will have their home equity in a safer, more liquid position, earning a good rate of return!

The Centsibles are covering their new mortgage payment using money they were putting toward qualified plan savings and are redirecting some of the increased positive cash flow they realized when they paid off their prior mortgage. Meanwhile, they have a new mortgage deduction of $18,000 a year, which will jump to $25,500 when they refinance in ten years (to harvest another $100,000 of equity). The deductible mortgage payment will help offset taxes when they start the strategic rollout of their qualified accounts. In essence, their deductible mortgage payment will be-come their retirement plan contribution, and their nonqualified re-tirement plan will now be kick-started with a huge boost from repositioned home equity.

So the Centsibles take $240,000 from the sale of their house and use $15,000 of this money to pay off a credit card they have been paying on for quite some time. At 15 percent interest, they have just freed up a credit card payment of $2,667 a year—money they now can reallocate toward their nonqualified retirement nest egg. As-suming that they can get a 7 percent return in their new tax-favored plan, the nest egg will grow nicely every year. By the time they are age 65—fifteen years after they started this strategic repositioning—they will have accumulated $1,282,026.

This is more than the amount they would have had if they left the money in their IRAs and 401(k)s (which would have amounted to $923,661, assuming a 7 percent rate of return). This assumes they disciplined themselves (socking away the amount they had been paying in monthly payments on their former mortgage before their previous financial planner advised them to pay it off). If they had spent that money rather than saving it, their retirement fund would have only $721,000 accumulated. Regardless, they still have to pay the taxes on all this money when they withdraw it!

The welcome difference is that now, at age 65, they can withdraw a hefty sum each year in tax-favored interest earnings, which is 50 to 60 percent greater than the net-after-tax income they would have realized if they had not rolled out their qualified plan funds. If they wish, they could pay off their mortgage anytime by taking it out of their right-hand pocket (their nonqualified plan) and putting it into their left-hand pocket (their home). *But by keeping a mortgage on their house, they continue to earn a return greater than the net cost of the interest they pay each year.* This is because they are earning 7 percent tax-free in a compounding account, while paying a net of 5 percent simple interest on their tax-deductible mortgage. This allows them to have tax-free income plus enjoy additional tax savings by continuing to maintain a mortgage throughout their retirement.

From age 65 forward, the earnings on their nonqualified retirement plan will give the Centsibles a total of $89,741 in annual income from their equity management retirement plan. Subtract the net after-tax cost of the mortgage interest ($17,000), and they will realize net spendable income each year of $72,741—considerably more than they would have netted by leaving their money in those taxable IRAs and 401(k)s (only $43,273 after tax).

The Faralongs: More Time and a Vacation Home, Too

Frank and Felicia's situation is similar to that of the Centsibles in that they are each 50 years old. They have similar homes, but the Faralongs still have a mortgage on their home of about $167,500. They refinanced four years ago to a fifteen-year mortgage in an attempt to pay off the house before they retired. They don't plan to retire until they are 70—five years later than Clark and Carrie. They also have their heart set on someday owning a beachfront condominium. They think this will be easier to acquire once they retire since their home will be paid off and they will have a nice nest egg.

Frank and Felicia, who are freelance commercial artists, both have SEP IRAs (a plan similar to a 401[k] specifically designed for the self-employed), with a total balance of $155,000. They are currently contributing $9,000 a year to their SEP IRAs. They avail themselves of our advice and refinance their house at 80 percent loan-to-value. It has a fair market value of $335,000. They obtain an interest-only mortgage at 7 percent. In addition, they agree it makes financial sense to begin an immediate rollout of their current retirement plans, despite the tax hit and penalty. So each year for the next eleven years, they will roll out $20,104 of that money into a nonqualified plan.

The Faralongs' tax-deferred retirement plans were previously earning 8 percent interest. If they would have left them there, those accounts would have grown nicely until each spouse reached age 70, but at that point they would be forced to take a minimum distribution. Instead, during each year of the phased rollout, they will pay the pre-59½ penalty of 10 percent while repositioning the remaining money into a nonqualified plan, earning an average of 8 percent.

Meanwhile, the refinancing of their primary home lowered their monthly payments by $265 a month ($3,176 a year), and they were able to eliminate $20,000 in credit card and other nonpreferred debt, freeing up another $500 a month ($6,000 per year). Next, Frank and Felicia go ahead and buy their beach condo for $385,000, taking out an 80/20 mortgage, at 7 percent interest on the first mortgage and 7.5 percent on the second to cover the entire purchase price. *This has also created enough tax-deductible interest that can completely eliminate the taxes and penalties on their SEP IRA rollouts and contributions!*

Until they retire at age 70, the payments on the beach condo plus the payment on their primary residence amount to somewhat more than what they had been paying on the conventional mortgage for their primary residence alone. But they will not experience an increase in their monthly outlay. Why? Their expenses have been offset by the tax savings on both mortgages, plus the credit card payments that were freed up, and a portion of their SEP IRA contributions.

By the time they are 61 years old, the Faralongs will have rolled out all of their qualified plan funds into nonqualified retirement plans earning 8 percent interest. As they approach their retirement target age of 70, they will have accumulated $1,080,066 in their nonqualified plans that could generate $86,405 of tax-free annual income. If they deduct the net-after-tax combined mortgage payments of $30,730, they will have $55,675 of spendable income. Compare this to their SEP IRA account, which would have been worth $1,167,255—but only $778,170 after tax. Let's assume they disciplined themselves once their house was paid off and socked away the equivalent amount of their house payments, earning 8 percent. In that case they would have an additional $287,828. The combined total would give them $116,406 per year of taxable interest income ($77,604 after tax) derived from both sources. So how are the Faralongs ahead?

Well, they will have logged twenty years of memories at their beach condo—and would still be enjoying weekends there. If they had waited until they retired to purchase the same beach house, assuming it appreciated at 7.2 percent, it would cost them $1,540,000! If they financed it then at the time of purchase (age 70), it would require a net-after-tax payment of $71,867 a year, thereby leaving them only a net spendable income of $5,739!

Another advantage of their nonqualified plan is, if they wish, they could tap into that money anytime they felt the need, because access to the money in their nonqualified plan is not restricted as in qualified plans—in other words, they are not forced to withdraw any money until they choose to.

Of course, this example has been kept simple for illustrative purposes—they refinanced their home and financed the beach condo only once at the beginning. In reality, the Faralongs should probably refinance these properties every three, four, or five years, as it appreciates over time. The Faralongs would catch on quickly to the power of equity management, I'm sure. If their properties appreciated conservatively, and they refinanced every five years or so, they could possibly reap an additional $1 million in their retirement fund. If their primary residence appreciated at 7.2 percent, it would double in value twice during that twenty-year period to $1,340,000. Under the same assumptions, their beach condo would be worth $1,540,000. So the combined value of both properties in twenty years could be $2,880,000. After subtracting the original mortgages they took out on each, they could have a net of $2,227,000 of additional equity to harvest and manage to dramatically enhance their retirement resources.

The Eager Family: A Ten-Year Sprint to a Worry-Free Retirement

At 55, Ed manages a chain of retail stores, and Elizabeth is a paralegal. They are viewing their future Social Security income as icing on the cake of their retirement planning, but they are still concerned about having enough of their own resources to live on should they retire in ten years. They want to put some giddyap into the money they have socked away in their IRAs and 401(k)s, because they have accumulated only $95,000 thus far. A year ago, they decided to capitalize on the steep appreciation in the value of their home. They sold it and were able to net $385,000 of cash out. They parked that money temporarily in several CDs earning 5 percent interest, and they moved to a town home they are renting.

We convince the Eager family that they were practically throwing their $1,500 away in rent every month when they could own a similar town home for about the same outlay per month. So they buy a town home for $250,000 with an 80/20 mortgage and are now paying slightly more in monthly mortgage payments than they had paid in rent. The mortgage also gives them additional tax deductions they had missed out on since selling their home, so their monthly outlay is actually less than when renting.

Meanwhile, using our strategy, Ed and Elizabeth begin converting their CDs for a better payout and investing the money in a non-qualified retirement plan. Ten years from now, the money initially parked in the CDs (which would have been taxed-as-earned, representative of *crawling* toward retirement) will have been *sprinting*, and will be available to them under tax-favorable circumstances.

As the final maneuver in a worry-free strategy, they begin right away (at age 55) repositioning their 401(k) contributions of $15,000 a year, because their new mortgage can now give them the same tax benefits. In the meantime, they will wait four and a half years before starting to roll out their IRAs and 401(k)s, which have been earning an average of 8 percent tax-deferred. Once they reach 59½, those accounts will be worth a total of about $130,000. At that point, they would no longer be subject to the 10 percent early withdrawal penalty. They will begin a strategic rollout of $25,887 a year from those IRAs and 401(k)s, repositioning that money, too, in their nonqualified, tax-free retirement plan. Since they still will have some tax savings from their mortgage, the Eagers will have to pay only about 8.5 percent in taxes on the money they roll out! This nets them $23,675 a year to transfer to their plan. Hence, they will successfully offset the majority of the taxes that would otherwise by payable.

So, although they would have to pay some taxes each year while they repositioned their retirement contributions (as well as on the balance of the money they transfer out of their qualified plans), the Eagers understand that the tax hit should be largely offset by their tax-deductible mortgage interest. Let's assume that as the next five years speed by (from age 60 to 65), the Eager family earns a steady 8 percent a year tax-free on the money in their new plan. By the time they reach their scheduled retirement age of 65, they can look forward to the strong possibility of being able to withdraw $89,000 a year tax-free from their nonqualified plan.

This retirement income, together with their Social Security benefits (which should total about $125,000), would be approximately ten times the amount required to meet their mortgage payments (which would total about $12,000 per year after tax). There is enough left over for Elizabeth to realize her dream of going to law school part-time so that by the time she is in her early 70s, she can become an attorney for her local Legal Aid Society. Ed, meanwhile, is embarking on a new part-time career as a small-business consultant.

The Gainsworthys: Golfing and Gallivanting in Their Golden Years

These 60-year-olds live in the suburban house where they raised their children. George continues to work as a sales executive, while Gail continues as a college administrative assistant. With their children grown and living elsewhere, the Gainsworthys are empty-nesters. No longer wanting nor needing so much room, they have thought about downsizing—moving to a smaller condominium that requires less maintenance.

Both George and Gail want to work until they are 70. But they also want discretionary spending money to enjoy the cultural offerings of the city, to travel, and to visit their grandchildren. At retirement (or when they make a transition to different employment), they will receive income from their defined-benefit pensions, in addition to eventual Social Security benefits. By the time they are each 70, they think they will be ready to completely retire, and then they would like to add golfing and traveling to their leisure menu.

The one thing that stopped them from carrying out their plans was a concern about the tax consequences of selling the family home. After a consultation with a trained financial professional, however, they were assured they could sell it without incurring a capital gains tax, and with Uncle Sam's approval.

So the Gainsworthys take advantage of the substantial appreciation in home values and sell their suburban house without triggering a taxable event—thanks to the $500,000 exemption. Then, rather than buying their new condo with cash and having equity tied up in it with no rate of return, they finance 100 percent of the purchase price with an interest-only first mortgage of $180,000 and a second mortgage of $45,000. This generates a mortgage interest tax deduction for them, while allowing them to reposition all of the money they receive from the sale of their house into a nonqualified retirement plan, earning an average of 7 to 8 percent interest.

The Gainsworthys also have a large sum of money trapped in IRAs and 401(k)s ($350,000). They don't need the money right now since they are both still working, but they don't like the idea of being clobbered with taxes down the road when they do need it. Rather than postpone the inevitable, they have arranged a ten-year strategic transfer of this asset into a nonqualified plan. Part of the taxes they would pay on this rollout is washed away by their new mortgage interest deduction. They also have a CD that in three years will reach a maturity value of $50,000. Realizing they would rather sprint than crawl with this money, they decide to reposition the CD to their tax-free nonqualified plan in the third year.

By the time they reach 70, George and Gail have had ample time to accumulate a very generous nest egg. And they will be able to enjoy it to the hilt. They can withdraw enough money income-tax-free ($70,000 or $90,000 per year—depending on whether they averaged 7 percent or 8 percent on their nonqualified account) to gallivant around the globe, sampling exotic golf resorts, dining at fine restaurants, attending concerts in town, or taking their grandchildren to amusement parks. This extra tax-free income added on top of their defined-benefit pensions and Social Security income will really make a meaningful difference—one that will allow them to stay active, excited, and worry-free about outliving their money.

For the sake of simplicity, I have touched only on a few points in the Centsible, Faralong, Eager, and Gainsworthy cases. I'll come back and visit these cases again in Chapter 12. (If you would like to study any or all of the actual comprehensive plans—each comprising approximately sixty pages in length using our proprietary software that was created for clients like these hypothetical couples—you are invited to visit our Web site at this address: www.MissedFortune.com/LCMCaseStudies.)

POSITION YOURSELF TO REAP THE
GAINS OF YOUR EARNING YEARS

As you can see, there are probably an infinite number of scenarios in which it would behoove people to reposition retirement resources under tax-advantaged circumstances by utilizing strategic rollouts with mortgage interest offsets. In each of these four cases, couples were able to fulfill their dreams without surrendering their right to retire as they saw fit. They could choose their retirement age, as well as determine for themselves the age that was right for them to tap into their retirement plans. They could decide how much or how little they wanted to reposition each year in pursuit of their own goals, while optimizing their assets.

With most of the strategies suggested, if you are 50 or older, you, too, potentially can withdraw up to $60,000 per year (depending on the mortgage interest offsets that can be created) out of an IRA or 401(k) with possibly no tax consequence. Even if you could cut your taxes by only 50 percent—or 25 percent—wouldn't it be worth investigating the possibility? You'll see in subsequent chapters how you can arrange to eventually replenish some or all of the money you might give up in taxes while performing a strategic qualified plan rollout or conversion. Remember, with a nonqualified retirement plan, you don't have to be bound by a government-designed formula. And, as you will see shortly, you don't have to saddle your heirs with taxes either.

That's my wealth optimization strategy in action. Doesn't this sound like true financial freedom?

REMEMBER THIS:

- Approaching retirement, scrutinize each element of your retirement plans to maximize savings before age 59½ by minimizing taxes and capitalizing on employer contributions.
- *Rollovers only postpone taxes.* Prepare a strategic *rollout* of qualified money in IRAs, 401(k)s, or similar qualified plans into nonqualified plans that allow tax-free distributions.
- Waiting to withdraw money from qualified plans until you reach age 70½ can cost you.
- Take advantage of lower-income years to increase strategic rollouts from IRAs or 401(k)s while in a lower tax bracket.
- Inspect last year's Schedule A to better plan for offseting the tax on every rollout dollar with tax deductions, especially with mortgage interest.
- My two-part strategy—rolling out money now from qualified retirement plans that can be repositioned in tax-free alternatives, and offsetting the tax on the rollouts with mortgage interest—can be done separately, but works best when combined.

CHAPTER 10

Establish an Individual Retirement Abode (IRA)

How to Invest in Your Second-Home Dream and Retirement Savings—At the Same Time

WHAT IF YOUR NEST EGG were a "nest"? What if you spent your leisure time relaxing at a vacation home instead of re-viewing dry account statements? I am about to show you how some of the cash you're currently putting into qualified retirement plans could be shifted into investing in a second home, where you could enjoy the same tax and appreciation benefits as your quali-fied plans—plus the precious, fleeting opportunities to build mem-ories with family and friends.

Too often, people assume that a second home—a cabin in the mountains, a cottage by the beach, a condo at a resort develop-ment, a fractional share in a luxury hotel, even an RV—is not prac-tical to pursue until they meet their retirement planning goals.

Yet when financial strategists like myself ask clients what they would most like to do once they retire, we hear over and over again the same kind of reply: "I'd love to build that cabin in the moun-tains we've talked about for so many years," or "We've always wanted to have a comfortable motor home and travel around the country visiting the national parks." What I'm about to demonstrate is that your dream cabin can double as a nonqualified retirement plan.

When I tell audiences about my "Individual Retirement Abode (IRA)," I always get such an enthusiastic response that I know I've touched a matter close to people's hearts. People also smile when I use the terms "401 Cabin" and "401 Condo" (my friend Don Blanton coined the term "401 Condo") to refer to this opportunity to see second homes in an all-new light. It doesn't take long for people to learn that I am a huge proponent of second homes (or boats or RVs or anything else that qualifies as a secondary residence), not merely because they can be a superior investment, but because they encourage quality family time away from the stress of everyday life.

Why wait for your golden years to enjoy the pleasures of a vacation home? You can buy that dream home or timeshare or vehicle right now and achieve your financial retirement goals. What's more, your life from now until retirement will be enriched a thousandfold by the experiences you store up along the way.

After all, consider what the real objectives are behind your retirement plans. Along with securing a comfortable living, most people are hoping to afford opportunities to create lasting memories with family and friends—exactly the kind of moments found at a family cabin or other second home.

What sounds more appealing? Would you rather enjoy summer sunsets by the lake and winter mornings on the ski slopes now? Or would your prefer to spend your weekends watching TV, waiting until you turn 65 to invest in a second-home getaway (at which time you realize you're getting clobbered with taxes and spending four times as much on your vacation condo as you would have if you had bought it a few years earlier)?

With my sweetheart, Sharee, and our six children, we have spent memorable times in our cabin in the mountains of central

Utah and at our condo in St. George, Utah. Each is an oasis of peace, beauty, and outdoor fun, where we fish, barbecue, ride ATVs, and play golf. We were lucky enough to find these incredible properties for reasonable prices some years ago. We purchased our cabin that sits on twenty acres of wooded property for just over $100,000. It's now worth almost triple that amount. We purchased our three-bedroom condo at a spa resort for $138,000 and it is now valued at more than double that. We were able to buy each property with no cash down (out of our pocket). I know there are many families out there who have put aside a lot of money in retirement savings, but how do you put a dollar value on the joys of our Individual Retirement Abodes, compared with staying home every weekend, filing your 401(k) and IRA statements for the same amount?

The only stumbling block might be a myopic perspective. If so, adjust your attitude, continue reading, and you'll see that a second home is possibly within your reach.

VACATION AND INVESTMENT ALL IN ONE

The popularity of second homes has soared in recent years, especially since the tax law reforms of 1997 allowed home sellers to exclude up to $500,000 in capital gains from taxation. According to the National Association of Realtors, "Homeowners did not have to buy expensive homes to avoid capital gains tax anymore. Instead, buying a smaller/less expensive primary residence and a second home (whether used as a vacation home or an investment vehicle) with the tax-free gain made second-home buying more financially attractive to homeowners than ever before."[*]

Many homeowners buy second homes to diversify their investments, since real estate can achieve gains during a period when the stock market declines. For example, from 2000 to 2004, existing

---

*Keunwon Chung, "Second-Home Boom," *Real Estate Insights*, March 2006, /www.realtor.org/resortsweb.nsf/pages/REISecondHomeResearch?OpenDocument.

home price appreciation increased 55 percent, while the Standard & Poor's (S&P) 500 Index declined 15 percent.[*]

"MY OTHER HOME IS A YACHT"

Have you seen the bumper stickers on cars with slogans such as "My other car is a Harley-Davidson"? Boomers might well have a sign on their front lawn saying, "My other home is a yacht." As more people are discovering, when your boat or motor home can qualify under the Internal Revenue Service definition of a "primary or secondary residence," you can deduct the mortgage interest on it just as you deduct the mortgage interest on your primary home.

The definition in the IRS code is: "a house, condominium, co-operative, mobile home, house trailer, boat, or similar property that has sleeping, cooking, and toilet facilities."[**] This means that *interest on a loan taken out to buy a fully equipped boat or RV qualifies as tax-deductible, provided you hold a title or similar ownership papers.*

A cottage or condo that you use a certain number of weeks a year but rent out other times may be regarded, under certain guidelines and parameters, as a second home for tax purposes. That may also be true for a timeshare or fractional interest property at a resort, a suite in a condominium hotel, or even a share amounting to several weeks a year in various properties owned under the banner of a destination club. Rental property deductions are declared on a different schedule of your tax return, but the end result is the same. Your professional tax preparer will help you with the appropriate way to deduct qualified mortgage interest.

When considering investing in a second home, most people ask themselves, "What will this second home cost us?" But after understanding the financial and personal advantages of a second home, the question really becomes, "What will it cost us if we pass up this

---

[*]Ibid.
[**] http://wwirs.gov/publications/p936/ar02.html d0e532.

opportunity to invest in a second home?" Given the appreciation in value of second homes in communities across the country, it may be smarter to buy your dream vacation hideaway at today's prices, using leverage (that's the *drag* that actually makes your money soar, remember), than to wait a decade or more when prices could be considerably higher.

ANOTHER FORM OF EQUITY MANAGEMENT

The secret is to see your 401 Cabin/Condo/RV/Timeshare as another way of managing equity. (Section 163 of the Internal Revenue Code addresses the deductibility of the interest for secondary residences. While I have created terms like 401 Cabin to describe the subject, there is not a reference in Section 401 of the Internal Revenue Code that refers to this strategy.) Think of the arrangement as similar to the glass and the pitcher. You have the use of the glass, which may very well appreciate as so many second homes have in the past few years, while you retain the use of the money in the pitcher.

Whether you dream about a pied-à-terre (a part-time, modest dwelling) in the city, a cottage by the sea, or a sailboat in the Gulf of Mexico, the plan is the same as with your primary home, as outlined in Chapter 8. You obtain a tax-deductible loan to cover the cost of your second home. At the end of each year, the mortgage interest you have paid on it lowers your taxable income on your federal return. (The law allows you to deduct interest on a total of two properties—a primary and a secondary residence.) It does not matter whether you deposit several thousand dollars a year in a qualified retirement account or make payments in the same amount on a second-home mortgage; both are deductible.

Meanwhile, you can use the cash you remove from the second home as it appreciates and invest it. At the end of, say, twenty years, you likely will have accumulated enough money to pay off the second home if you wish, although I will recommend a better, tax-free alternative to optimize that equity in the next chapter.

Those who already own a primary and a secondary home can still buy a third (in the names of your children if necessary for them to take advantage of the tax break, or you can borrow from a family-empowered bank, which I will discuss later).

Fig. 10.1

"401 Cabin" Individual Retirement Abode

Readers of my book *Missed Fortune 101* may remember John and Susie Wannacabin, whom I introduced in connection with an Individual Retirement Abode. Let's assume they are both 50 years old. The couple socks away $500 a month into qualified retirement plans in hopes of accumulating enough money to buy a weekend getaway house in the countryside within a few hours' drive from their primary home. For a moment, let's assume their retirement accounts do quite well, earning an average of 11.25 percent for the next twenty years. Their $500 per month at that rate over twenty years grows to $450,000.

At last, they reach age 70 and decide the time has come to act on their retirement dream. Alas! When they examine their finances, they see that their $450,000 is fully taxable, and since they are in the same 33.3 percent tax bracket, they will net only $300,000. Then they go real estate shopping in the country, and are dismayed; because of home value appreciation, the cabin they could have built or bought twenty years earlier for $100,000 will now cost $400,000. They are still $100,000 short like they were thirty years ago!

HOW MY INDIVIDUAL RETIREMENT ABODE (IRA) WORKS

Contrast John and Susie's dismay with the human as well as financial benefits Sharee and I have gained by owning our mountain cabin. As I said, it cost $100,000. During the first five years of ownership, it appreciated to over $200,000 (that's about 15 percent annually). However, let's be more conservative and use simple math for our example. Even at an average appreciation rate of 7.2 percent, after twenty years, the cabin would be worth at least $400,000. The rule of 72 tells me that my property will double in value every 10 years at 7.2 percent. During that twenty-year period, let's say we pay 6 percent on our interest-only mortgage, meaning it costs us $500 each month, or $6,000 a year.

Because second-home mortgage interest is tax-deductible, we enjoy both the wonderful time at our cabin, plus the same tax deduction that the Wannacabins get on their tax-deferred retirement plan. We both save $2,000 in taxes (33.3 percent of $6,000), and our net outlay is $4,000. But the Wannacabins, or anyone else who is socking away money in an IRA or 401(k) as they are, would have to earn a lot more interest on their $500-per-month investment in order for it to grow to the same amount our cabin will be worth after twenty years. Unfortunately, those with qualified plans will then net much less because they will owe tax on their plans—they will need an even greater return to match the same amount we will realize. Meanwhile, after twenty years we will still owe only $100,000 on our interest-only mortgage, since the same math illustrated in Chapter 8 applies here. So, subtracting the $100,000 mortgage balance, our net gain from the cabin appreciation would equal at least the same amount that the Wannacabins would realize after tax.

Fig. 10.2	INDIVIDUAL RETIREMENT ABODE (Purchase of a $100,000 cabin with an interest-only mortgage at 6%) VERSUS A Traditional IRA (Depositing $500 per month [$6,000 per year] tax-deductible)			
End of Year	[1] Traditional IRA at 7.2%	[2] Traditional IRA Net After 33.3% Tax	[3] $100,000 Cabin at 7.2% Appreciation less Mortgage	[4] Difference [3] - [2]
1	$6,202	$4,135	$7,200	$3,065
2	$12,866	$8,577	$14,918	$6,341
3	$20,025	$13,350	$23,193	$9,842
4	$27,718	$18,478	$32,062	$13,584
5	$35,982	$23,988	$41,571	$17,583
6	$44,862	$29,908	$51,764	$21,856
7	$54,403	$36,269	$62,691	$26,422
8	$64,654	$43,103	$74,405	$31,302
9	$75,668	$50,445	$86,962	$36,517
10	$87,502	$58,334	$100,423	$42,089
11	$100,216	$66,810	$114,854	$48,043
12	$113,876	$75,917	$130,323	$54,406
13	$128,553	$85,702	$146,906	$61,204
14	$144,323	$96,215	$164,684	$68,468
15	$161,266	$107,511	$183,741	$76,230
16	$179,470	$119,647	$204,170	$84,523
17	$199,029	$132,686	$226,070	$93,384
18	$220,044	$146,696	$249,547	$102,852
19	$242,622	$161,748	$274,715	$112,967
20	$266,881	$177,921	$301,694	$123,774

STOP AND SMELL THE ROSES

Too often financial planners concentrate solely on financial assets but ignore the human assets—the people we care about—who are the reasons we are so keen on acquiring something like a vacation home.

By designing a strategy for your 401 Cabin or Individual Retirement Abode, you can also be taking a major stride toward a more gratifying life's journey. You're crafting a center where family members can get together for an annual (or more frequent) reunion, a spot where you can celebrate holidays, anniversaries, and birthdays.

I may be in the business of financial consulting, but I believe everyone needs to stop now and again and smell the roses. Buying a vacation home now is a quality-of-life choice, not just a tax break—view a family retreat as an investment, not an expense. A vacation home is often where people kick off their sandals or ski boots and have time to take pleasure in the company of two, sometimes three generations of family. Those roses could be the ones you plant in the garden at your vacation property.

Back in Chapter 2, Misconception #9 was: "I view retirement as a time for finally doing what I've always wanted to do." That's the mistake the Wannacabins made, and that's the difference between my family and the Wannacabins. My family has reaped a priceless bonus—a collection of memories to share, captured in living color in a drawerful of home videos and snapshots. The Wannacabins? They've got a drawerful of black-and-white account statements.

Statistics suggest that my family's choice of a 401 Cabin or 401 Condo within a few hours' drive from our primary residence is typical of the vacation homes bought by the majority of U.S. vacation home buyers.* But perhaps you envision a slightly different scenario as your perfect vacation getaway, so let's look at other options.

UNDERSTANDING TIMESHARES OR FRACTIONAL VACATION OWNERSHIP

The timeshare concept typically means that instead of owning 100 percent of a property, you own a piece of vacation real estate

---

*www.realtor.org/Research.nsf/files/2ndHOHilites06WebFile.pdf/$FILE/2ndHO Hilites06WebFile.pdf.

such as a unit in a hotel or resort for a period of time. Your ownership is still considered real estate when you buy a deeded timeshare
(take note, some plans don't convey ownership), so you can take
out a loan to pay for it and get a tax deduction on the interest. In
addition to the purchase price, you also pay a portion of the maintenance fees.

You don't always have to go to your own timeshare place; you
can join a timeshare or fractional exchange program for a fee (RCI
and Interval International are among the biggest), which allows
you to trade your time period at a specific place for time in one of
thousands of other timeshare properties all over the world. It is a
great way to add both a lodging guarantee as well as flexibility to
your vacation options. This choice is often priced much lower than
the 100 percent ownership of a similar property would be.

Way back in 1976, I bought a timeshare in a unit at the Snowbird Resort in Utah. For $3,500 I was entitled to spend a week a year
in a two-bedroom property close to the ski slopes, and I also received thirty free ski lift tickets every year for five years. It was an
incredible deal. After five years, Snowbird was charging about $50
a day for a lift ticket, so those free passes ended up being worth
more than the timeshare cost us. We had a great time during our
winter stays at Snowbird, and I eventually sold the timeshare for
$10,500.

Timeshares (sometimes called fractionals because you are buying a percentage of the year, rather than a week) have come a long
way in the past thirty years. Today you can buy timeshares in
campgrounds, cruises, and other types of property. You typically
have the choice of fixed weeks (the same ones every year) or float-
ing weeks (a week that you must reserve sometimes as much as one
year in advance). Major hotel chains like Marriott and Hyatt have
joined the timeshare business. With some plans, you can even
trade your timeshare for points you can then use for something like
an airline ticket or cruise.

The most important piece of advice I have for timeshare buyers is to *maximize your trading power by purchasing your primary timeshare in a top resort in a popular area.* That way, in an emergency you can list your place with an exchange club, or rent it out—even at the last minute. Destinations such as Hawaii or coastal California[*] will always be in demand, and there are many top-rated resorts throughout the world.

Fred and Felicia Fortunate: The Florida Home Alternative

Let's imagine a couple I'll call Fred and Felicia Fortunate who live in Fort Wayne, Indiana, most of the year. Their idea of a great weekend getaway is escaping to a villa on Florida's southwest coast near Fort Myers. Like the snowbirds they are, they love to bask in the Florida sun and relax by the pool while there's still an icy winter up north.

Fred is an executive with a salary of $300,000 that puts him in the top tier of income nationwide. He and Felicia, both in their 50s, have $3,000 in discretionary money each month that they could allot for a qualified retirement plan. Instead, they have bought a two-bedroom villa for $500,000 in a resort development in Florida. They were able to obtain an interest-only mortgage with the interest pegged at 7.25 percent.

For the next fifteen years, the Fortunates expect to spend at least forty-five days a year in their Florida second home—a two-week vacation in the winter and long weekends other times of the year. It's where they hope their children, now in college, will want to come for special times like Thanksgiving or Christmas. Their Individual Retirement Abode in Florida will cost them about $3,000 a month in mortgage payments that are tax deductible (a net cost of $2,000 a month in a 33.3 percent tax bracket). They hope that the property will appreciate at an average of 10 percent a year.

When Fred finally retires in fifteen years, the Fortunates think they probably will move to Florida full-time. But rather than sell

---

[*]http://www.tug2.net/advice/faq.htm.

their current first home in Fort Wayne, they plan to refinance it in five years, hold on to it, and rent it out on a long-term lease upon their retirement, as recommended by a smart financial planner who has been tutored in my wealth optimization strategies. If their new interest-only mortgage is for $600,000 at 7.5 percent, that would mean gross payments of $3,750 on that home each month.

As a result, the Fortunates will have two tax-deductible properties. The mortgage payments on their Fort Wayne house should be covered by the $4,000 a month rent they expect to collect on it. Meanwhile, they took the separated equity from their Florida house and invested it in properly structured, maximum tax-advantaged insurance contracts, a strategy I will outline in detail in Chapter 12. They calculate that this investment should earn them an average of 7 to 8 percent (compounding tax-free) over the fifteen years before retirement—enough to offset their after-tax mortgage payments. Upon retirement, they will live extremely comfortably on withdrawals from their nonqualified retirement plan, whether they sell one of the properties or continue to own it as a rental income property, managing the equity successfully as it appreciates.

Tim and Tammy Traveler: The Timeshare Alternative

Tim and Tammy Traveler, also in their 50s, have a different but equally attractive vision. Currently, they live and work in Tyler, Texas, where their combined income is $72,000 a year. Their idea of the perfect vacation is to visit different U.S. resorts in beautiful settings where the outdoors beckon. They like to settle into a place for a week to explore, hike, ski, play golf, and get into new hobbies such as bird-watching.

The Travelers, too, are converts to the idea of the 401 Cabin but they worry that their modest income will not be enough to afford one. Besides, they don't want to decide yet on just one location. They are now getting serious about socking away as much as 20 percent of their income for retirement and have budgeted $1,200 a month for that purpose. Rather than putting all of that into qualified retirement accounts, they decide to start smelling roses while they still have a lot of energy. So they allocate up to half of their discretionary long-term savings to achieving their goal. The best getaway for their lifestyle turns out to be a multiple-week timeshare or fractional ownership. After a fabulous stay in a condominium in one of the ski and summer resorts on Lake Tahoe on the California-Nevada border, they pay $45,000 to buy a winter-week and summer-week timeshare interest at a new development. They obtain an attractive loan to cover all or almost all of the purchase with a monthly payment of under $600—which is largely deductible.

Last February, the Travelers spent one week in Tahoe skiing. They have deposited their additional week and next year's weeks in a timeshare "bank" and are trading them for weeks in other time-share locations. During the first two years of ownership, this has al-lowed them to enjoy a week in Hawaii during the spring, another exploring San Francisco during July, and a third in Mexico during late fall.

The Travelers are thrilled that they can spend all this time dis-covering new places, while getting tax-deductible interest on the loan they obtained to purchase their fractional ownership. They use $550 a month to pay their mortgage and put the rest in a safe retirement fund. Because they enjoy running their own business in Tyler, they don't know when they might retire, but they know that if their lifestyle changes, they can sell their timeshare. Then they can combine the proceeds from the sale and the side fund into a comfortable new nonqualified retirement savings plan to enjoy tax-free income (see Chapter 12).

Robert and Rochelle Rover: The RV Alternative

The Rovers are both 60 and they have yet another kind of re-tirement dream. Over the past twenty-five years, these two, who are high school teachers, have raised their three children in a big home they've paid off in a suburb of Raleigh, North Carolina. They have taken learning vacations to spots like Washington, D.C., and they have seen historic parts of Europe and Asia. But now they are in the grip of wanderlust. They have more house than they need, so they would like to sell it, especially since it has appreciated greatly since they bought it years ago. With the proceeds, they want to buy both a pied-à-terre in town and a motor home. They would use the RV to visit their children and grandchildren, who live in different parts of the country, and to explore the byways of North America.

Until now, they thought they needed to wait until they reached retirement at age 65 to fulfill this dream. However, a retirement planning specialist has told them about the 401 Cabin and my wealth optimization strategies. They realize they can begin right now to enjoy both the cultural life of Raleigh and travel as they please. Theirs can be a cabin on wheels: The motor home they have longed for can be used to meander all over the map. They can buy it immediately, while they are still healthy and active enough to drive from place to place, especially during their summer vacations. Since they are over 59½, they can roll out some of the funds, if necessary, from their qualified retirement plans without the 10 percent penalty.

The first thing the Rovers do is sell their house for $400,000. While they had always anticipated using all of the proceeds from that sale to buy a pied-à-terre and an RV outright, the retirement specialist has shown that they will be much better off not to pour all their equity into their new living quarters—the condo and the RV—where it would earn no return.

Instead, the retirement specialist has prepared an equity management and transfer plan not just for the house money, but for their other assets, including the pension they will each get from their teaching jobs, a deferred annuity, and mutual fund holdings. The aim is to reposition available home equity so that it is tax-deductible, while restructuring their current and future financial portfolio to maximize earnings, eliminate unnecessary taxes, and create a sizable estate for their children, who are their heirs, to inherit.

They have chosen a two-bedroom condo for $250,000 in Raleigh. They obtain an Option ARM mortgage to pay for it. After moving into their new condo, they take out a second loan to purchase a new thirty-seven-foot luxury motor home for $150,000 (economy models to mid-range class A motor homes are generally priced from $80,000 to $250,000), which will be their ticket to ride all over the continent. They have used only $80,000 of their $400,000 home equity to purchase their condo and motor home. The loans total $320,000, and at 7.5 percent interest, the payments are approximately $2,000 a month, or $24,000 per year. But their net (after-tax) payments will likely total only about $16,000 per year. In the meantime, the Rovers are enjoying annual earnings of $24,000 or more from their invested home equity at 7.5 percent or more.

The Rovers are on track to roll out almost all of the savings that are trapped in their qualified retirement plans over the next ten years. They will enjoy the mortgage interest offsets that will allow them to withdraw up to $24,000 a year with no tax consequence, compared to what they would have had if they had paid cash for the condo and motor home. The one plan they have been advised to keep is a Roth IRA, since they can start withdrawing money from that at any time tax-free. Both Robert and Rochelle also will be able to collect their Social Security benefits for everyday living expenses.

As teachers, both have defined-benefit pensions. When Rochelle meets with a benefits officer for her pension, she is asked to choose between a 100 percent no-survivor benefit or one of several joint and survivor annuities, which would give her a reduced amount and provide for a survivor. These are two of the options I outlined in Chapter 9.

To the surprise of the benefits officer, Rochelle selects the no-survivor option. "Don't you want to share this benefit with your husband?" he asks. The expected answer is, "Of course I do." But the Rovers' retirement specialist has crunched the numbers in advance for Rochelle, showing her that a survivor option would have slashed the amount of money due her by thousands of dollars a year—in other words, it would have been the most expensive life insurance policy she could have imagined. The no-survivor option maximizes her pension. Meanwhile, with the help of the retirement planner, she and Robert can prepare for the future by self-insuring themselves using a private life insurance policy that is more flexible and just as generous. What's more, by using my strategies, these life insurance policies pay for themselves. Money that would have otherwise gone to pay income tax covers the premiums.

The rest of the Rovers' assets—traditional IRAs, CDs, annuities, mutual funds—will be strategically rolled out and invested in a nonqualified plan using properly structured maximum tax-advantaged life insurance. I discuss how to do this in detail in Chapters 11 and 12. The nonqualified plan sets them on a worry-free course through their golden years. The Rovers will be able to withdraw a handsome sum of money each month tax-free to pay for their RV loan, their condo fees, and their living expenses. Their assets are also restructured so that when the Rovers pass away, their remaining funds blossom, providing an ample estate for their children or their chosen charities.

In every possible way, the Rovers are rolling!

(Because of the popularity of this concept, I have recorded a brief explanation of the Individual Retirement Abode, 401 Cabin concept. If you are struggling trying to explain it to someone who would rather listen and learn before reading this book, take them to www.MissedFortune.com/401Cabin to hear a concise description of the strategy.)

REMEMBER THIS:

- By putting off buying your vacation dream home, you miss creating family memories and could miss out on homes that could later appreciate beyond your reach.
- Mortgage interest can be tax-deductible on a second home as well as your primary residence.
- Dollars that would otherwise go into an IRA or 401(k) can alternatively be used to obtain a tax-deductible mortgage for a 401 Cabin or Individual Retirement Abode that qualifies as a second home.
- A part-time city dwelling, condo, town home, cabin, boat, yacht, RV, timeshare, or fractional deeded property qualifies as a second home under IRS rules when it has sleeping, cooking, and toilet facilities.
- Consider downsizing once your larger first home has appreciated greatly. Consider buying both a winter home and a summer home.

CHAPTER 11

Choose Investments That Pass the Liquidity, Safety, and Rate of Return Tests

A Scorecard for Stocks, Bonds, Money Markets, Mutual Funds, Annuities, and Maximum-Funded Insurance

IF YOU GIVE PEOPLE A FISH, you feed them for a day; teach them how to fish and you feed them for a lifetime." I'm a great believer in this adage. Until this point, I have concentrated on teaching you "how to fish" with a strategy that will optimize your wealth and make it last a lifetime. Now it's time to talk more about the ingredients that work best when you are using my recipe.

I hope that by now you grasp the basic principles: repositioning your savings in a nonqualified retirement plan and managing the equity in your home to dramatically enhance your savings. I hope you realize at this point that it makes sense to sprint toward your retirement goal via tax-favored investments on the contribution, accumulation, distribution, and transfer phases rather than to jog, walk, or crawl. The next question is: What are the smartest investments to use within this strategy?

You'll recall that in Chapter 6, I said that a wise investor always applies the LSRR or "Laser" test to point to investments that are both prudent and productive: Such investments offer *liquidity, safety,* and *rate of return*. While there are numerous investments that promise a high return, many also expose you to high risks. Several are not liquid enough, and some of those that are safe do not offer a good enough rate of return to allow you to enjoy a comfortable retirement. Because your retirement money and home equity is what I call "serious cash," you want to reposition it in investments that are neither volatile nor speculative.

I stand with almost all retirement specialists in believing that the closer you get to retirement, the greater the portion of your serious cash you should put into low-risk, safe investments. But I feel that many planners steer you toward investments that do not meet all three requirements. Some instruments flunk one or another LSRR test. Furthermore, I know that your retirement money really thrives when you can access it without triggering any tax.

Let's tour the main places to park your money: One is the securities market, which includes stocks, bonds, and mutual funds; another is real estate; a third is banks, which offer CDs and money market funds; and another includes annuities and insurance.

In the 1980s, the stock market became a subject of contempt and scorn. But in the 1990s, people got excited as they watched the market climb steeply, despite warnings that eventually there would be a correction. You could have thrown a dart at a dartboard of stock symbols and made money if you had bought in 1990 and held for ten years; the overall rate of return was 12.9 percent compounded annually. Unfortunately, the average investor return during that decade was only 2 to 3 percent, because the average holding period was 2.9 years. People try to time the market—and the vast majority of them fail.

When people lose faith in the stock market, the money they had parked there often migrates to real estate or conservative, less volatile instruments such as bonds, annuities, CDs, and money market accounts. That's why real estate went through the roof in the first years of the new millennium. And what happens if it turns out to be a bubble of "irrational exuberance" just like the stock market was earlier? Real estate values could go soft as they did in different regions at different times. That's why I recommend separating equity from your property, so you can invest your money in a more reliable place no matter what happens.

What about CDs and money market funds? Everyone piled their cash into those vehicles in high-interest periods such as the late 1970s and early 1980s, but it was a terrible place for money in the late 1990s and early 2000s.

To assess systematically the best choices for serious cash, let's examine the pyramid in Figure 11.1. It covers sixteen categories of investments. Those with the highest risk are at the top, while the least risky are at the bottom.

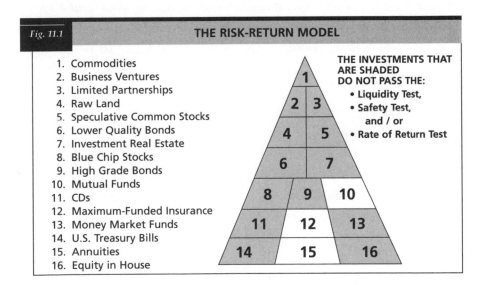

Fig. 11.1 THE RISK-RETURN MODEL

1. Commodities
2. Business Ventures
3. Limited Partnerships
4. Raw Land
5. Speculative Common Stocks
6. Lower Quality Bonds
7. Investment Real Estate
8. Blue Chip Stocks
9. High Grade Bonds
10. Mutual Funds
11. CDs
12. Maximum-Funded Insurance
13. Money Market Funds
14. U.S. Treasury Bills
15. Annuities
16. Equity in House

THE INVESTMENTS THAT ARE SHADED DO NOT PASS THE:
• Liquidity Test,
• Safety Test, and / or
• Rate of Return Test

Apply the test of *liquidity,* and you can eliminate five investments. You may not be able to obtain cash from them when you need it, which is the time frame for an investment defined as liquid. That disqualifies business ventures, limited partnerships, raw land, investment real estate, and equity in your home.

Next is *safety*. That knocks out five more investments—commodities, speculative common stocks, lower quality bonds, and even blue-chip stocks and high-grade bonds—that lack some type of guarantee with regard to either principal or interest. Most financial planners are in agreement that these do not constitute the right place for retirement funds.

Finally, there is *rate of return*. I define this as a net profit after tax that will be in excess of the net cost of the funds used in order to maximize potential. This eliminates CDs, since the interest on them is taxed as earned, reducing the yield relative to the net after-tax interest rates charged on mortgages. The same problem cancels out money market accounts. If you deposit equity separated from your home into a side fund that is a money market account or CD, you will have a hard time earning more on it after tax than the net cost of your tax-deductible, simple-interest mortgage. U.S. Treasury Bills, however safe, also do not yield a high enough rate of return.

That leaves three possible investments for serious cash:

- mutual funds
- annuities
- maximum-funded life insurance contracts

Some, but not all, of the choices in each of these three categories are liquid, safe, and have a good rate of return. Let's analyze each to see which best suits your objectives.

THE UPS AND DOWNS OF MUTUAL FUNDS

There are now over 15,000 mutual funds available to investors, and the universe keeps on expanding.[*] Some, but not nearly all,

---

[*]http://www.ici.org/stats/latest/2006_factbook.pdf.

mutual funds meet all three of the tests for liquidity, safety, and rate of return. Depending on recent experience, experts may praise or condemn mutual funds, since the numbers indicate many equity mutual funds showed double-digit gains in the 1990s, only to experience a wrenching correction with the bursting of the tech stock bubble in 2000.

Different kinds of mutual funds hold different baskets of securities. Thus at different times in the economic cycle, funds holding only money market instruments (Treasury Bills and the like) may perform better than stock or bond funds. Or, as was the case in the 1990s, diversified stock funds—whether devoted to large-cap or small-cap, value or growth, U.S. or overseas securities—can be a much better investment than bond or money market funds. In general, when the stock market goes down, bonds, money markets, and interest rates will go up; when the stock market flourishes, bonds, money markets, and fixed instruments gradually go down. The Federal Reserve's manipulation of interest rates and tax rebates also affects fund performance.

While the market in general goes up over the long term, there will be numerous ups and downs in the short run. It's like a person with a yo-yo walking up a flight of stairs. If such an image does not connote safety to you, I would suggest that your choice of a place for serious cash should not be in mutual funds that invest in speculative venture capital companies or other high-risk securities.

We all want the highest return at the lowest risk, so first you must ask yourself what your risk tolerance is. Based on the answer, you may decide how much of your nest egg you are willing to invest in a mutual fund aiming for good performance in a growth environment versus one aimed at performing well in an income environment. A growth environment of stocks and some bonds may fluctuate considerably within a given period of time while climbing over the long term. An income environment would include investments in bonds, money markets, and other financial instruments that primarily generate needed income or dividends for use in the immediate future.

Series 1 of Figure 11.2 is the performance over ten years of one of the biggest diversified mutual funds, the Vanguard Total Stock Market Index Fund. Its stated aim is to track the performance of a benchmark index that measures the investment return of the over-all stock market.

As you see, the fund had seven gain years and three loss years. During the loss years, there was a substantial reduction—over 10 percent in two cases, over 20 percent in one—in the value of the portfolio. The loss years seem to be more than offset by the many gain years. This fund started out well and ended well, with the losses tucked in the middle years. However, anytime you experience a 10 or 20 percent loss in a portfolio after the fund has grown to a sizable amount represents a serious dollar loss, because of the fund's growth in value in the years before the loss was incurred.

Fig. 11.2		STARTING WITH $100,000 If You Were Approaching Retirement, Which Series Would You Prefer?			
Year	SERIES 1 - TAXABLE TOTAL STOCK MARKET Indexed Value*		SERIES 2 - TAX FREE INDEXED VALUE* 17% cap 1% guarantee	SERIES 3 - TAX FREE INDEXED VALUE 12% cap 2% guarantee	
1	$120,960	20.96%	$117,000 17.00%	$112,000 12.00%	
2	$158,446	30.99%	$136,890 17.00%	$125,440 12.00%	
3	$195,300	23.26%	$160,161 17.00%	$140,493 12.00%	
4	$241,801	23.81%	$187,389 17.00%	$157,352 12.00%	
5	$216,242	-10.57%	$189,263 1.00%	$160,499 2.00%	
6	$192,521	-10.97%	$191,155 1.00%	$163,709 2.00%	
7	$152,168	-20.96%	$193,067 1.00%	$166,983 2.00%	
8	$199,873	31.35%	$225,888 17.00%	$187,021 12.00%	
9	$224,897	12.52%	$254,169 12.52%	$209,464 12.00%	
10	$238,346	5.98%	$269,369 5.98%	$221,990 5.98%	
	Average Return 9.07% Net After Tax Return 6.05%		Average Return 10.42% Net After Tax Return 10.42%	Average Return 8.30% Net After Tax Return 8.30%	

*Fund Performance from 1996 through 2005

The average return during this ten-year period was 9.07 percent or 6 percent after tax (upon withdrawal) if it was a qualified account, assuming the investor was in a 33.3 percent tax bracket. A

$100,000 investment at the beginning of the above ten-year period would have an ending value of $238,346—not completely regaining the value it achieved at the end of the first four years (which was $241,801).

Recovering from market downturns can take one, two, three years or longer. A 25 percent loss has to be followed by a 33 percent gain to break even. A 50 percent loss has to be followed by a 100 percent gain to break even. After the serious drop in market value (which happened during the three-year period ending 2002 to this fund), this fund's portfolio would require a 59 percent gain during the three-year period ending 2005 to arrive at a net gain of zero percent over the last six years of that ten-year period. The value of the fund after four years was $241,801, but it lost 37 percent down to $152,168 during years 5 through 7. Years 8 to 10 would have to have gained 59 percent to come back to the $241,801 value the fund achieved during the first four years (a period of unprecedented growth). Often when investors look at a chart like the one for the Vanguard Total Stock Market Index Fund, they see only the year-by-year history and they think they are getting a much higher return than they actually are. During the down years, many people get heartburn reading their quarterly statements!

Suppose you owned this fund and it was established as an IRA or 401(k) and wanted to start taking income. If you were confident it would continue to earn an average of 9 percent, you could take approximately $21,000 per year of income from your $238,346 nest egg. However, after tax, in a 33.3 percent tax bracket, you might net only about $14,000 to spend. In a bit, I'll show you how you can keep your money in a stronger house of bricks, while participating during the good years but protecting yourself during the bad years when the house of straw (stocks) gets blown down. If you had your return linked to the market without actually being in the market, using this example, you could have achieved whatever the market did up to a cap of 17 percent as shown in Figure 11.2, Series 2, during years 1 to 4 and year 8 (even though the market did better). But you would have avoided a loss during years 5 to 7 with a guaranteed return of at least 1 percent. Based on that model, your fund would have been worth $269,369 at the end of ten years or an average annual return of 10.42 percent. If you choose the right investments (which I am about to disclose), you could very possibly withdraw $21,000 a year in retirement income—totally tax-free.

What if you had your return linked to the market without actually being *in* the market and your money was credited with whatever the market did up to a cap of 12 percent, as shown in Figure 11.2 Series 3, during years 1 to 4 and years 8 and 9? And as a trade-off to being capped at 12 percent during the good years, you would have avoided a loss during years 5 to 7 with a guaranteed return of at least 2 percent? Based on that model, your fund would have been worth $221,990 at the end of ten years, an average annual return of 8.3 percent. I'm about to show you that if you choose the right investments, you could very well withdraw tax-free retirement income greater than the net after-tax income you would realize from the Series 1 fund.

Which would give you peace of mind, especially during retirement: a more consistent, stable return averaging 7, 8, or 9 percent compounded annually that is tax-favored during the harvest? Or a range of returns entailing some gut-wrenching loss years as well as some great gain years that end up being taxed when finally withdrawn, thereby reducing the value by possibly one-third when you need the money the most?

Another problem, even with broad-based mutual funds, is that when you convert fund shares to cash to meet living expenses, you may need to pay close attention to your timing. It is always tempting to hold off in a down market until you can recapture some of your previous "paper" profits. This can create turmoil for you during retirement because you are trying to take a stable income out of a volatile market.

Is the risk inherent in mutual funds worth the reward? Most people are not able to time the market, although investors continue to try. Historical results show that returns achieved by individual *investors* who constantly try to time when to buy and when to sell do not equal the *investment* returns achieved by buying and holding the same investment through the ups and downs. As discussed previously, in the unprecedented upward spiral decade of the 1990s, various studies showed that while some mutual funds gained as much as 12.9 percent per year average in a bull market, individual investors averaged only about 2 to 3 percent.

It is not so much *which* fund you own; it is *how long* you own it that counts. According to Dalbar Reports, an equity fund is held only about 2.9 years on the average. This brings us back to the #1 Boomer Misconception: thinking you can use long-term investments for short-range goals.

Warren Buffett, the investment world's "sage of Omaha," once wrote that his favorite holding period was "forever."* Not many heed his advice, however. To minimize the impact of volatility and emotions, I usually advocate *indexed* investments or *fixed-portfolio* investments for serious cash. But financial jellyfish tend to ignore this advice. I will talk more about these investments shortly.

The primary advantage of mutual funds is that they pool money from many small investors, allowing them to diversify their holdings over a variety of publicly held companies in various industries throughout America or the world. By reading fund literature you can choose mutual funds that mesh with your investment objectives and then go about your business, allowing professional managers to pick specific stocks and bonds. In a diversified fund you thus spread your risk over more holdings than your personal amount of capital would be able to buy efficiently.

The disadvantage of mutual funds, whether they are in qualified tax-favored retirement plans or not, is that taxes must be paid either on the front end or on the back end. If you have a nonqualified account, you invest after-tax dollars at the beginning; and any dividends or

---

*http://www.berkshirehathaway.com/letters/1988.html.

capital gains will be taxed as realized. If you have a mutual fund in a qualified IRA or 401(k) account, the taxes are deferred while you buy and accumulate shares but the money you pull out is taxed during the distribution or transfer phase. Tax advantages are not available on the back end except in the case of Roth IRAs or certain tax-free or tax-exempt bond mutual funds.

THE PLUSES AND MINUSES OF ANNUITIES

A large proportion of Boomers encounter annuities when an advisor pitches one version or another to them as a good place for retirement money. I define an annuity as a savings account with an insurance company. It's deemed a fairly safe investment because insurance companies have high legal reserve requirements that make them even less prone to failure than banks. Because it is similar to a savings account, it passes the liquidity test.

With a traditional annuity, the insurer promises to pay you a specific amount of money over a period of time when it is annuitized. If they do annuitize it, most people choose monthly payments for a set number of years or for the life of the annuitant. Recently, more people have been using annuities simply as savings accumulation vehicles and then accessing money only as needed with periodic withdrawals, rather than annuitizing it for a set monthly income. There are three basic types of annuities: *fixed*, *variable*, and *indexed*. In each group there are two versions: *immediate* and *deferred*.

When you deposit premium dollars into a deferred annuity, whether it is fixed, variable, or indexed, your money accumulates in a tax-favored environment. Even if it is not a qualified plan, the money grows tax-deferred. But if you take money out before you are age 59½, you are assessed a 10 percent penalty, just as you would be on an IRA or 401(k), and you must pay tax on your gain.

If you are beyond 59½, the money you withdraw is taxed as ordinary income, but it receives LIFO, last in, first out, treatment.

This means the last money you earn in an annuity is the interest credited most recently on your account. The IRS regards your distribution as being the last money earned, and treats it as the first money you are withdrawing. Thus, you are taxed on 100 percent of your distributions (assuming interest-only withdrawals) from the first day you start distributions. There is no way to avoid this. Even if you make principal and interest withdrawals you must still count the interest earned each year as the first money you withdraw for tax purposes.

A *fixed* annuity offers you a rate of return based upon the generally fixed account portfolio of the insurance company—but the return can fluctuate. A *variable* annuity pays a return that varies according to the performance of the underlying stocks, bonds, or money market fund. If it is an *indexed* annuity, it is linked to an index such as the S&P 500; you get a minimum guaranteed return, even if the market loses, but you get to participate indirectly in any gains in the market up to a ceiling or cap. The interest credited fluctuates according to the index to which it is pegged.

An *immediate* annuity is one that begins to pay you a certain amount immediately or within one year. Let's look at a single premium immediate annuity (SPIA). You deposit one lump-sum payment and you receive immediate income distributions. The taxable portion of the annual distribution is averaged during the period the annuity is calculated to pay out. SPIAs are among the investments that can make a good side fund. I will talk about the need for side funds in Chapter 12.

A *deferred* annuity is one in which you delay receiving income payments until a certain point or you use it simply for accumulation until you withdraw your money. So a deferred annuity has two phases—an accumulation phase, when you invest money in it and it accumulates tax-deferred, and a distribution phase, when you start to withdraw the money, either as a lump sum, periodic withdrawals, or as a specific amount over a period of time, such as monthly retirement income. For instance, if you have $100,000 in an annuity, and it credits 10 percent interest, you could pull out $10,000 of interest a year without depleting the principal part of your annuity. The principal that you invested is called the "basis" on a deferred annuity. On your tax return, you report the $10,000 you receive as an interest withdrawal; thus it is 100 percent taxable from your first withdrawal in this example. You get a tax break only when you begin to deplete the principal, because it was created with after-tax dollars.

Historically, during the last three decades, fixed annuities have credited between 5 and 9 percent for an average of about 7 percent, resulting in a net after-tax return of about 5 percent. So annuities pass the rate of return test.

Lately, investors have bought variable annuities that aim to get tax-deferred growth by using a variety of mutual funds. You can choose to assign your variable annuity to the mutual fund management team of your choice. The annuity may also include insurance, to make sure your heirs will collect more than the account's current value in the event of death and/or if the investments perform poorly. There is, of course, a price for such protection—this kind of variable annuity may carry annual expenses of approximately 2.25 percent of assets.

Some variable annuities provide that your heirs will get back the amount invested, in the event you lose money on the annuity during your lifetime. Other annuities are now sold giving heirs back at least the amount invested plus 5 or 7 percent in annual interest. Some may even pay heirs the highest value determined on a particular date each year. However, the rising death benefits may have a cap at a certain age, such as age 80. Death benefits may also be reduced if you withdraw any money from the annuity.

Insurance companies offer other options with regard to survivor benefits. If you die before withdrawing all the funds in an annuity without a life insurance component, the remaining balance will be paid to your heirs at face value. That is, your beneficiaries get the exact amount remaining or accumulated in the annuity, either as a lump sum or in installments over a period of time. Your beneficiaries typically must pay the appropriate income tax due on that money.

Because of the risk inherent in an annuity linked directly to securities or other variable instruments, I believe financial advisors should never recommend putting home equity into such an investment. Home equity is serious cash and you should use it for more stable or fixed investments that contain guarantees.

If you feel annuities meet the liquidity, safety, and rate of return test for your objectives, and you want to participate indirectly when the market is going up without the inherent risk incurred when money is actually in the market, I would recommend indexed annuities. Indexed annuities contain a safety net or guaranteed minimum interest rate they will credit regardless of what the market does. So your principal is generally not at risk. Your return is linked to an index such as the Dow Jones or Standard & Poor's. Some indexing products allow you to participate up to a certain percent with no cap, while others allow 100 percent participation (or higher) in whatever the index achieves during a specified time frame up to a cap. Understand that there is a cap or maximum limit because your money is actually not at risk in the market. So the insurance company is required to buy options in the market or employ other strategies in order to credit you a return that is based on whatever the index does—even though your money is not actually exposed to market risk.

TAX-FAVORED HARVESTS

In the course of my thirty-plus years as a financial consultant I have found that many people simply look for the highest gross rate of return on investments without figuring in the tax considerations that will reduce the return. I hope I have convinced you by now that you don't want retirement investments that are tax-deferred but that have big slices carved out by taxes on the back end—the distribution and transfer phases. You certainly don't want to postpone taxes until later if you think they will be higher than they are now, and you want to be careful to not take profits that could unnecessarily push your tax bracket high enough to make your Social Security taxable.

I believe the best investments for long-range goals such as retirement are financial instruments with no tax on the back end, so that they provide the most money at the time when you will likely need the money most. For the highest *net spendable income*, I recommend certain properly structured maximum-funded life insurance contracts. I sometimes refer to them as "investment-grade" insurance contracts. Please study Figure 11.3, which illustrates a comparison of various retirement planning vehicles. The features that I feel are important to maximize your retirement income and tax benefits are listed on the left.

As you study the four categories, remember, that traditional IRAs/TSAs/401(k)s are like *jogging* toward retirement with the wind at your back at the beginning of the race. Roth IRAs and 401(k)s are like *jogging* toward retirement with the wind at your back at the end of the race. Nonqualified annuities are more like brisk *walking* toward retirement. But you'll shortly see why properly structured, maximum tax-advantaged life insurance contracts are like *sprinting* toward retirement when used in conjunction with successful equity management.

Fig. 11.3	COMPARISON OF VARIOUS RETIREMENT PLANNING VEHICLES			
	QUALIFIED PLANS, IRA/TSA/401(K)	ROTH IRAS	NON-QUALIFIED ANNUITIES	INSURANCE CONTRACTS
Current tax	Pre-tax or deductible	No deduction	No deduction	No deduction
Earnings taxed	No	No	No	No
Withdrawals taxed	Yes	No	Yes, gain only	No*
Death benefits taxed	Yes, spouse no	No	Yes, gain only	No
Amount at death	Account value	Account value	Account value	Death benefit
Limits on amounts and timing	Yes	Yes	No	No
Effect on Social Security benefit	May make it taxable	None	May make it taxable	None

*If policy remains in force until insured's death

LIFE INSURANCE AS A RETIREMENT INVESTMENT

A lot of Americans do not realize they can go to the same AAA-rated life insurance companies that issue annuities and establish a maximum tax-advantaged insurance contract, which can be structured so that *retirement money can be withdrawn tax-free*. They also don't generally understand that these companies are not much different from a conservative mutual fund asset management company.

This is another part of my strategy for wealth enhancement that runs contrary to the beliefs of conventional financial advisors. Remember, all the dogs barking up the same tree doesn't make it the right tree. Just because a financial consultant may deal primarily with brokerage houses or securities dealers does not make that person an expert on retirement planning for the greatest net spendable income. My approach is the opposite of the way most people, as well as some financial planners, view life insurance. Instead of using it for a maximum death benefit, I use it for *maximum living benefits*.

Insurance companies are experts in managing risk. When they accept and hold money set aside for future needs, they are responsible by law for investing that money wisely to achieve a safe rate of return. Many life insurance companies invest their capital in a conservative portfolio primarily consisting of high-grade bonds. They also may invest a small percentage of assets in mortgage loans on real estate and sometimes in stocks and other investments.

Chances are you have never had a reason to look at the financial statement of a highly rated life insurance company. If you had, you would discover that they are structured in a way that's similar to conservative, income-oriented mutual funds with some growth potential. Typically, about 90 percent of an insurance company's general account portfolio will be comprised of 70 percent in AAA and AA bonds and 20 percent in mortgages on shopping malls and office buildings.

Because the portfolio of an insurance company is more

conservative and is likely less volatile than most mutual funds, it will likely earn a lower rate of return with less deviation. Most insurance company portfolios earn from 7 to 9 percent, while most growth mutual funds try to achieve an average return of 10 to 12 percent, taking into account periods of both gains and losses.

"Whoa!" You're probably thinking: "If I can get to 10 to 12 percent from mutual funds over a ten- or twenty-year period, why wouldn't I choose them and pay the tax on the gain rather than accept an average return of only 7 to 9 percent?"

The quick answer is: *The 7 to 9 percent is tax-free and thus can be equal or better than the gains on mutual funds after taxes*. More important is that the insurance contracts I recommend are more stable and less volatile than other choices, and can provide you with a higher net spendable income and greater net accumulation value. You can sprint into retirement. You won't be paying tax on your harvest. For these reasons, wise investors who wish to sleep soundly at night are turning more to insurance companies for tax-favored long-term savings and capital accumulation.

SOME BACKGROUND ON INSURANCE INVESTING

Insurance is a trillion-dollar industry here in America and is probably one of the most stable sectors in the American economy. During the 1930s, at the same time some banks, stocks, and real estate were tanking, some of the most durable and safe investments were in life insurance contracts. But until recently, they were not attractive as retirement investments. Until the 1980s a typical whole life insurance policy may have credited only about 2.5 to 3.5 percent return on the cash values that would accumulate. Nevertheless, well-managed and highly rated life insurance companies, as a general rule, are some of the best money managers in the world.

If you looked at an insurance company's portfolio the same way you perused a mutual fund's holdings, you might choose a top-rated insurance company to manage your money. You would be putting your faith in the managers' ability to earn future rates of return similar to those achieved in the past, just the way you would be when investing in a mutual fund. One difference is that in order to qualify for maximum tax-favored treatment, your account would have to include a death benefit.

The most fundamental change I recommend in making life insurance a retirement fund is for you to purchase the *lowest death benefit* required by tax law, and pay the *highest premiums* you can afford. This permits you to invest the greatest amount of "excess" cash in the policy beyond the true cost of the insurance itself. This is the reverse approach taken by most people who buy life insurance primarily for a death benefit. By focusing on the tax-favored living benefits, this investment better deserves the term "life insurance." *People who come to me now don't necessarily want "insurance"; they simply want a safe, liquid investment with a good rate of return as well as tax-favored treatment of the withdrawals.*

A former brokerage firm, E. F. Hutton, is often credited with being the first to fully harness the unique treatment of life insurance under the tax code:[*] life insurance is the *only* instrument that accumulates money tax-free, that allows you to access that money tax-free (including the gains), and that transfers the money tax-free—and in addition blossoms in value for heirs if the person insured happens to die before using all the money. Over the past several decades this innovative use of life insurance has been redefined by new tax laws and rulings.[**] The result is that insurance contracts can be structured so they produce a much better rate of return than the old 2.5 to 3.5 percent. Insurance companies usually can afford to pay higher interest rates than banks and credit unions because their portfolio of investments doesn't turn over quickly.

---

[*]Internal Revenue Code, Section 72(e) 7702 and Section 101.
[**]See the discussion of TEFRA, DEFRA, and TAMRA in Appendix A.

WHAT IS THE DIFFERENCE BETWEEN TERM LIFE INSURANCE AND CASH-VALUE INSURANCE?

Before getting into the nuts and bolts of how maximum tax-advantaged insurance works, let me offer some insight into life insurance in general.

At one time some people viewed life insurance as a necessary evil—something for which you tried to pay the smallest premium possible so that your family had some economic protection. The objective was to create an immediate estate in the event of premature death, helping cover the economic loss suffered by the beneficiaries. There are two basic categories: Policies that provide only a death benefit are classified as *term insurance*, while those that provide a built-in savings component in addition are classified as *cash-value* or *permanent insurance*.

All insurance is based on the concept that each individual pays a premium based on the desired coverage. It is priced per $1,000 of coverage per year, usually payable monthly. The cost varies with factors such as age, insurability, health of the insured, type of policy, and also mortality, which is calculated using a standard table. Term insurance premiums generally increase with age, since mortality rates increase as people grow older. Some don't want to pay a higher premium each month. They pay a level premium based upon the average required to cover mortality and expense charges over a five-, ten-, or twenty-year period, or perhaps for a lifetime. Another way to pay a level premium is by electing decreasing term insurance, in which the death benefit goes down as the person gets older. Term insurance may be a good way to meet specific needs but it has no cash accumulation value or living benefits.

Insurance companies try hard to keep their risks to a minimum in order to be more profitable and reward those with healthy lifestyles. Those who don't have healthy lifestyles are penalized with a "substandard" rating and charged a higher premium. They may even be declined altogether. People who lead somewhat healthy lifestyles may be rated "standard." Those deemed very healthy—no tobacco, no excessive alcohol use, height and weight within certain guidelines, a nonhazardous occupation, regular exercise—are rewarded by being rated "preferred" or even "ultra-preferred."

A UNIQUE WAY TO SAVE FOR RETIREMENT

Let's concentrate on cash-value life insurance. You pay an average premium over the lifetime of the policy. The excess premium paid over and above the costs of mortality and the sales and administration expenses builds up equity in the policy. The excess money accumulates with interest, and then begins to accrue the cash values that can be used for living benefits. If death occurs, cash values are absorbed into the policy's death benefit, or they can be added on top of the face amount of the policy.

There are five varieties of cash-value policies, including *whole life, variable life*, and three kinds of *universal life—fixed, variable*, and *indexed*. Whole life can be an effective method of purchasing insurance on a long-term basis. The insurance company invests the excess premiums in a long-term portfolio, thus creating additional cash accumulation or dividends that can be reinvested with the company for additional growth.

Cash-value insurance thus provides a liquid fund that can be used at will—in an emergency, for investment opportunities, or to supplement retirement income. A unique feature is that the cash values accumulate tax-free. They can also be accessed without tax under certain provisions of the contract, which I will explain shortly. Life insurance death benefits are also free of income tax under most circumstances[*] no matter how large, although they may be included in the total valuation of the deceased person's estate. An important element is that insurance proceeds are not subject to the claims of creditors of the deceased unless they were

---

*Internal Revenue Code, Section 101.

assigned or pledged as such, or unless the beneficiary was jointly responsible. However, if a policy's beneficiary is the estate of the insured, rather than the spouse, children, trust, or other party, then the creditors may have a claim.

Let me restate the unique advantage of life insurance: It is the only investment that:

- allows you to accumulate money tax-free;
- enables you to access your money tax-free; and
- blossoms in value and transfers tax-free when you die.

Provided the required premiums are paid, a permanent life insurance policy contract contains guaranteed cash values. These values are supported by company monetary reserves. They also contain maximum guaranteed premium schedules designed to keep the life insurance in force until a certain age under a guaranteed interest rate. Of course, most contracts credit *more* than the rate guaranteed.

Because many financial planners are familiar with life insurance only as protection against financial loss in the case of untimely death, they may not be educated on the remarkable power it offers as an investment. Robert A. Miller, the marketing director of the major company AIG Life Brokerage, has declared, "We are overlooking the potential role of life insurance in a comprehensive retirement plan."[*]

In fact, it may not be the investment you thought you were looking for. Most people do not object to life insurance benefits; they just don't want to pay for them! In a moment, I will show you how to use otherwise payable income taxes so that Uncle Sam pays for your life insurance.

I often compare life insurance to a tin can that you stuff with money and bury in your backyard. If you have an investment

---

[*]"Maximum Tax Advantaged Life," *Sales Insights*, Vol. 4, No. 7 (July 2005).

instrument that earns 8 percent a year but is as readily accessible as the nearest drive-up bank window, chances are you are going to dip into that account from time to time, even with its good rate of return. But if you have the same amount of money in a tin can soldered shut and buried where it is not quite that accessible, it is a case of "out of sight, out of mind." After, say, ten years, I daresay most Americans would have more money in the tin can, even though it has not earned a nickel in interest.

The real secret to accumulating wealth is not the rate of return—but rather the ability to put money aside, keep it aside, and put it to work for you.

What is now typically called universal life insurance, when structured properly to perform like an investment, achieves this. Take an insurance contract . . . squeeze it down to the minimum death benefit that really just comes along for the ride and satisfies tax code requirements . . . load the policy with cash . . . overpay the premiums normally required to cover mortality and expense charges . . . and you wind up with a great deal of equity in the policy. This tremendous excess of cash, stored in the insurance company's internal portfolio, earns interest and compounds through the years.

As you continue to over-fund the contract, the mortality and expense charge associated with the death benefit usually drains out just a small portion of the overall amount, often giving up only about one of the percentage points of the rate of interest earned. So during the life of my insurance contracts, the average gross return has been between 8 and 10 percent. After deducting the costs, most of which are necessary for tax-favored treatment of the gain, at the end of the day (so to speak), the net internal rate of return, cash on cash, has averaged between 7 and 9 percent. What I mean by "the end of the day" is that, down the road when I use the money for tax-free retirement income, or when I eventually pass away, looking back retroactively to day one of each of my insurance contracts, I would had to have gotten a 7, 8, or 9 percent return compounded annually on my premium deposits to generate the benefits I have enjoyed.

I would rather have a tax-free return with this kind of performance over a taxable return that could be a few points higher. Why? The small portion of my accumulated cash that is paying the costs of buying this life insurance is money that would otherwise have gone to the government in taxes on a taxable investment. That's why I think of it as Uncle Sam indirectly paying for my life insurance.

PICK THE TYPE OF LIFE INSURANCE CONTRACT THAT FITS YOUR NEEDS

There are basically five categories of cash-value life insurance. Let's examine each.

Whole life is often thought of as traditional cash-value life insurance. Sometimes it is called *permanent* life insurance. It provides guaranteed survivor benefits, cash values, level premiums, and possibly dividends. The most basic version is often called ordinary, or straight, life. Newer whole life policies have lower costs than older ones due to upgraded mortality rates. (Mortality rates are tables of the death rate by age within the population as computed by an insurance company.) *The cash-value accumulations grow tax-deferred. The dividends of a whole life policy are tax-free.* The projected return is based on a long-term portfolio of assets. A policyholder can access cash values via withdrawals or loans.

Variable life includes a death benefit created by term insurance with an equity investment side fund. The insured may choose the investment vehicle used for cash accumulations. The values are dependent upon the return on the vehicle chosen. The premium is a specified amount based upon the insured's age and the face amount of the policy. Among the investment options are money market funds, accounts that have guaranteed or fixed interest rates, government securities funds, corporate bond funds, total return funds, and growth funds. Variable life also typically carries the highest costs. As your investment objectives change, you may switch from one portfolio to another.

I do not recommend that homeowners invest home equity in variable life contracts because the underlying portfolios may fluctuate and lose value, thus being too risky for serious cash. Instead, I believe home equity should be invested in more stable fixed or indexed insurance contracts that contain guarantees.

Universal life insurance is more flexible than whole life. Both premium payments and insurance death benefits can be varied to meet your needs, within certain parameters. As you pay premiums, a portion of the money pays the pure term insurance rates. The balance goes into a side fund on which interest is paid. If the premium paid is not sufficient to cover the cost of the term insurance, the balance comes out of the side fund. You may elect to pay premiums higher or lower, subject to some limits. You may even skip premium payments without losing coverage if there is enough cash value in the savings portion of the contract. Universal life generally contains low mortality costs due to updated mortality rates. Cash values grow in a tax-advantaged environment and can be accessed tax-free via withdrawals or loans. Cash values and accumulated earnings can transfer tax-free to heirs.

There are three kinds of universal life contracts. *Fixed universal life* is the most conservative and generally has the lowest expense charges. "Fixed" doesn't mean a fixed interest rate; it means you get interest based on the insurance company's relatively fixed general account portfolio. A large company with high ratings may have about 70 percent of its assets invested in high-grade bonds, 20 percent in mortgage-backed securities, and the remaining 10 percent in a combination of stocks, real estate, cash, and short-term investments or policy loans.

A fixed universal life policy will typically have a guaranteed minimum interest rate, usually around 4 percent. In my experience very few companies have credited only the guaranteed rate. You will know what the minimum is because under National Association of Insurance Commissioners (NAIC) rules, you are asked to sign an illustration showing the projection of the policy benefits based on the premium payments that you will likely make. The illustration may be based upon the interest rate credited by the company at the time you take out the policy. But the illustration must also show the worst-case scenario using the minimum guaranteed interest rate on the cash values from the start of the policy. This illustration also assumes that the maximum mortality charges allowed are assessed throughout the life of the policy. That low a return is unlikely, but the idea is to show you what *could* happen. Actual mortality charges are usually less than the maximum, and policies usually far outperform the minimum interest guarantee.

Fixed universal life tends to respond slowly to market swings. A five-year history of a highly rated company's returns typically will show less than a half-percent swing from year to year.

Variable universal life insurance blends the premium flexibility of fixed universal life with the investment flexibility of variable life. You can select from various investment funds as you can with variable life and you can also choose to adjust the premiums higher or lower, within limits. You may even choose to skip a premium payment without losing coverage if your policy has accumulated adequate value.

Variable universal life differs from fixed in that generally all cash values except the part needed to cover mortality and expense charges are *not* under the umbrella of the insurance company. Instead, the cash values are usually invested in equities. As a result there is no guaranteed minimum interest rate and if the investments suffer a loss during a specified time period and the portfolio does not contain sufficient cash, policy owners may have to make additional premium payments to make sure the mortality and expense charges are covered.

Comparison studies that I have done over a fifteen-year period indicate that a variable universal life policy typically must outperform a fixed universal life's internal rate of return by about 3 percent in order to match the fixed policy's net return. One of the reasons is that the administration fees on a variable contract are greater. I recommend choosing a variable universal life contract only if its expected net return is higher than the *net* expected return on a fixed contract.

I urge you to be very cautious before choosing variable universal life. It is volatile and exposed to market downturns, which could occur when you need liquidity the most. These qualities make variable universal life an *inappropriate* choice for your home equity. I think your home equity belongs in more stable or fixed contracts. Also, *I discourage this choice among elderly clients, who usually want a stable return.* Younger investors, on the other hand, might consider taking on a variable universal life policy's greater risk for nonserious cash (money other than home equity or money that guarantee of principal is not critical) in pursuit of possible greater growth over twenty or thirty years.

Indexed universal life offers you a guaranteed floor along with the chance to participate indirectly in upswings within the broader market. The interest rate you are credited with is linked to the performance of an index such as the S&P 500, which tracks a basket of diversified large-company stocks in the U.S. stock market. Over the long term the S&P 500 Index has outperformed high-grade bonds, CDs, and the rate of inflation. Indexed universal life provides a return approaching that of such an index, but with a ceiling cap. Yet it also protects you by guaranteeing a minimum interest rate, usually 1 to 3 percent, even if the index you are linked to declines.

With an indexed universal life policy, your cash values remain under the protective umbrella of the insurance company. You get the benefit of being linked to a market index without being *in* the market. I have found that such policies can net you about 1, 2, or 3 percent better over the long haul than the fixed ones. These policies carry slightly higher expense charges than a fixed but lower than a variable universal life policy.

Fig. 11.4	EXAMPLES OF 3 TYPES OF UNIVERSAL LIFE MAXIMUM-FUNDED INSURANCE CONTRACTS				
30-Year Historical Crediting Interest Rates					
	Guaranteed	Lowest	Average	Highest	Interest Rate Required to Achieve Same Accumulation Values
Fixed	4%	4.75%	7.5%	13.75%	7.44%
Variable	None	<30%>	10%	35%	10.52%
Equity Indexed (Linked to S&P 500)	1%	1%	8.5%	17%	8.20%

To get an idea of the range of performance you might expect from these different life insurance contracts when they are structured to perform primarily as investments rather than solely as death benefit protection, refer to Figure 11.4. It compares the guarantees plus the highs, lows, and average returns of a fixed, variable, and indexed universal life contract along with the rate of return each would need to match the same bottom-line results over the long haul—namely, thirty years.

HOW AN INDEXED INVESTMENT PERFORMS IN A VOLATILE MARKET

If you were to look at the market over an extended time frame, it will generally show two years of growth for every one year of loss. Let's look at an example of how indexing works in a volatile market.

Most insurance companies use an index like the S&P 500. The most common way of linking the interest-crediting rate on the cash value of an indexed life insurance policy to the market is the point-to-point method. When you pay a premium into the policy, the net amount (after deducting the mortality and expense charges for the life insurance) is shortly thereafter linked to the index. Whatever the index is at one year from when your premium was linked will determine your return. If the S&P 500 went up from 1,350 to 1,500, it would represent an 11 percent growth. Most companies have a floor (guarantee) and a cap of what you can earn. If the cap is 12 percent, in this example you would be credited with the full 11 percent gain.

A nice feature in many indexed contracts is the "locked in gains and annual reset." If the S&P 500 takes a turn downward the next year to 1,275, it would represent a negative 15 percent change in the index. However, the cash value inside the insurance policy would still be credited with a 0 to 3 percent gain even though the market went down! And the 11 percent gain you earned the year prior is locked in due to the locked-in-gains feature. If you were *in* the market instead of being linked *to* the market you would be down 5.5 percent from where you were two years before. Let's say the S&P 500 Index increases the next year to 1,410. If the insurance policy has an annual reset feature, you started over at 1,275 and would benefit from the growth to 1,410 the third year. That represents a 10.5 percent gain for the third year.

Let's review the actual credited return you would have received during the three-year period. The first year you were credited 11 percent. The second year, when the S&P 500 lost 15 percent, you didn't lose anything. You received the guarantee of, let's say, 2 percent in this case. Remember, the 11 percent growth, from the year prior, was locked in. At the beginning of the third year the policy crediting rate was determined by a starting point that was reset at 1,275. Thus when the S&P 500 Index went up from 1,275 to 1,410 you were credited 10.5 percent! That represents an average of 7.9 percent over the three-year period. Had you been *in* the market, you would have experienced only an S&P-indexed growth from 1,350 to 1,410 over the three years (not to mention the heartburn you probably experienced when the market went south). The annual average return each year for those three years represents a measly 1.5 percent compounded annually!

So you can see, when money is actually invested in the market, the returns can be very small during certain time periods, whereas returns that are linked to an index with a guaranteed floor coupled with a ceiling can provide more stability and, often, a better return. Most of the indexed universal life policies that I own have a 100 percent participation rate (guaranteed) and then a cap of what I can earn. Most of these caps range from 10 to 17 percent. A 100 percent participation rate means that if the index goes up 8 percent I would receive 100 percent of that growth. If the index went up by 15 percent and the cap is 12 percent, I would receive the maximum crediting rate of 12 percent.

I'm not a gambler, but if I were invited to play in a casino and the owner stated, "Hey, you can play here all day and the house will cover all your bets. At the end of the day, if you end up in the loss column, we will assure that you will at least leave with 1, 2, or 3 percent more than you started with. If you end up in the win column, you can keep everything up to a maximum of 12 percent." Hmm, I wouldn't mind playing that kind of a game.

The majority of insurance policies that I own use the one-year point-to-point method. Some have different strategies, such as the one-year monthly average, one-year monthly average multiple index, one-year monthly cap, and two-year point-to-point method. The most widely used index is the S&P 500 but some companies allow you to link to the Dow Jones Industrial Average Index and the Nasdaq Composite Index as well. Some companies allow you to link to global indexes such as the Dow Jones EURO STOXX 50 and the Hang Seng Index. The companies that use multiple indexes let you diversify between each index by allowing you to have an indexed return of 50 percent of the index that performs best over the time frame, 30 percent of the index that comes in second place, and 20 percent of the index that comes in third place. One of my indexed universal life policies uses the S&P 500 and the two global indices; 75 percent of my crediting rate is determined from the index that performs best, 25 percent from the index that comes in second, and the index that comes in last will be left out for that time period.

Based on the actual history of the S&P 500 Index during the thirty-year period ending in 2005, if you had received a 1 percent guarantee during the loss years and 100 percent of the gains up to a cap of 17 percent during the positive growth years, you would have experienced a 9.62 percent average annual crediting rate (see Figure 11.5). During the last fifty years or so, if you would have received a 2 percent guarantee during the loss years and 100 percent of the gains up to a cap of 12 percent during the positive growth years, you would have experienced a 7.9 percent average crediting rate using a one-year point-to-point method. Using a two-year point-to-point method, you would have experienced an 8.3 percent average crediting rate.

Fig. 11.5	ILLUSTRATED RATE ON AN INDEXED UNIVERSAL LIFE (17% Cap and 1% Guaranteed Floor)					
YEAR	**S&P 500 GROWTH**	**INDEX ALLOCATION**	**YEAR**	**S&P 500 GROWTH**	**INDEX ALLOCATION**
1976	15.74%	15.74%	1991	13.40%	13.40%
1977	-2.98%	1.00%	1992	10.53%	10.53%
1978	-2.63%	1.00%	1993	8.08%	8.08%
1979	6.41%	6.41%	1994	2.48%	2.48%
1980	18.63%	17.00%	1995	17.13%	17.00%
1981	6.71%	6.71%	1996	25.96%	17.00%
1982	-6.89%	1.00%	1997	28.82%	17.00%
1983	36.91%	17.00%	1998	24.53%	17.00%
1984	0.48%	1.00%	1999	22.55%	17.00%
1985	17.06%	17.00%	2000	7.68%	7.68%
1986	26.16%	17.00%	2001	-14.53%	1.00%
1987	22.10%	17.00%	2002	-17.70%	1.00%
1988	-7.74%	1.00%	2003	-4.09%	1.00%
1989	23.51%	17.00%	2004	18.30%	17.00%
1990	4.40%	4.40%	2005	7.59%	7.59%

Index Allocation Average Annual Crediting Rate = 9.62%

a. 30 years of S&P 500 performance using annual point-to-point averaging of the 4 set allocation buy dates set by the company with a 17% Cap and a 1% guaranteed floor.

b. The 4 set allocation dates are Febuary 15th, May 15th, August 15th and November 15th.

Let's assume you maximum-funded an indexed universal life policy from age 55 to age 60 or 65, and then let the cash values accumulate in this fashion for a total of thirty years through age 85. If you experienced a 9.62 percent average gross crediting rate, your net internal rate of return, after the cost of the insurance is deducted (which is absolutely necessary for it to received tax-advantaged treatment when you take retirement income), would likely be about 8.5 percent. Likewise, if you experienced a 7.9 to 8.3 percent average gross crediting rate, your internal rate of return would likely be about 7 percent.

WHY I CALL IT "PROPERLY STRUCTURED, INVESTMENT-GRADE" LIFE INSURANCE

You may have observed how I stress the phrase "properly structured" life insurance contracts. A contract must meet the minimum death benefit requirements established by law, based on the insured's age and gender. Federal guidelines dictate the amount of money you can invest in premiums without exceeding the definition of a life insurance contract. This will make the accumulation of cash values and the death benefit not subject to tax.[*]

In the past, whenever Congress has made major changes to the tax code, especially with regard to life insurance, it has grandfathered policyholders who already had a policy in force. It might be wise to establish a life insurance policy now that will accommodate the total amount of money you hope to sock away eventually, just in case Congress decides to change the rules again. If it does, the hope is that existing policies would be grandfathered. There can be no guarantee of this, but if precedent holds, as it did most recently in 1988,[**] grandfathering is likely.

Unfortunately, many life insurance agents don't totally understand the legal guidelines known by the acronyms TEFRA, DEFRA,

---

[*]See Appendix A for details on the Tax Equity and Fiscal Responsibility Act of 1982 (TEFRA) and the Deficit Reduction Act of 1984 (DEFRA), which govern the parameters of a properly structured universal life insurance contract.
[**]See Appendix A for details in the 1988 Technical and Miscellaneous Revenue Act (TAMRA).

and TAMRA. It is crucial for you to have someone who does understand all these ins and outs if you expect your policy to perform at its optimal level for living benefits, rather than death benefits.

If you want a contract that I would consider to be investment-grade, I believe it must meet several criteria. First, it must be structured properly so it can perform as an investment rather than just as a death benefit policy. It also needs to be structured so it can be maximum-funded as soon as possible under federal guidelines, yet maintain flexibility in case circumstances change.

Second, you need to be certain that due diligence has been taken in selecting an appropriate insurance company. There are different agencies that rate life insurance companies, including Standard & Poor's, A.M. Best, Fitch, Moody's, and Weiss. They use various methods and scales, often confusing the public, Congress, and the Government Accountability Office. For instance, the highest rating assigned by Standard & Poor's is AAA, while A.M. Best uses A++. I use Vital Signs, a financial strength reporting system that quickly and reliably qualifies an insurance company's financial strength in a variety of easy-to-understand reports. Vital Signs assigns each company a "Comdex score" from 1 to 100 based upon combined data from rating agencies and the insurance company itself. For insurance contracts that will be maximum-funded, I generally recommend companies that have a Comdex score of at least 70 or higher. Ask your agent for the various ratings of the insurance company being recommended or for a combined Comdex score.

Third, I feel it is necessary for an insurance company to maintain liquidity, so I select companies with sufficient cash or cash equivalent on hand. Insurance companies typically have a much greater surplus or solvency ratio than other financial institutions such as banks and credit unions. In really tough economic times, I would want my money to be easily accessible should I decide to liquidate my funds. Remember, the size of an insurance company does not determine its strength. A company can be very large yet have excessive liabilities. A good insurance agent, consultant, or planner who is trained to follow the strategies in this book can help you find the best company and insurance instrument for your needs.

Indeed, life insurance contracts function as the ideal tin can. And I'm about to show you the best of all worlds, where not only can you stash money in this tin can, not only will it likely stay put, but it will grow at a rate of return equal to or greater than the return achieved by other more risky, more volatile taxable investments.

Once you see how well such a contract works, I think you will want to do what most of our clients do and *what I do with my own money*: reposition your discretionary dollars into this remarkable wealth enhancement tool. The long-term performance of a properly funded life insurance contract, from the standpoint of a cash-on-cash, tax-favored, internal rate of return, is usually much better than many IRA and 401(k) investments, not to mention taxable investments such as mutual funds, CDs, and money market accounts or even tax-deferred annuities.

Boomers can follow my lead and *sprint* toward retirement by repositioning IRA and 401(k) contributions or rolling out their accumulations and depositing them in a maximum tax-advantaged life insurance contract. If it makes fiscal sense you may choose to optimize your assets by repositioning some or all of your home equity into such a contract as well.

In the next chapter, I go into detail on strategies that you—like the Centsible, Eager, Faralong, and Gainsworthy families I introduced in Chapter 9—can use with maximum tax-advantaged life insurance to maximize your wealth and enjoy your harvest years in a tax-free environment.

(If you would like to listen to an audio recording explaining the success formula for choosing the right investments, structuring your life insurance to perform as a superior investment, and accessing your money tax-free at retirement, please go to my Web site at www.MissedFortune.com/SuccessFormula.)

REMEMBER THIS:

- Some mutual funds, annuities, and properly structured maximum tax-advantaged insurance contracts are the only investments that meet the "Laser" test of liquidity, safety, and rate of return on serious cash.
- Invest your serious cash such as home equity only in stable or fixed investments that contain guarantees.
- While mutual funds may achieve overall before-tax gains greater than annuities, CDs, money market funds, or maximum-funded life insurance in the long run, their return is *not* guaranteed. The after-tax retirement income from a mutual fund will likely not meet or beat the tax-free income stream that can be achieved with a maximum-funded insurance contract.
- Of the three forms of annuities—*fixed*, *variable*, and *indexed*—and two versions of each, *immediate* and *deferred*, variable annuities are not stable enough for serious cash such as home equity, while certain single-premium immediate fixed annuities work well as side funds while funding an insurance contract.
- Money invested in nonqualified deferred annuities is tax-deferred during the accumulation stage but is taxed on distribution.
- Certain cash-value life insurance—such as properly structured, maximum tax-advantaged universal life policies—are the only investments in which you can contribute, accumulate, and withdraw money tax-free and which blossom tax-free when transferred to your heirs.

CHAPTER 12

Insure That Your Retirement Income Lasts as Long as You Do

How Maximum Tax-Advantaged Life Insurance Contracts Pay for Your Retirement

YOU'RE PROBABLY FAMILIAR with the term "multitasking." With the twenty-first century has come the idea that one personal computer can be utilized for accomplishing several tasks, sometimes simultaneously, including searching the Internet, downloading a brand-new album of music, and answering e-mail.

In the same way, life insurance is a multitasking financial instrument. When a life insurance contract is structured properly, it can be a superior tool for tax-advantaged capital accumulation, distribution, and transfer. At the same time, it plays its traditional role as a provider of financial protection for your family and your heirs.

I realize that when you started reading this book, you didn't necessarily want to buy life insurance. That's okay. But I've never had a widow or widower turn down an insurance check. Sometimes when a client says, "Sure, I want a great way to sock away retirement money in these contracts that outperform other investments, but I don't need life insurance," I am tempted to reply: "Fine. After the policy is structured so you have a great investment, please make *me* the beneficiary."

TIME TO CONNECT ALL OF THE DOTS

At this point I want to connect the dots—the strands of information this book has offered about managing home equity, rolling out your qualified retirement plans into a better alternative, and obtaining maximum tax-advantaged life insurance, which can be the optimal alternative. This is my strategy for enhancing your wealth and providing a comfortable retirement plan that lasts as long as you do in a tax-favored environment. To show how to achieve these goals, I'm going to return to the families we met in Chapter 9.

You'll recall the four Boomer couples and their retirement timetables:

- Clark and Carrie Centsible, 50 years old, plan to retire at 65.
- Frank and Felicia Faralong, 50 years old, plan to retire at 70.
- Ed and Elizabeth Eager, 55 years old, plan to retire at 65.
- George and Gail Gainsworthy, 60 years old, plan to retire at 70.

Once again, for simplicity's sake, I make the following assumptions:

- Each individual has a spouse.
- Each couple is in the 33.3 percent tax bracket.

- The couples earn between $70,000 and $115,000 a year and have various tax deductions (mortgage interest, charitable contributions, state and local taxes, and exemptions).
- Each couple annually files a joint tax return assuming the 2006 tax brackets.
- Each couple has qualified plans worth varying amounts.

DETERMINE HOW BIG YOUR NEST EGG IS NOW

The first step in retirement planning is to figure out how much money you want to sock away in your nonqualified retirement funds. (I call this the "back door" approach to life insurance, since the "front door" approach begins with your decision on how much money you want or need in actual insurance benefits.) This does not have to be the final number, since there are ways to add assets later on. However, it is useful for you to prepare now with a specific amount in mind. Depending on how much money you want to invest, a computer software program can determine how much life insurance you must obtain in order to comply with federal guidelines so your account remains tax-favored in all phases.

For example, the 50-year-old Centsibles had $125,000 invested originally in a qualified plan. By age 60 it had grown to a value of $245,000 assuming a 7 percent return with no further contributions. They withdrew money gradually over a five-year period starting at age 60 from their qualified plan, paying the taxes along the way rather than postponing the tax bite later on, and earmarked that money for a new, nonqualified plan. Because of mortgage interest offsets, they cut their tax liability on their retirement withdrawals almost in half. They separated equity that was trapped in their house on two occasions. We then created an indexed universal life insurance contract to accommodate both their IRA/401(k) funds and the equity they removed from their house within the boundaries set by various tax laws.

Imagine their nonqualified retirement plan with two large buckets that will be filled from deposits from two different faucets: One faucet is the cash contributions totaling $354,522 for their first bucket they started at age 50 and $327,869 for their second bucket they started at age 60. The other faucet is the component that provides *lift* for the Centsibles' future—compound interest. The concept is illustrated in figure 12.1.

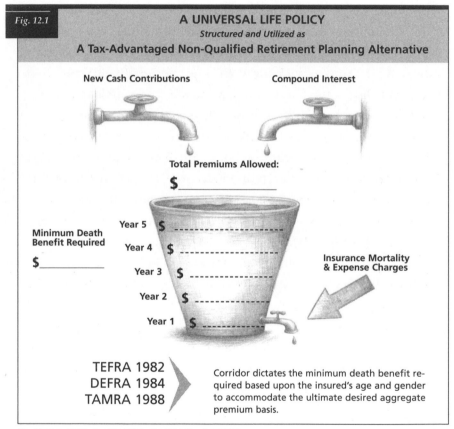

Fig. 12.1

A UNIVERSAL LIFE POLICY
Structured and Utilized as
A Tax-Advantaged Non-Qualified Retirement Planning Alternative

New Cash Contributions   Compound Interest

Total Premiums Allowed:

$_____

Minimum Death Benefit Required

$_____

Year 5 $ ----------------------------
Year 4 $ ----------------------
Year 3 $ ----------------
Year 2 $ -------------
Year 1 $ ----------

Insurance Mortality & Expense Charges

TEFRA 1982
DEFRA 1984
TAMRA 1988

Corridor dictates the minimum death benefit required based upon the insured's age and gender to accommodate the ultimate desired aggregate premium basis.

Tax Citations: IRC Section 101, IRC Section 72(e), Rev. Rul 66-322, 1966-2 CB 123, TEFRA Section 266, DEFRA Section 221

Thus the Centsibles' buckets have the potential to accommodate a combined total of $682,391 of deposits if filled to the brim with both sources of funds they will reposition. However, the compound interest can accrue far beyond that amount. The total of the allowable deposits is called the *maximum basis*. In the case of the Centsibles, who have fifteen years before they plan to retire, it can be filled during the first eleven to twelve years of each policy.

If they wanted to, the Centsibles could choose to fill their buckets all at once, as a lump sum. They would still benefit from tax-free accumulation and tax-free death benefits after they made that contribution. However, their access to the cash, including the interest earned, might be subject to tax unless certain other guidelines are met. That's why we recommend that they stretch their premium contributions over a longer period of time.

Like most of our clients, the Centsibles are interested in death benefits, but only as a secondary objective. They understand that these death benefits are simply coming along for the ride, while the main goals here are to grow their cash with the highest net rate of return on premiums paid, and to harvest the money tax-free after they retire. In such cases, the life insurance bucket should be just big enough under the federal rules to handle the maximum allowable amount of total contributions they likely will make within the given time frame.

When the premiums paid into this policy reach its limit before the end of the eleventh year, the Centsibles are required under the federal definition of life insurance to stop contributing. If they still have more money to reposition at that time, they simply take another bucket and start to fill it—that is, they take out a new, additional policy, providing they pass the physical exam required for life insurance and are approved by the insurance company. The second bucket has the same advantages as the first, as long as the tax laws are the same.

Is there a cost for doing this? Naturally, there is. The small spigot attached to the bottom of the bucket represents the mortality and expense charges associated with a universal life policy. Over a period of time the spigot potentially may consume from 0.5 percent to 3.0 percent credited during the life of the policy. These costs closely resemble those for term insurance. But there's a big and welcome difference: If the bucket fills up with premiums far greater than the actual pure term insurance premiums, the bucket (the policy) accumulates excess cash value. Over time, the compound interest that piles up and thus adds to this cash can more than compensate for the continuing costs of owning the policy. Meanwhile the costs allow the investment to be regarded under federal guidelines as life insurance and therefore remain tax-free, giving the policy a much greater effective rate of return.

I think an indexed universal life insurance contract is the best choice for people like the Centsibles. The result is that over a twenty- or thirty-year period, when the Centsibles need to access their money for retirement living, they could very well achieve a net, internal rate of return, cash on cash, of 6.5 to 8.5 percent on their buckets, which means a policy that credits an average of 7.5 up to 10.5 percent interest. They also get survivor benefits, which come along for the ride. In my mind, the small amount of cash that pays for the life insurance is "free," because it is paid for with money that otherwise would have gone to Uncle Sam in taxes, if the original funds had been placed in a taxable investment. Any investment has costs attached to it. Isn't it great to find one where, in effect, Uncle Sam is paying those costs?

You may be asking yourself, "Isn't it awfully late in the game for me to start a program like this?" The answer is: absolutely not. The federal guidelines say that no matter how old you are, the spigot on the bucket can be designed to drain out about the same percentage of your interest. Thus a Boomer, or even someone older than a Boomer who qualifies for an insurance policy, can structure it to achieve close to the same net rate of return on premium dollars placed in the bucket as a 20-year-old. The 20-year-old simply receives more of a death benefit in his policy for the same size bucket than the 50-year-old. However, people like the 50-year-old Centsibles usually have more money to invest, so the insurance is usually commensurate.

Because this strategy aims to help you reach your goal of the greatest amount of capital at the highest net rate of return possible, *you should take only the minimum death benefit required to fund it.* Then you should fill the bucket to the maximum level as soon as you can.

If, during the funding phase, your situation changes and you see that you may never be able to fill the bucket to the brim, you can still maximize the return and minimize the cost. You do this by reducing the size of the survivor benefit. That can be done simply and quickly. If you cut the insurance in half, the effect is to cut your bucket in half. You should use a trained professional to do this, rather than risk going beyond IRS guidelines. There also may be some surrender charges that will be deducted from your policy.

WHAT'S THE GUIDELINE SINGLE PREMIUM?

There are two phrases you will hear when dealing with maximum-funded life insurance. One is *guideline single premium*. This is the total amount of money that you can put into one policy during its first eleven years or so, according to current tax laws. You do not have to take that many years to fill your bucket; you can put the maximum in as one big lump sum. However, when you do this, your withdrawals will be taxable.

The second phrase is *guideline level premium*, which is the guideline single premium divided by eleven. This is the approximate amount you can put in each year if you were wanting to fill your bucket in eleven equal installments, even though you aren't forced to take eleven years to do this.

If you really want your policy to zing, you should fill your bucket in four or five years. But once you do, you must stop, because you've reached the limit of your guideline single premium. Meanwhile, your money earns interest over the next several years. What happens if you decide you want to add to your nest egg? You can start a new bucket (fund a new life insurance policy).

Let's use Ed and Elizabeth Eager, both 55 years old, as an example. Their deposits to their nest egg total $640,218; that's their guideline single premium. They can put $60,750—their guideline level premium—into their bucket every year for the next eleven years to fill it up to its maximum level. In fact, they are permitted to continue putting in $60,750 a year for the rest of their lives and still comply with the tax laws (even though they are not required to).

The Eagers want to fill their bucket as fast as they can over the course of ten years—filling up their buckets 75 percent full ($478,000) during the initial five years. The law permits that. If they wanted, they could deposit as much as $129,000 per year. However, they would totally fund their bucket in the first five years, so they would have to stop contributing thereafter. In this case, they have complied with the guidelines and they will be able to start withdrawing money for retirement income, tax-free, when they reach their planned retirement age of 65. They can decide to start taking income sooner or later than that, if they choose.

Does this sound tricky? It can be a bit complicated, which is why I urge you to use a qualified life insurance specialist who is versed in my strategy. Such a person can structure a policy to perform correctly as a maximum tax-advantaged insurance contract in full compliance with Internal Revenue Code guidelines.

BE PATIENT FILLING YOUR BUCKET

It's important to understand that if you use a life insurance contract for investment for retirement purposes, you must meet certain requirements. You must have a commensurate amount of life insurance coming along for the ride, and you have to fill your bucket over a certain period of time in order to then withdraw money from it without being taxed. As I said in the last chapter, you still can squeeze the survivor benefits way down, load the contract with cash, and then access it tax-free as long as your contract is in compliance with the various laws.

For *universal* life, the kind I usually recommend, you can meet the federal guidelines by funding your contract to the max over a period of just a few years. If you are under the approximate age of 50,[*] you can deposit the maximum in your policy in the course of as few as three years and one day (a total of four installments). If you are over the approximate age of 50, you can fund your policy to the maximum level in four years and one day, or a total of five installments.

You should realize that when just 5, 10, or 20 percent of your total bucket is filled after one year, the spigot costs will drain out a much higher percent of the cash value in the bucket than when the contract is fully funded. During the first few years, the net rate of return will usually not be within 1 percent of the gross rate of return. For example, by the fifth year your gross rate of return might have averaged 8 percent, while your net average rate of return might be only 5 percent. That's okay. You should choose investments based on which ones generate the most at the time you will likely need the money most. Down the road, retroactive back to the first year of the policy, if you averaged a gross crediting rate of 9 percent, you might average a net rate of return within about 1 percent—which would be about 8 percent—meaning the insurance was paid for by that difference, which qualified your account to be tax-free. You need to let your bucket feel the *lift* of compound interest, and the *thrust* of tax-free accumulation, and that takes time.

My two sons, Emron and Aaron, are professional planners in our firm. They explain the concept as follows: If you built a five-story office or apartment building, you are going to incur certain costs (mortgage payments, utilities, taxes, insurance) whether you

---

[*]Some insurance company actuaries design certain life insurance products one way and other products another way under different parameters and interpretations of the TEFRA, DEFRA, and TAMRA tax citations. They also differ a little from one insurance company to the next. So the breakpoint at which a policy needs to comply with TAMRA using four years of premium installments versus five years of premium installments can be around ages 47, 48, 49, 50, 51, 52, or 53 depending on the insurance product and company.

get tenants (renters) or not. If you rent out the first floor or just part of a floor, it will likely not cover those costs. When you fill two floors with renters, you may cover most or all of your costs. When you fill three floors, you will likely cover your costs and may have positive cash flow and a profit. When you fill up the fourth and fifth floors of your building, the profits really begin to add up, and if left to accumulate (especially tax-free) it's only a matter of time when the costs associated with the building are very small in comparison to the profits that you have accumulated. Similarly, an insurance contract, as it is maximum funded over the first five years and it grows thereafter, can become an incredible capital accumulation vehicle that can generate a handsome tax-free income stream.

Therefore, it is important to be patient as your bucket fills up. Keep in mind that this is a long-term investment, and you need not worry about the net rate of return achieved in the early years of a contract. The Centsibles realize this. Since they begin when they are only 50 years old, and they don't plan to retire until they are 65, they know they will eventually enjoy great benefits that will generate a hefty rate of return retroactively to the first day of the contract. They understand that their investment can far outperform other investments. They have the discipline to expect a long-term investment like this to reap a long-term, tax-free reward.

WHAT IF YOU OVER-FUND YOUR CONTRACT?

There is a way out for those who put too much money too soon into an insurance contract. The law allows you to "perfect" the contract within sixty days of the end of the policy anniversary. Thus, even if you happened to violate the federal premium limit, you could request a refund of the overage that was paid into the contract, and then redeposit the money during the first sixty days of the next year. Otherwise, you wind up with what is called a Modified Endowment Contract (MEC). When you create a MEC, your

money can accumulate tax-deferred, but it is taxable when you start to withdraw it.

When you "perfect" a contract you can avoid a MEC. However, when a refund is made during the sixty-day window after the policy anniversary, the excess interest earned that is refunded over and above the premium will be taxable.

HOW FLEXIBLE IS UNIVERSAL LIFE INSURANCE?

One reason a properly structured universal life insurance contract can be so attractive as an investment is that its premiums as well as its death benefits are extremely flexible. You can choose to have either a *level death benefit* or an *increasing death benefit*.

For those who want to maximize their internal rate of return as soon as possible and who regard the death benefit as coming along for the ride, it makes sense to choose a *level death benefit*. The options get somewhat complex here.

In such a case the death benefit remains the same as the size of the bucket grows. The bucket gets filled up as you pay new premium dollars into it, and as the money there is credited interest. The total amount is the cash value of the policy.

As your bucket grows with cash value, the cash value can actually qualify as part of the original death benefit required under federal guidelines. The amount of insurance that the company is at risk to pay is the difference between your cash value and the original required death benefit. Ultimately, the differential can become so nominal that the net rate of return is within 1 percent of the gross rate of return, retroactive to the first day of the policy.

Here's an example, using George and Gail Gainsworthy. You'll recall that they had quite a bit of money trapped in IRAs and 401(k)s as well as equity from the sale of their house. They were able to strategically roll out money from both these sources and reposition that money in an indexed universal life insurance contract. In five years, George reaches age 65. Imagine that the life insurance contract for

him is designed to accommodate a total of $681,500 of premiums (a maximum of $130,000 a year for the first five years to comply with federal law and still be accessible tax-free). It thus carries with it a minimum death benefit (required by law) of $1,510,000 and in its tenth year has $1,004,191 in cash value. In this case, the true insurance risk paid by the company is the difference between $1,510,000 and the $1,004,191 cash value, or $505,809.

Although the cost of the life insurance portion itself—the cost per $1,000 of death benefits—goes up each month as a person gets older, the amount of actual insurance you are paying for goes down. The result is an enhanced rate of return. Your money grows more effectively as the insurance cost gets smaller. In the fifteenth year, the cash value might be $1,461,775, which, if subtracted from the original death benefit of $1,510,000, leaves just $48,225 of insurance for which you are paying at that age.

However, IRS guidelines require that the death benefit stay ahead of the cash values by a certain percentage. So in actuality the life insurance death benefit in the fifteenth year has increased to $1,534,864. In the twentieth year, the cash value might grow to $2,157,971, at which point the death benefit will have increased to $2,265,870 to stay in compliance. This continues until George is age 100, when the cash value might be $10,332,231, at which point the death benefit would be $10,538,876. Thus when choosing the level death benefit option, that policy may end up actually having a slowly increasing death benefit, just to stay ahead of the cash values that are growing inside the contract. I know this sounds confusing. It behooves you to use an agent who can maneuver through the thicket of regulations and options while keeping your desire for an optimal *investment* in the forefront. You should make it clear to your agent that you are deliberately choosing a minimum death benefit to allow for maximum funding of the contract to enhance its rate of return within federal tax law guidelines.

Let's look very briefly at the *increasing death benefit* option. This is a wise choice for those whose first goal is to maximize the money

paid to survivors—that is, the amount that you leave behind to your heirs. Without going into all the details, the point here is that the tax-free retirement income—the *living* benefits—will generally not provide as much money when you opt for an increasing death benefit unless it is structured properly. For a more detailed explanation of these options, please refer to my previous books, *Missed Fortune* and *Missed Fortune 101*.

People switch their policies from a level death benefit to an increasing death benefit when circumstances change. One example is in the event the insured develops an illness that will likely shorten his life. For now, let's concentrate on properly structured contracts with a *level* death benefit. It is simply helpful to keep in mind that these contracts are flexible. Your agent should be able to explain how to adjust a death benefit if you need to make a change.

HOW THE GAINSWORTHYS OPTIMIZE THEIR RETIREMENT MONEY

Let's look at the Gainsworthys as an example of how older Boomers net a greater gain through the use of insurance contracts as their nonqualified retirement alternative. They are each 60 years old and expect to completely retire at age 70.

As you'll recall, the Gainsworthys began receiving income from their defined-benefit pensions in addition to Social Security benefits when they qualified. They had $350,000 in IRAs and a 401(k). They also had $230,000 in funds remaining from the sale of their house and subsequent purchase of their condo. They were able to reposition that money into a nonqualified retirement plan using an indexed universal life insurance contract. Thus the size of their bucket (the guideline single premium) is $681,500 and the minimum death benefit for George would be $1,510,000. He and Gail did a strategic transfer of $130,000 into the life insurance contract each year for the first three years, and lesser amounts in subsequent years in compliance with federal guidelines.

At the end of the fifth year, George and Gail are 65 years old and still going strong. So the Gainsworthys decide to allow their money to grow for five more years and continue to complete a strategic rollout from their qualified plans. If the cash value of their life insurance contract earned an average gross rate of 8 percent interest, at age 70 they would have a cash-value balance of $1,004,191 once the mortality and expense charges (the spigot on the bucket) are deducted.

Since they have arrived at their target retirement age of 70, they start to withdraw a reasonable amount of money to pay for traveling and golf. (They consider this and their Social Security income a bonus on top of their defined-benefit pensions.) If their net rate of return after the spigot drains its allowance is anticipated to be within 1 percent of the gross rate, they can withdraw about $70,000 a year without depleting the principal. For approximately the first ten years in this case, they can access this amount tax-free because it is deemed a return of their basis up to the amount they paid into the contract (see Figure 12.2).

Let's listen in as George and Gail question their insurance professional, who has been specially trained in how to structure a maximum-funded insurance contract about their strategy:

George: This is great! From the age of 70 until the age of 80, Gail and I will gallivant around the globe, take our grandkids to Disney World and other fun places, and have a wonderful time.

Gail: But what happens once we reach the age of 80, which we have every intention of doing?

Expert: Under current assumptions, you could still have $1 million of cash value in your insurance contract. I assume you want further withdrawals to be tax-free, just as they were the first ten years until you've withdrawn your basis. You can likely continue to take out $70,000 a year, but instead of labeling it "withdrawal," you label that annual income as a "loan."

Fig. 12.2			TAX-FREE ACCESS VIA WITHDRAWALS AND LOANS								

Yr	Age	Annual Premium Outlay	Annual With-drawal	Annual Loan Amount (a)	Annual Loan Repayment (b)	Interest Charged To Loan (c)	Total Loan Balance	Interest Earned on Loaned CV (d)	Net Loan Cost (c)-(d)	Accumulation Value	Surrender Value	Net Death Benefit
1	61	130,000	0	0	0	0	0	0	0	126,353	68,445	1,510,000
2	62	130,000	0	0	0	0	0	0	0	262,214	204,306	1,510,000
3	63	130,000	0	0	0	0	0	0	0	408,255	350,347	1,510,000
4	64	47,802	0	0	0	0	0	0	0	481,189	423,281	1,510,000
5	65	39,967	0	0	0	0	0	0	0	551,377	493,469	1,510,000
6	66	40,202	0	0	0	0	0	0	0	627,443	574,747	1,510,000
7	67	40,453	0	0	0	0	0	0	0	709,657	662,172	1,510,000
8	68	40,720	0	0	0	0	0	0	0	798,576	756,303	1,510,000
9	69	41,005	0	0	0	0	0	0	0	894,900	857,839	1,510,000
10	70	41,310	0	0	0	0	0	0	0	1,004,191	972,341	1,510,000
11	71	0	70,000	0	0	0	0	0	0	1,002,493	978,299	1,438,110
12	72	0	70,000	0	0	0	0	0	0	1,001,292	983,661	1,366,734
13	73	0	70,000	0	0	0	0	0	0	1,000,736	989,196	1,295,830
14	74	0	70,000	0	0	0	0	0	0	1,001,076	995,193	1,225,359
15	75	0	70,000	0	0	0	0	0	0	1,002,380	1,001,756	1,155,288
16	76	0	70,000	0	0	0	0	0	0	1,004,284	1,004,284	1,085,263
17	77	0	70,000	0	0	0	0	0	0	1,007,621	1,007,621	1,058,002
18	78	0	70,000	0	0	0	0	0	0	1,011,369	1,011,369	1,061,937
19	79	0	70,000	0	0	0	0	0	0	1,015,313	1,015,313	1,066,078
20	80	0	51,459	18,541	0	371	18,912	371	0	1,038,300	1,019,388	1,071,303
21	81	0	0	70,000	0	1,778	90,690	1,778	0	1,114,253	1,023,563	1,079,275
22	82	0	0	70,000	0	3,214	163,904	3,214	0	1,191,605	1,027,702	1,087,282
23	83	0	0	70,000	0	4,678	238,582	4,678	0	1,270,345	1,031,764	1,095,281
24	84	0	0	70,000	0	6,172	314,754	6,172	0	1,350,407	1,035,654	1,103,174
25	85	0	0	70,000	0	7,695	392,449	7,695	0	1,431,902	1,039,454	1,111,049
26	86	0	0	70,000	0	9,249	471,698	9,249	0	1,514,600	1,042,902	1,118,632
27	87	0	0	70,000	0	10,834	552,532	10,834	0	1,598,567	1,046,036	1,125,964
28	88	0	0	70,000	0	12,451	634,982	12,451	0	1,683,778	1,048,796	1,132,985
29	89	0	0	70,000	0	14,100	719,082	14,100	0	1,770,074	1,050,993	1,139,496
30	90	0	0	70,000	0	15,782	804,863	15,782	0	1,857,309	1,052,446	1,145,311
31	91	0	0	70,000	0	17,497	892,361	17,497	0	1,945,538	1,053,178	1,130,999
32	92	0	0	70,000	0	19,247	981,608	19,247	0	2,036,124	1,054,516	1,115,600
33	93	0	0	70,000	0	21,032	1,072,640	21,032	0	2,129,648	1,057,008	1,099,601
34	94	0	0	70,000	0	22,853	1,165,493	22,853	0	2,226,601	1,061,108	1,105,640
35	95	0	0	70,000	0	24,710	1,260,203	24,710	0	2,325,040	1,064,837	1,111,338
36	96	0	0	70,000	0	26,604	1,356,807	26,604	0	2,425,229	1,068,422	1,116,927
37	97	0	0	70,000	0	28,536	1,455,343	28,536	0	2,527,012	1,071,669	1,122,209
38	98	0	0	70,000	0	30,507	1,555,850	30,507	0	2,630,470	1,074,620	1,127,230
39	99	0	0	70,000	0	32,517	1,658,367	32,517	0	2,735,452	1,077,085	1,131,794
40	100	0	0	70,000	0	34,567	1,762,934	34,567	0	2,841,791	1,078,857	1,135,693

Assuming an 8 percent gross return

George: Why?

Expert: Because under IRS provisions, loan proceeds are not considered as earned, passive, or portfolio income, so this money is still tax-free. We have simply changed the nomenclature.

Gail: Will the insurance company let us do that?

Expert: The company is willing to lend you the equivalent of the interest your contract is earning. It works the same way it would with a CD at a bank. If you had that much cash residing in a CD, I know the bank would be willing to make you such a loan, because the bank is holding that big CD as collateral. The insurance company treats your money in the same fashion.

George: But aren't we incurring a debt that we will be charged interest on?

Expert: Please look again at this table [Figure 12.2, on previous page], which I have printed for you. Notice that you start to have a loan balance at the age of 80. However, you don't have to pay it back during your lifetime. Your loan balance grows each year that you take your money as a "loan," but it remains open until death.

Gail: Then what happens?

Expert: The insurance company deducts the loan balance from the death benefit. But as you can see, the interest you have been accumulating on the cash value can replenish some or all of the reduced death benefit. If you look at the numbers, by the time you are each 90, your insurance ledger shows you having plenty of money to cover your loan, even though you have continued to "borrow" money to prolong your comfort. Yet all the money that maintains your enjoyable retirement is still tax-free. It stays that way as long as the policy has enough cash value remaining in it at death to cover the mortality costs.

George: Really? What's the catch here? Are we doing something illegal?

Expert: Absolutely not. You are simply taking advantage of the various federal guidelines that govern life insurance. We must adhere to these guidelines even as we create a contract that performs as a superior retirement vehicle. Among my responsibilities is to make sure the contract stays within the guidelines so it does not trigger unnecessary tax. Part of your responsibility is to read and understand the disclosures on the NAIC [National Association of Insurance Commissioners] illustrations that you are required to review and sign, so you know what to expect.[*] You should also be accountable and responsible to follow through with your intended premium payments into the plan or ask to have adjustments made to the policy to best meet the goals and objectives that you outlined at the inception of your plan. We build tremendous flexibility into each plan, but it will perform only as intended if the funding of the plan and interest crediting rate are in harmony with the assumptions. It can perform better or worse than illustrated depending on these variables.

Gail: We certainly will make sure everything is clear to us and that we follow through with our intended premium payments or make any necessary adjustments.

George: This sounds like a retirement alternative that would work wonderfully for us!

---

[*]Under National Association of Insurance Commissioners rules, you are asked to sign an illustration showing the projection of the policy benefits based on the premium payments that you will likely make. The illustration may be based upon the interest rate credited by the company at the time you take out the policy. But the illustration must also show the worst-case scenario using the minimum guaranteed interest rate on the cash values from the start of the policy. This illustration also assumes that the maximum mortality charges allowed are assessed throughout the life of the policy. That low a return is unlikely, but the idea is to show you what *could* happen. Actual mortality charges are usually less than the maximum, and policies usually far outperform the minimum interest guarantee.

HOW BENEFITS BLOSSOM FOR YOUR HEIRS

What happens if you set up a nonqualified retirement plan using maximum tax-advantaged insurance contracts and the insured person dies? That retirement plan blossoms. The minimum death benefit required under Internal Revenue Code guidelines is dictated by the guideline single premium (the total of premiums anticipated to be paid into the policy) and the age and gender of the insured. For example, for a healthy, preferred-rated male desiring to deposit a total of $100,000 into a maximum-funded life insurance contract, the minimum death benefit may vary depending on the specific contract. However, the minimum death benefit is approximately:

- $330,000 if you are age 50
- $270,000 if you are age 55
- $225,000 if you are age 60
- $180,000 if you are age 65

Remember, you can get a lot more life insurance for $100,000 of premium, but that's not the objective. We are trying to do the opposite—*take the least amount of life insurance and deposit the most premium we can into the policy to optimize the rate of return and tax-favored treatment it receives.* If you wanted to calculate the approximate amount of insurance that would come along for the ride for a $500,000 guideline single premium, simply take five times the amount shown above. A $1 million bucket would provide about ten times the death benefit shown above. If you are a female at the same ages, your rate of return would not necessarily be greater, you would simply receive about 17 to 19 percent more insurance benefit because your mortality is better.

An additional benefit is that the life insurance proceeds are transferred to the beneficiary free of income tax. In other words, you get a great rate of return but at a cost none of us wants to incur anytime soon! It should at least be comforting to know that your

beneficiaries will be taken care of in the event of an untimely death.

What would you do if your employer suddenly said, "I want to offer you some free life insurance benefits. How much would you like?" Most people would answer: "As much as I can get!" My point is that with a nonqualified retirement plan, you get life insurance that comes along for the ride that can end up not costing you anything. You can pay for it out of tax you would otherwise fork over to Uncle Sam.

WHY THE FARALONGS ARE BETTER OFF USING INSURANCE CONTRACTS

Let's see how Frank and Felicia Faralong, who are both 50 years old, will do in terms of retirement savings, using maximum-funded, tax-advantaged life insurance contracts compared to various other investment alternatives.

Imagine that the Faralongs want to compare repositioning the same amount of money into mutual funds, IRA/401(k)s, municipal bond funds, or annuities, all of which are often touted by financial consultants as good places to park retirement funds. The Faralongs, instead, decide to reposition the same amount of money into an indexed universal life insurance contract. What would be the difference in the coming years, as they reach their retirement age? How do they fare in the years after they reach 70 and draw on their retirement savings for living expenses in each of the five alternatives?

As Figure 12.3 shows, some of the investments have very good rates of return, including those that are tax-favored until accessed at the retirement age of 70. But those after-tax returns do not match the after-tax value of the insurance contract. What's more, the Faralongs' insurance contract really sails along nicely when they begin to make withdrawals. The investments in mutual funds, bond funds, annuities, and the like start to head into negative territory compared to the withdrawals or loans that they are able to take tax-free.

Fig. 12.3	INDEXED UNIVERSAL LIFE COMPARED TO VARIOUS ALTERNATIVES
	prepared for Frank and Felicia Faralong

	TAX TYPE	INTEREST RATE	MANAGEMENT FEE	PREMATURE DIST. TAX	SALES CHARGE
Municipal Bond Fund	Exempt	7.00%	1.00%	0.00%	0.00%
Annuity	Deferred	8.00%	0.50%	10.00%	3.00%
Mutual Fund	Taxable	11.00%	1.00%	0.00%	3.00%
IRA/401(k)	Qualified	9.50%	1.00%	10.00%	3.00%
Master Choice	**Tax Favored**	**9.62%**			

		AFTER TAX VALUES				INSURANCE VALUES		
Year (Age)	Net Withdrawals or Payment	Municipal Bond Fund	An Annuity	Mutual Fund	IRAs & 401(k)s	Accumulation Value	Surrender Value	Death Benefit
1 (50)	$62,700	$66,754	$64,019	$64,604	$37,363	$55,103	$44,837	$1,012,753
2 (51)	$62,700	$137,823	$130,588	$133,229	$77,866	$116,542	$94,026	$1,012,753
3 (52)	$43,522	$193,069	$180,303	$186,365	$110,346	$165,579	$129,512	$1,012,753
4 (53)	$11,694	$218,001	$199,655	$210,013	$126,589	$188,912	$148,503	$1,012,753
5 (54)	$12,007	$244,878	$220,315	$235,455	$144,384	$214,907	$174,498	$1,012,753
6 (55)	$12,341	$273,848	$242,385	$262,825	$163,873	$243,823	$203,414	$1,012,753
7 (56)	$12,700	$305,073	$265,980	$292,268	$185,215	$276,016	$235,607	$1,012,753
8 (57)	$13,084	$338,726	$291,218	$323,939	$208,579	$311,714	$271,305	$1,012,753
9 (58)	$15,505	$377,132	$320,283	$360,076	$235,349	$353,316	$313,068	$1,012,753
10 (59)	$15,945	$418,489	$351,343	$398,915	$264,632	$399,741	$360,948	$1,012,753
11 (60)	$14,586	$461,074	$401,375	$438,771	$347,722	$449,706	$412,368	$1,012,753
12 (61)	$0	$490,882	$422,766	$466,079	$376,948	$490,832	$458,505	$1,012,753
13 (62)	$0	$522,618	$445,638	$495,087	$408,630	$536,010	$511,765	$1,012,753
14 (63)	$0	$556,405	$470,092	$525,899	$442,975	$585,574	$569,410	$1,012,753
15 (64)	$0	$592,376	$496,239	$558,630	$480,208	$640,007	$631,925	$1,012,753
16 (65)	$0	$630,674	$524,195	$593,397	$520,569	$699,951	$699,951	$1,012,753
17 (66)	$0	$671,447	$554,085	$630,328	$564,323	$765,947	$765,947	$1,012,753
18 (67)	$0	$714,856	$586,044	$669,558	$611,754	$838,710	$838,710	$1,012,753
19 (68)	$0	$761,071	$620,214	$711,229	$663,172	$918,651	$918,651	$1,074,822
20 (69)	$0	$810,274	$656,749	$755,494	$718,912	$1,006,222	$1,006,222	$1,167,217
21 (70)	$-91,380	$765,371	$598,109	$705,447	$680,276	$1,098,642	$1,001,779	$1,166,576
22 (71)	$-91,380	$717,564	$535,411	$652,284	$638,392	$1,196,292	$996,754	$1,152,272
23 (72)	$-91,380	$666,667	$468,374	$595,813	$592,989	$1,299,574	$991,201	$1,134,155
24 (73)	$-91,380	$612,479	$396,698	$535,828	$543,769	$1,408,874	$985,136	$1,111,935
25 (74)	$-91,380	$554,789	$320,062	$472,109	$490,412	$1,524,633	$978,608	$1,085,333
26 (75)	$-91,380	$493,368	$239,233	$404,424	$432,571	$1,647,361	$971,712	$1,054,080
27 (76)	$-91,380	$427,976	$154,674	$332,527	$369,868	$1,776,910	$963,859	$1,052,705
	$-362,876							

Notes:

a. The values shown above are an after tax reflection based on a tax rate of 33.33%.

b. Prior to age 59 1/2 a premature distribution tax is assessed to applicable accounts.

c. Any tax deferred or qualified accounts do not reflect any possible surrender charges.

d. Values shown are based on non-guaranteed interest rates shown above. Actual results will be different and may be more or less favorable.

e. This illustration must be accompanied by an illustration from Fidelity & Guaranty to confirm its validity.

Fig. 12.3 continued	INDEXED UNIVERSAL LIFE COMPARED TO VARIOUS ALTERNATIVES prepared for Frank and Felicia Faralong

	TAX TYPE	INTEREST RATE	MANAGEMENT FEE	PREMATURE DIST. TAX	SALES CHARGE
Municipal Bond Fund	Exempt	7.00%	1.00%	0.00%	0.00%
Annuity	Deferred	8.00%	0.50%	10.00%	3.00%
Mutual Fund	Taxable	11.00%	1.00%	0.00%	3.00%
IRA/401(k)	Qualified	9.50%	1.00%	10.00%	3.00%
Master Choice	Tax Favored	9.62%			

		AFTER TAX VALUES				INSURANCE VALUES		
Year (Age)	Net Withdrawals or Payment	Municipal Bond Fund	An Annuity	Mutual Fund	IRAs & 401(k)s	Accumulation Value	Surrender Value	Death Benefit
28 (77)	$-91,380	$358,357	$66,214	$256,155	$301,895	$1,913,529	$954,833	$1,050,509
29 (78)	$-91,380	$284,237	$-27,179	$175,031	$228,209	$2,057,623	$944,542	$1,047,423
30 (79)	$-91,380	$205,326	$-128,044	$88,857	$148,329	$2,209,534	$932,805	$1,043,282
31 (80)	$-91,380	$121,312	$-236,978	$-2,708	$61,736	$2,369,737	$919,541	$1,038,028
32 (81)	$-91,380	$31,867	$-354,627	$-100,988	$-48,688	$2,538,626	$904,556	$1,031,487
33 (82)	$-91,380	$-63,679	$-481,687	$-206,476	$-203,397	$2,716,416	$887,440	$1,023,260
34 (83)	$-91,380	$-165,913	$-618,912	$-319,700	$-372,804	$2,903,445	$867,867	$1,013,039
35 (84)	$-91,380	$-275,303	$-767,116	$-441,227	$-558,305	$3,100,054	$845,479	$1,000,481
36 (85)	$-91,380	$-392,351	$-927,176	$-571,667	$-761,428	$3,306,593	$819,880	$985,209
37 (86)	$-91,380	$-517,592	$-1,100,040	$-711,673	$-983,848	$3,523,412	$790,633	$966,804
38 (87)	$-91,380	$-651,600	$-1,286,734	$-861,947	$-1,227,397	$3,750,868	$757,260	$944,803
39 (88)	$-91,380	$-794,989	$-1,488,363	$-1,023,241	$-1,494,084	$3,989,316	$719,229	$918,694
40 (89)	$-91,380	$-948,415	$-1,706,122	$-1,196,364	$-1,786,106	$4,239,089	$675,934	$887,888
41 (90)	$-91,380	$-1,112,580	$-1,941,302	$-1,382,183	$-2,105,871	$4,500,494	$626,687	$851,711
42 (91)	$-91,380	$-1,288,237	$-2,195,297	$-1,581,630	$-2,456,012	$4,777,131	$574,033	$765,118
43 (92)	$-91,380	$-1,476,191	$-2,469,611	$-1,795,703	$-2,839,418	$5,070,415	$518,269	$670,381
44 (93)	$-91,380	$-1,677,301	$-2,765,870	$-2,025,476	$-3,259,247	$5,381,973	$459,835	$567,474
45 (94)	$-91,380	$-1,892,488	$-3,085,830	$-2,272,100	$-3,718,959	$5,713,755	$399,426	$456,563
46 (95)	$-91,380	$-2,122,739	$-3,431,387	$-2,536,811	$-4,222,344	$6,067,875	$337,823	$337,823
47 (96)	$-91,380	$-2,369,107	$-3,804,588	$-2,820,934	$-4,773,551	$6,440,958	$269,634	$269,634
48 (97)	$-91,380	$-2,632,721	$-4,207,646	$-3,125,895	$-5,377,123	$6,833,900	$192,950	$192,950
49 (98)	$-91,380	$-2,914,788	$-4,642,948	$-3,453,220	$-6,038,034	$7,247,576	$106,797	$106,797
50 (99)	$-91,380	$-3,216,600	$-5,113,074	$-3,804,550	$-6,761,731	$7,682,879	$10,094	$10,094
	$-2,464,616							

Notes:

a. The values shown above are an after tax reflection based on a tax rate of 33.33%.

b. Prior to age 59 1/2 a premature distribution tax is assessed to applicable accounts.

c. Any tax deferred or qualified accounts do not reflect any possible surrender charges.

d. Values shown are based on non-guaranteed interest rates shown above. Actual results will be different and may be more or less favorable.

e. This illustration must be accompanied by an illustration from Fidelity & Guaranty to confirm its validity.

By the time they reach an age that we now consider elderly (age 85), the Faralongs have had fifteen years of tax-free harvest amounting to over $90,000 a year and don't have to worry about their money running out before they do. Even if Frank Faralong

does pass away at age 85, his insurance contract blossoms into a tax-free transfer to Felicia of just under $1 million, while all of the other investment alternatives were totally depleted to nothing at three to seven years earlier.

According to my calculations, the mutual funds, bond funds, or annuities would be as much as $3 million to $5 million in the hole if Frank Faralong lived to the ripe age of 99, which is how long the insurance contract could have generated a $90,000 tax-free income before becoming depleted. Otherwise, a slightly reduced income of $80,000 per year (starting at age 70) would continue a total of seventy years—if Frank lived to age 140 or longer (remember, that is the approximate life expectancy for a newborn girl if you are thinking about the impact of this strategy for your granddaughter)—never depleting the $1 million principal—based on the same assumptions. Also, the insurance contract is the only alternative that will blossom into an income-tax-free transfer to heirs when the policyholder dies. The other investments may be subject to both income tax and estate tax when they transfer at death, leaving the heirs of the Faralongs with a lot less money.

This, then, is the ultimate and unique value of the sprint into retirement. While other investments may get the *lift* of compound interest and the *thrust* of tax-free accumulation, they don't provide a tax-free harvest the way maximum tax-advantaged life insurance does. Other investments would be hard-pressed to last as long as you do if they had to generate the same stream of net spendable income. Add to these advantages the *drag* of leverage in the form of tax-deductible mortgage interest by repositioning the lazy, idle dollars trapped in your house earning zero return, and you have a strategy to accumulate tax-favored money on the front end and to enjoy tax-free income on the back end, during retirement.

(To view, study, or download the complete asset optimization plans—approximately sixty detailed pages for each of the four cases—prepared for the Centsibles, Faralongs, Eagers, and Gainsworthys, you can go to: www.MissedFortune.com/LCMCaseStudies. Each plan contains a com-

prehensive series of reports, charts, and colored graphs to illustrate the concept in a simple but detailed manner. Readers of *The Last Chance Millionaire* are also entitled to listen to a voice-stream explanation or view a video explanation of each of the four case studies introduced in Chapter 9 and revisited here in Chapter 12, through our Web site.)

FREQUENTLY ASKED QUESTIONS ABOUT MAXIMUM TAX-ADVANTAGED LIFE INSURANCE

What happens if Congress passes new laws about insurance?

People often ask me at public seminars if my strategy exploits loopholes in current tax law. The answer is that these are not considered loopholes. But some are concerned about the possibility that on top of the changes made to the tax code and to the definition of insurance in the 1980s, Congress or the IRS will at some point in the future enact new laws that make the strategy more difficult or less attractive.

I can't predict what any agency or Congress will do. However, in the past when changes were made, anyone who already had funds put away on the basis of old laws were protected by grandfather clauses. That's a good argument for establishing your bucket as soon as possible. The same goes for the tax-deductibility of mortgage interest. Even if the gain in an insurance contract became taxable, such as with a MEC, it usually is still better than an annuity or IRA/401(k) tax-deferred investment, because they don't blossom in value when a death occurs unless life insurance was intentionally attached.

I know that Congress and the IRS are aware of the strategies for tax-free accumulation of cash values as well as tax-free access. As a matter of fact, some members of Congress avail themselves of such contracts. I doubt either Congress or the IRS will do anything to hurt the finances of soon-to-be retirees, especially because so many studies in recent years indicate that Boomers especially need all the

retirement help they can get. Also, both the insurance industry and AARP are lobbies with a great deal of clout.

How can I be sure a mortgage or an insurance contract is in compliance with current IRS rules?

Naturally, it is crucial that when you take out a mortgage or contribute to an investment instrument, you comply with the Internal Revenue Code. My reading of the code and my thirty-plus years of dealing with such issues with other tax experts indicate that the strategies I've set forth here are compliant. I have an entire division of my firm that deals with nothing but proper compliance with insurance contracts. Any instrument that deals with your serious cash should be undertaken with a reputable agent, broker, or sales professional who understands and can show you the applicable part of federal and state laws. In Appendix A, I have included a review of TEFRA, DEFRA, and TAMRA so you can get some understanding of the most recent federal changes. However, you should always seek advice from a competent tax advisor who understands—or can find out—the parameters and guidelines for tax-deductible mortgage interest through various options of either refinancing a home or when purchasing a new one. The same holds true when using various insurance products to comply with IRS guidelines—consult an expert.

What about health issues that might prevent me from qualifying with an insurance company?

A top-drawer insurance professional usually has direct or indirect relationships with enough companies and access to various kinds of policies to most likely find a policy under which you can be insured even if you have had serious illnesses in the past, such as cancer or a heart attack, or have current health issues such as obesity, diabetes, smoking, or a family history of certain diseases. My firm deals primarily with thirty-six life insurance companies and we have several dozen more at our disposal. We have successfully written policies for people over the age of 75 with a variety of past

and present risk factors. One 79-year-old male client was recently approved for a life insurance contract, but with a rating that was three times higher for the insurance component than a normal 79-year-old due to recent health history that included a prostate cancer episode that was cleared up with surgery, three blocked heart arteries that were opened up with angioplasties, and adult-onset diabetes that was being controlled with diet and exercise. The TEFRA and DEFRA insurance guidelines allowed us to reduce the amount of insurance required when structuring the policy to perform as an investment, thus enabling him to realize the same internal rate of return that a healthy 30-year-old male would get.

In the event that you are deemed uninsurable because of poor health, you can still get a life insurance policy to use as a nonqualified retirement plan by using your spouse, one of your children, or another family member as the "insured." That is the insurance industry's term for the individual covered by the insurance. A critical requirement when applying for life insurance is that there must be an insurable interest between the person insured and the beneficiary named in the application—meaning the beneficiary would suffer an economic loss if the insured died due to the relationship between the two. Meanwhile, you can remain the "owner." The owner is the person who has the power to make changes in the contract, the person who owns all the cash value and interest, the person who assumes all tax liabilities, and the person who can take advantage of the tax benefits.

What should I know about surrender charges?
Annuities and life insurance can be subject to *surrender charges.* When you cancel a policy, the insured and the owner "surrender" it to the company and relinquish all benefits. In the early years of a contract, you are usually charged a fee that is a percentage of the cash value. If you withdraw some of your cash value, you make a *partial surrender.* Surrender charge formulas are stated in the contract. When you withdraw some, rather than all, the cash value, you give up a portion of the cash value and the death benefit could

be adjusted. A partial surrender permanently reduces the size of the insurance contract.

When I refinance my house and when I roll out my IRA or 401(k) into a nonqualified retirement plan, how can I be certain that I get both the best mortgage and the best insurance contract structured to optimize my wealth? I have outlined a general strategy here, but each person's circumstances are different, and different families have varying timetables for their retirement. You should always seek trusted and competent legal and accounting help when you embark on such a plan. If you were traveling by automobile from San Francisco to New York City, it would behoove you to take advantage of road maps and road signs. If you are going to reposition serious cash, you want to make sure that the financial services provider you are working with is knowledgeable in how to structure your plan properly to meet your objectives.

Again, if this book was given or recommended to you by a financial professional, you may choose to seek his or her services, as well as advice from your personal tax advisor. If you are not acquainted with a professional trained in the strategies contained in this book, don't despair. There is a network of professional financial planners and mortgage planners who understand how to design plans that help people responsibly achieve their goals. For help in locating a properly trained TEAM (The Equity Alliance Matrix) member, please visit www.MissedFortune.com/TEAMprofessionals. (If you choose to work with a financial planner or mortgage planner that is not a TEAM member, it would probably benefit you to insist that they at least read *The Last Chance Millionaire* and *Missed Fortune 101* before attempting to create an asset optimization plan for you.)

WHAT IS A SIDE FUND?

Side funds are temporary parking places for the short term (two to four years). They can include single premium immediate annuities, advance premium deposit funds, money market funds, CDs, Ginnie

Mae funds, or short-term trust deed notes secured by real estate. (A trust deed note is the promissory note that a mortgage company has you sign when lending you mortgage money. The note is secured by the deed on your house. It protects the lender with a lien against the property.) A side fund can be inside an insurance policy or outside it. When complying with the TAMRA regulation (as explained in Appendix A) to avoid a Modified Endowment Contract (in order to preserve tax-free access to funds), it may be necessary to use a temporary side fund outside of an insurance policy while filling up the bucket (insurance policy) to the maximum guideline single premium limit.

WHY MAXIMUM TAX-ADVANTAGED INSURANCE IS THE BEST INVESTMENT FOR RETIREMENT

The revolutionary strategy I promised in Chapter 1 to lay out for you is tax-advantaged at every stage in building your retirement plan, from the contribution phase through accumulation and distribution. By rolling out your IRAs and 401(k)s and by developing an equity management plan that delivers more serious cash for you to sock away, you can launch a plan with maximum-funded life insurance contracts at its heart—contracts designed to be sufficiently liquid and safe, and to pump out a rate of return that takes flight and stays aloft into perpetuity.

Isn't this a superior alternative to IRAs and 401(k)s? Imagine the peace of mind that comes from knowing that if you live until age 100, your wealth won't decline, but can soar beyond the $1 million mark in available resources. Imagine living your golden years on a spendable income of $50,000, $80,000, or $120,000 and more a year. Imagine the satisfaction of knowing that your heirs or your favorite charity could be endowed with $1 million or more income-tax-free! Your last chance turns out to be your best chance of becoming a millionaire.

REMEMBER THIS:

- Certain universal life insurance contracts can be used to optimize retirement savings and also offer death benefits that can be paid for indirectly with otherwise payable income tax.
- Structure insurance contracts as optimal retirement vehicles by over-funding the policy and squeezing down the death benefit within the limits dictated by federal guidelines.
- Be patient while accumulating cash in life insurance contracts to maximize living benefits and minimize costs.
- Choose to take the internal rate of return distributions on maximum tax-advantaged life insurance in adherence with federal guidelines, and the money can last into perpetuity.
- To avoid unnecessary income tax on retirement income and maintain flexibility, access your money using *loans* rather than withdrawals at the optimal time.
- Connect the dots: Combine the *drag* of leverage by separating money trapped in your house and reposition it in properly structured maximum tax-advantaged life insurance that gets the *lift* of compound interest and the *thrust* of tax-free accumulation to reach financial independence.

Make "At-Retirement Planning" Different from "For-Retirement Planning"

How to Approach Retirement with 50 Percent More in Savings and Create an Income Stream That Will Last as Long as You Do

IMAGINE FOR A MOMENT that you are watching a movie about your life. The opening scenes depict your childhood, adolescence, and young adulthood. You watch your college graduation, your wedding, and the births of your children flicker by. You see your career highlights and the big moments in the adult life of your children—*their* weddings and the births of your grandkids. You brace yourself for the vignettes about your retirement.

What follows? A sunset as you and your spouse prepare to stretch out in a deck chair to observe it? Stop there! Hit the "reset" button. Wouldn't you rather envision a glorious sun*rise*?

The so-called golden years don't have to be the end of something. Instead they can be the *beginning* of a bright future, filled with adventure. Just because other Boomers have bought into the timid version of life after retirement, it doesn't mean *you* need to

see things that way. Let me touch on just a few issues that often come up in my discussions with clients as their expected retirement date approaches.

USE *LIFT, THRUST,* AND *DRAG* TO MAKE YOUR MONEY SKYROCKET

When financial planners sit down with their clients, they often repeat the same advice: "You don't need the money yet. Continue to postpone tax. Keep shoveling your money into IRAs and 401(k)s."

Are you tired yet of the conventional advice? With a wake-up call, let's review the alternative strategies we've discussed so far:

- Back in Chapters 4 and 5, I showed why it is never a good time to postpone tax. You'll have to pay some taxes eventually, and if you assume taxes will go up—and most people do—it is smarter to pay them as you go.
- In Chapters 6 and 7, I challenged the conventional wisdom that suggests Boomers should celebrate the day they can burn their mortgage.
- My strategy for equity management, as outlined in Chapter 8, is *don't* start that fire. Use the *lift* of compound interest and the necessary *drag* of leverage to maximize what is probably the greatest asset you have acquired during your lifetime.
- Fill up that pitcher I talked about in Chapter 7. Separate those lazy, idle dollars locked inside your house, earning nothing. Take out the biggest mortgage you've ever had (or use a HELOC) to offset taxes with preferred, tax-deductible mortgage interest. Chapter 8 is a guide to choosing a mortgage that can make your wealth soar.

- The next step is to discover the *thrust* of tax-free accumulation. Shift your retirement assets into a nonqualified plan.

- First, plan to do a *strategic rollout* of your IRAs and 401(k)s, as outlined in Chapter 9.

- You can also use OPM to acquire the vacation home you always wanted, as shown in Chapter 10.

- My strategy for designing your personal nonqualified retirement plan employs maximum tax-advantaged life insurance contracts (the key to tax-free retirement distributions), as I discussed in Chapter 11.

- I recommend that you find an insurance expert who can help you choose the best life insurance companies and contracts. Have that person properly structure maximum-funded life insurance with the goal of liquidity, safety, and a predictably stable rate of return.

- Create a plan such as those described in Chapter 12—a plan that allows you to access your money tax-free during retirement and can last into perpetuity.

- Use tax-advantaged 100-cent dollars as your seed money for funding your home equity retirement plan and *sprint* toward retirement, flying high enjoying 100-cent dollars during your harvest.

- Remember money has to have a lodging place—a home. You should have your money tucked safely in houses made of bricks (stable, predictable investments), yet be able to participate indirectly in the markets of real estate (houses of sticks) and stocks (houses of straw). In other words, maintain the ability to take advantage of real estate and stock market gains without having your money directly at risk if those markets experience losses. That way, even if the big, bad wolf blows the straw or stick houses down, you can be left standing strong, with your money secure.

Fig. 13.1

WHY COAST WHEN YOU CAN FLY?

Do you remember Misconception #10? "I think of retirement as a time to coast." That's what too many financial planners suggest. But I say why coast when you can use *lift*, *thrust*, and *drag* to fly? It would be a pity to ride into the sunset, only to die three years later because you stopped being in motion. This can be the most invigorating, active time of your life. It's the moment to redefine your life and ratchet up the excitement.

See if you have some value you can market. Review your experience and your wisdom, and you may find ideas to start another career or a consulting business that can help others. Retirement is a great time to live your life differently from how you have up to this point.

For younger readers, this is where you say to yourself, "I'm not going to make the mistake my Boomer parents made." If you are those parents, I want to reemphasize some of the lessons I have offered. It behooves you as you approach age 59½, age 62, and beyond to prepare for liftoff: Take the steps to jump-start a positive shift in your finances and your life. By the time you are 65 or 70, you can be moving confidently in a totally new direction—toward the optimization of all your assets.

ELIMINATE THE BARRIERS TO WEALTH

People come to my seminars with the mentality of "I'm too old." I hope I have helped you reach the stage where you have reduced the confusion and isolation that leave you powerless to change. You should now feel secure in your ability to incorporate these new strategies. I hope that now you understand how to eliminate what I listed in Chapter 1 as the greatest barriers to wealth.

Let's go over them one by one:

• *Fear—Not having enough money accumulated for retirement.* You can overcome this fear now because you have discovered resources you might not have known you have. There's a nest egg sitting under your own roof. Your home is what's sacred, not your house. When you separate lazy, idle dollars trapped in your home, you unleash your money to work for you at a return greater than the cost, which is what banks and credit unions do. You create positive cash flow for income above the net cost of borrowing. At the same time, you dramatically reduce your taxes, because a mortgage or HELOC is usually tax-deductible.

• *Fear—Outliving your income after retirement.* Once you understand the power of compound interest, tax-free accumulation, and leverage, you can launch yourself into an environment of double-digit returns. Why quibble about paying 5, 6, or 7 percent tax-deductible interest when you can do exactly what the wealthy do—use that *drag* to earn the equivalent of 12, 15, or even 20 percent? With a better rate of return, you don't have to be concerned about outliving your money. Investments that are tax-free during the harvest provide you with 50 percent more net spendable income. The same income that might have drained your IRA or 401(k) by the time you are 80 or 85 now lasts as long as you do, and can even blossom for your heirs when you die.

• *Fear—Losing your ability to earn and save.* Security does not reside in your job or even in your investments; it resides in you as an individual. You can apply your creativity to put your talents and

ingenuity to work. The world respects usefulness. You can contribute value, not by sitting on a couch and watching the world go
by, but by devising new ways to be useful. A woman I learned about
from my literary agent, Jillian Manus, knitted as a hobby. When a
dog she loved died, she figured out how to weave the dog's hair
into her knitted goods as a way of remembering him. Soon, she
wrote an entire book about her technique and made thousands of
dollars teaching others how to do the same thing.

  • *Fear—Consuming instead of conserving retirement resources.*
By increasing the rate of return on your money and making it tax-
advantaged, you don't deplete your retirement savings, you grow
them. By repositioning assets, you harness the *lift* of compound
interest. By optimizing them via the *drag* of leverage and the
thrust of tax-free accumulation, you can enjoy a stable income
forever.

  • *Fear—Losing your health and mobility.* People who know they
have money in reserve that is constantly being replenished do not
worry as much as others do about the cost of health care. This is
not the place to show you how to improve your health as you age.
But you have learned by now that your health and well-being do
not need to cost you an arm and a leg. Physical health is tied to
mental, emotional, and spiritual health and they are all influenced
by your financial well-being. Even if your health fails, you can better manage big medical bills when your resources are sufficient to
cover major expenses.

  • *Fear—Dying too soon and leaving others without adequate resources.* None of us is getting out of here alive. But it is comforting
to know that if you die prematurely, the same tax-free investments
(your life insurance contracts) will blossom for your loved ones.
And remember, one of the secrets of longevity is holding on to your
curiosity about new things. Barring life-threatening diseases, we
tend to live as long as we think we will live.

  • *Fear—Having resources dwindle due to taxes and inflation.*
When your assets are safely housed in stable investments that are

tax-advantaged on the seed and the harvest, you can enjoy a net spendable retirement income that can be 50 percent greater than IRAs and 401(k)s (qualified plans that can quickly lose air like an inner tube when the valve stem is open). Your income can last into perpetuity, no matter how long you may live. What's more, tax-free retirement income can create a hedge against monetary inflation and allow you to maximize your retirement income without affecting Social Security and Medicare benefits.

• *Fear—Not having enough resources to care for your parents physically and financially as they age.* As members of the Sandwich Generation, Boomers may be called upon to come to the aid of elderly parents. Throughout this book, I have shown you ways you can afford such an expense. The book also includes ideas that might come in handy in supporting your parents. One is through a reverse mortgage, described in Chapter 7. Your parents may be candidates for a rollout of some of their own retirement money into insurance contracts.

• *Fear—Using up resources to pay for long-term health care.* I'm convinced that people who worry less about their resources age with better health than others who are burdened with financial concerns. But regardless of what may lie ahead, you have a plan in place. You have the resources to buy long-term care coverage. If you don't wish to do that, you have money that is liquid when you need to access it quickly. You can use your resources to self-insure your future needs, or you can even obtain a reverse mortgage.

• *Fear—Having to work to make ends meet.* It's a lot more fun to work because you want to, not because you have to. You can increase your usefulness by choosing a new career after you have "retired." You will never become bored, because you can utilize your unique talents and follow your personal interests.

In summary, abundance often leads to more abundance. Now that you have clarity, balance, focus, and confidence, you can take the financial wobbles out of your life and propel yourself with far greater velocity than before.

PROTECTING ASSETS AND INSURING YOUR FAMILY'S FUTURE

There are often expensive milestones in a family's lifetime, things like college tuition or long-term care during our senior years. While you may be familiar with conventional financial planning options for these situations, I would urge you to consider that the alternative strategy we've been discussing for retirement planning—setting aside funds in maximum tax-advantaged insurance contracts—can be used to cover a range of family financial needs, as well.

Some conventional financial consultants advocate that Boomers put aside thousands of dollars a year in qualified savings plans so they can fund their children's college tuition. The trouble with these plans, which sometimes are referred to as Coverdell savings accounts or 529 plans, is that like the Roth IRA and Roth 401(k), they have too many strings attached.

Rather than these conventional plans, I would recommend putting the money for college tuition into maximum tax-advantaged insurance contracts. Not only will the money accumulate tax-free, but when the money is needed for college expenses, it can be accessed tax-free. Furthermore, in the event that the premium payor (who is usually the insured) dies before being able to fully fund the plan, it will immediately blossom in value, creating a college fund with tax-free life insurance proceeds. In other words, it is self-completing. Even if your children's situations change and the fund is not needed for college tuition, what better way to accumulate money for the eventual benefit of your children and grandchildren? After learning what I have taught you in this book, you can probably figure out a way to find tax-advantaged dollars to fund your children's college education plan—they may be sitting under your own roof.

Sooner or later, you also will likely consider whether you should invest in long-term care insurance or not (this is insurance that helps cover costs should you or your spouse need long-term care in a nursing facility). This is often a tough decision for those

approaching or already in retirement. But be aware. Sometimes these policies are pushed using hard-sell tactics and they can carry expensive premiums. Sometimes proponents will show frightening examples of how expensive it can be should you or a loved one need to spend years in a nursing home. According to statistics I have seen, about 90 percent of all nursing home stays are actually less than sixty days.

Naturally, I am all in favor of peace of mind. But I would advise that you make the purchase of long-term care insurance a logical decision, rather than an emotional one. If you were to need long-term care in a nursing facility, it could be financially devastating—possibly draining a retirement nest egg in seemingly no time at all. But sometimes the smartest way to save for all but the most catastrophic situations is to self-insure your future with that same money invested in nonqualified retirement plans.

Look at it this way: When purchasing health insurance, you want to protect yourself from devastating major medical expenses. You tend to purchase only the features and benefits that will alleviate your biggest concerns. Similarly, you may not need to put a crimp in your lifestyle with the often large premiums for long-term care insurance. Look at your health history and your parents' health history to help you determine the likelihood that you will require long-term care. Then purchase only the protection you feel you need and can afford. A professional long-term care insurance specialist can help you make the right decision.

What about homeowner's insurance? That's a no-brainer. It is wise to insure your home. But how much insurance should you get? If you apply for a mortgage, you'll find that most lenders protect themselves by requiring fire insurance at the very least. As those who have been through a catastrophe like Hurricane Katrina or Hurricane Rita know, homeowner's insurance does not necessarily protect you against certain kinds of disasters. Also, specific insurance (such as flood or tidal wave insurance) can sometimes be bought only at a very high cost, if at all, depending on location.

Even if you have it, sometimes it takes a long time to get reimbursed—time that could have been spent more profitably on rebuilding or relocating. So make your decisions regarding the scope of your homeowner's insurance wisely. And regardless of how extensive your homeowner's insurance is, it makes much more sense to reposition your cash outside your home, where you can tap it by simply making a phone call, as explained in Chapter 8.

I would also recommend that you visit with a professional estate planning attorney that specializes in living trusts. You don't have to have a large estate to benefit from the protection and peace of mind that a properly drafted (and funded) living trust can provide. A living trust can help avoid probate and unnecessary estate tax. It can provide more privacy with regard to your financial affairs. It helps preserve love and harmony in a family during the distribution of assets after the death of parents. It can help preserve assets within the family after the death of a spouse, especially if the surviving spouse remarries. And it can reduce liability exposure.

SEIZE YOUR GREATEST FINANCIAL OPPORTUNITIES

I hope you have also discovered as you've made your way through this book how to seize your greatest opportunities:

- To get equity separated from your greatest asset, your house.
- To turbocharge your retirement money by harnessing the power of the three marvels of compound interest (lift), tax-free accumulation (thrust), and leverage (drag).
- To become your own banker by using Other People's Money.
- To seek the best investments with liquidity, safety, and rate of return.
- To take ownership of your retirement by doing a strategic rollout of your IRAs and 401(k)s.

- To find ways to stay in motion and package your wisdom by capitalizing on your lifetime of experience.

You have learned to identify your greatest strengths and unique abilities, such as your work ethic, and your ability to discipline yourself in cultivating your own specific Perpetual Life of Asset Nurturance, or PLAN. You have found the freedom to dispel the myths that parents, especially those who lived through the Great Depression, have instilled in you about money.

Perhaps in the past you have wanted to implement new ideas, but you became tense at the thought of making changes in your family's balance sheet. Finance is an area that can make people clench their teeth! Knowledge brings clarity; clarity helps you relax your financial muscles and paves the way for action.

Most of all, I hope you have new self-reliance to move forward optimistically, thanks to the new direction you have received. You see the brightness of a future in which you live longer than you originally thought, and have enough wealth to enjoy your retirement years in financial comfort. You look forward to the things you can still accomplish with a feeling of peace.

My aim has been to empower you with insight so that you feel more capable and less stressed in dealing with wealth enhancement strategies. You should be ready to implement the strategies with a three-part mantra that says: "I can do this! I can do it right now! I know what tools I need to accomplish this."

COMMENTARY ON THE WORKING PAPERS STUDY BY THE FEDERAL RESERVE BANK OF CHICAGO: "THE TRADEOFF BETWEEN MORTGAGE PREPAYMENTS AND TAX-DEFERRED RETIREMENT SAVINGS"

One of our own federal banks—Chicago's Federal Reserve Bank—has determined that by accelerating mortgage payments instead of stashing money in tax-deferred accounts, more than one in

three Americans are making the "wrong choice," and are giving up potentially important arbitrage gains.

The mortgage overpayments, the Fed's recent report says, are a "misallocation" of funds that costs people $1.5 billion a year. If consumers changed their allocation by *not* sending excess payments to their mortgage company, and instead put that money in some form of tax-advantaged savings, they would reap a median gain of between *11* and *17* cents per dollar.

This is the *very first time* the Fed has compared these two kinds of "savings," write the authors. They conclude that "many households have significant amounts of money" in both tax-favored and taxable accounts, but that a "large proportion" of American taxpayers apparently are *not* taking the smarter route to asset allocation, which would put substantially more money in their retirement savings.

I am delighted to see that the Fed's own experts now believe deductible mortgage interest can be an excellent choice for many taxpayers to use in structuring their retirement funding strategy, even though I do not agree with the report's narrow focus on only qualified plans such as IRAs and 401(k)s.

What's more, the paper says arbitrage is a "rather conservative" way of optimizing retirement wealth. Taxpayers gain when interest rates go up, since the newly invested amount earns higher rates than the mortgage debt costs. Should interest rates go down, taxpayers still come out ahead, because they are "likely to exercise their option to refinance," thus "reducing the downside risk of the arbitrage strategy."

The Fed report ends by saying that despite the risks (and remember—there are risks associated with all investment strategies), saving retirement money in a tax-deferred plan "has the additional benefit of providing a good hedge against the combination of housing price risk and liquidity risk."

Finally, the Fed says that taxpayers with incomes over $100,000 a year who use mortgage-deductible interest as part of an arbitrage strategy in retirement accounts would appear to have the most to

gain, and the authors find it "puzzling" that more people who are in "better financial shape" than the average taxpayer don't take advantage of this kind of strategy.

While I have no idea if the authors of this Federal Reserve paper have read my *Missed Fortune* books, it is gratifying to see government experts validate a key element of my wealth optimization program. (If you would like to read the entire study, it is available at www.MissedFortune.com/ChicagoFedStudy, and can be found in the "Working Papers" section of the Federal Reserve Bank of Chicago's Web site.)

THE OWNERSHIP SOCIETY

For a moment, let's take a look at the larger picture of America's personal finances. Back in Chapter 3, I talked about how crucial it is for all of us to take ownership of our retirement. When you take ownership in your home or any other aspect of your life, you take better care of it. When you take ownership of your financial strategies, you take better care of your money. When you use my strategy to *sprint* toward the finish line with funds that are tax-advantaged on all four phases—contributions, accumulations, distributions, and transfers—you are taking a step that will help turbocharge the growth of the *entire U.S. economy*.

Some people have suggested that my strategy might make congressional revenuers and proponents of higher taxes so alarmed that they'll start agitating to close "loopholes" that allow you to enjoy tax-advantaged optimization of wealth and equity management. There's a myth that revenuers will say, "We've got to stop that *Missed Fortune* guy from pushing for tax-free this and that—it will run the whole country into debt!"

I want to destroy that myth. In fact, as you and many others come to the same positive conclusions about these strategies, you may be instrumental in solving some of the major issues our global society faces.

By taking ownership in your retirement, you may be part of a movement of people who are doing better for themselves and are solving major issues that confront American taxpayers. According to a recent AARP article, "Home equity now represents at least half the net wealth of most American households, about $121,000 on average for a 49-year-old, and more than $144,332 for a 59-year-old."[*]

Look at what occurred between 2001 and 2006. In order to get the economy back on track, the government kept lowering interest rates until they reached a forty-year low. People told themselves that they *had* to refinance at the low rates. When they did pull out just a little of home equity, whether to finish a bathroom or for some other purpose, they stimulated the economy to such a degree that the revenue being taxed in those years provided more revenue for the government than if it had raised taxes.

What happens if America gets hold of the idea to reposition some of the 10 trillion lazy, idle dollars trapped in property and puts just a fraction of that into insurance contracts? Shortsighted revenuers may initially think, "Golly, we're giving them tax breaks; we need to close that loophole." But they soon will realize that showing retirees how to use billions of dollars otherwise earning zero return to finance their golden years will actually benefit the economy.

The huge population of Boomers who are not saving nearly enough for retirement will suddenly have plenty of money to spend. That shift would take the pressure off government-funded entitlements like Social Security and Medicare. Revenuers will see that these strategies solve the issue of where Americans will get the money to pay for their retirement. Yes, insurance companies would be major beneficiaries of this change. And guess where the insurance companies have to invest their billions? Into AAA- and AA-rated bonds and mortgages for shopping malls and office buildings. Imagine these billions being pumped into corporate and municipal bonds and mort-

---

*Ellen Hoffman, "House Party," *AARP Bulletin*, September 2004.

gages on property. Such investments will give the economy a tremendous jolt. Consumer spending will fuel additional economic gains. Federal and state governments will be able to collect vastly larger amounts of revenue in taxes than what they gave up. It's in their best interest to continue permitting people to take ownership of their retirement through tax-favored investments.

The message: If revenuers were to try to end these tax breaks, they would be shooting themselves in the foot—in both feet—since this combination of repositioning home equity into tax-free insurance contracts will generate so much more money than they had been collecting. This is a stimulus plan that will benefit municipalities, states, and corporations, propelling the economy into a better, more stable orbit.

Down the road, Boomers with much greater spending power would be buying big-screen TVs, airline tickets to visit grandkids, vacations and motor homes and everything else. Government could tax the consumption end through something like a national sales tax, rather than tax Boomers' savings.

As you reduce the need for government spending on social policies, government has more room to reduce things like the deficit. Individuals will have more money to donate to charity. Taking ownership of your own retirement is the best solution not only for the Faralongs, the Eagers, and the Gainsworthys, but for you, your spouse, and your children.

REMEMBER THIS:

- Overcome the barriers to a worry-free retirement now that you have the knowledge to roll out funds from IRAs and 401(k)s into nonqualified plans with properly structured, maximum-funded life insurance coupled with mortgage interest offsets.
- Think of retirement not as a time to coast but as a time to discover a fresh career based on your unique skills, hobbies, and passions.
- Use the same wealth-building strategies of equity management combined with investment in tax-free alternatives to fund nonqualified college tuition programs, to help out aging parents, and to self-finance late-in-life health care coverage for yourself.
- Retain a youthful attitude by taking courses to improve your computer skills and by sharing your hard-won experience and entrepreneurial ability through mentoring and volunteer work.

CHAPTER 14

Redefine Yourself for a Future of Abundance

Optimize *All* of Your Assets—Financial, Core, Experience, Contribution

WHO SAYS YOU'RE TOO OLD to run a marathon . . . or to become wealthy? Boomers are rewriting the record books on what can be accomplished at an "advanced" age. They are inspired by people like Jenny Wood-Allen of Dundee, Scotland, who made headlines a few years back when she completed the London Marathon at the age of 90, and like former President George H. W. Bush, who made a parachute jump out of a plane to celebrate his 80th birthday. By the time you are in that age range, I have no doubt there will be loads of people close to the age of 100 competing in all kinds of contests.

The Baby Boom generation views the world differently from how any previous age cohort did. As more Americans lead healthier lives, they are looking for ways to positively change their lives. You and your friends probably realize that even when you do choose to retire, you'll live for several more decades. When your balance sheet is as healthy as your body, you'll want to create real

meaning in your life during your golden years, to share your wisdom and to put your experience to work for the good of your community as well as yourself and your family.

BALANCE YOUR LIFE, NOT JUST YOUR CHECKBOOK

What concerns me occasionally is that even after I have helped clients save grundles of money, they still feel they must scrimp and save. I had clients who were naturally so frugal that they unscrewed every lightbulb in their bathroom except one to save money . . . and then the husband would cut himself shaving because he couldn't see well enough!

There is nothing wrong with being careful about your money after you optimize your assets. But this couple could have spent $100,000 a year without depleting their nest egg. Think of what else they could have done. They could have taken the cruise to Alaska they always talked about. They could have started a family foundation to make charitable gifts. But these two people worked until they were 70½, and once they retired, they realized they were total strangers to each other. Their working life consisted of going off to their respective offices in the morning, coming back home in the evening, and merely coexisting. They couldn't stand each other in retirement because they had not been *with* the other for fifty years. How sad!

Everyone needs to balance working hard with playing hard. More important is the need to pay attention to your spiritual and civic sides so that when you finally do leave your careers behind, you don't say, "I wonder what it was all for?" Once people recognize that they have both the time and the money to enjoy the fruits of their labor and their assets, they feel invigorated. Sometimes, though, they are unsure about how to kick off the adventure.

The most popular topic at self-improvement seminars is always the "how to get started" session. The way to get started is simply to start! Do you need some ideas on how to get started? You should ask

yourself what you have done that has given you the most satisfaction? What gives you energy? What do you know that most people don't? Do you think you have a book in you? You don't have to be an author to write one. You can share things by talking into a tape recorder. You can gather a group of people and begin a class based on your hobby, whether it is knitting or fantasy football.

Retirement is not a time to coast but to fly. And because the world loves usefulness, opportunities open up even when you are not seeking them. Once you're in motion you'll be amazed at how such opportunities abound.

EMPOWER YOURSELF WITH A FAMILY BALANCE SHEET

By thinking about the balance in your life you set the stage for what Lee Brower, president and founder of Empowered Wealth, LC, calls the Brower Quadrant. In his system there are four categories of assets: Human, Intellectual, Financial, and Civic. Human assets are your *core* assets. Intellectual assets come from your *experiences*. Financial assets are usually measured monetarily. And Civic, or Social, assets are the *contributions* we give back to society. I prefer to call this strategy a holistic approach to optimizing all the assets on your personal and family balance sheet. Until this point, I have focused entirely on the financial balance sheet. Now, I'd like to expand that balance sheet so that it includes your *Core, Experience,* and *Contribution assets*.

I'm an executive committee member and one of the founding quadrant living architects of the Brower Quadrant Living Experience. Nobody understands the power and impact of the Brower Quadrant Living Experience better than Lee. He teaches that there are three fascinating but little-known facts:

- In life, there's "True Wealth" and "false wealth."
- False wealth is seductive but has no real or lasting power.
- True Wealth is one of the greatest powers on earth when harnessed and employed correctly.

As I was completing *The Last Chance Millionaire*, Lee was completing his new book, titled *The Brower Quadrant—The True Wealth Phenomenon*. His book outlines a system that allows individuals, families, and businesses to be fully responsible for themselves and to experience true potential. It is not about being better, improving, or changing; it is about true transformation.

Quadrant Living has helped me with brilliant ideas and tools to help my clients become proactive High Impact Families—masters of their future—not victims of their past.

As I experienced personal and business success, I was troubled by the fact that just because I was able to implement tactical strategies to reduce and/or eliminate income, estate, and inheritance taxes there was no correlation between the planning and the overall happiness of the family.

For most of us, a life of affluence sounds ideal. Who wouldn't like to live a life of luxury? However, there are those that claim such luxury carries a price . . . a price that many do not want nor expect. That price may include the forfeiture of experiences that can only be learned firsthand because we want our children to have the opportunities and not the struggles. For an ever increasing number of families, that is exactly the price being paid. Even the less affluent—often unknowingly—sacrifice their family in the pursuit of a career and the trappings of our modern society. Is there a system that would allow for managing the capture and transference of true wealth in a responsible manner?

The answer is not found within the traditional system of financial and estate planning. One comes closer to discovering the answer upon recognizing how financial wealth relates to our True Wealth. True Wealth encompasses *all* of a family's assets . . . not just the material possessions. This includes everything that contributes to the individual health, happiness, and well-being of each and every family member. Our values, our unique abilities and talents, our experiences and education, our health and attitudes toward others are all essential components of True Wealth.

Affluent families are concerned with wealth preservation. However, the less affluent are just as "lost" in trying to make it, catching up with the Joneses, or attaining what they believe, or have been convinced, is an acceptable standard of living. In the process, both get caught up in trying to provide a lifestyle that is in line with what society perceives they need in order to be happy or considered successful. Those who have already achieved financial wealth and those still seeking financial status fall into the trap of neglecting their more important and lasting asset—the family!

Because I am one of the founding quadrant living architects, Lee asked that I write a foreword to *The Brower Quadrant*. If you would like a copy of this incredible work, you can purchase a copy at www.MissedFortune.com/QuadrantLiving at special pricing for readers of *The Last Chance Millionaire*.

Fig. 14.1

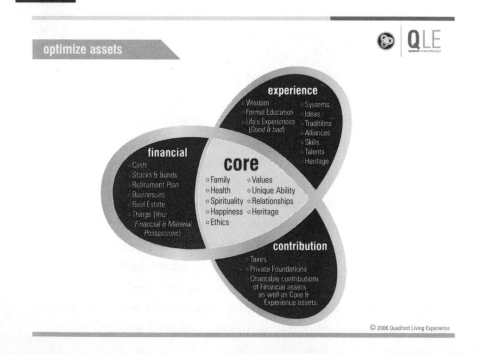

© 2006 Quadrant Living Experience

Please refer to Figure 14.1. It depicts the four quadrants in a manner different from my previous books, *Missed Fortune* and *Missed Fortune 101*. Notice the synergy and interaction of all quadrants with the core assets at the heart.

- Financial Assets: You now have in your hands a strategy for your financial resources. By following through on it, your family wealth should never dissipate, but grow into perpetuity to bless the lives of your children and grandchildren.
- Experience Assets: You have the power to share the knowledge, wisdom, experiences, education, reputation, alliances, skills, ideas, and good habits you have gained in your lifetime and pass them down to future generations.
- Contribution Assets: You can give back to society by setting up a family empowered "bank" that will keep the family's passion and purpose living on into perpetuity for charitable causes. Your family can also establish a formal charitable foundation.
- Core Assets: You can optimize family relationships, health standards, values, and heritage and also capture family genealogy, personal life histories, and unique abilities to pass on to future generations.

I urge you not to hesitate a moment longer to take advantage of this unique opportunity to redefine your life beyond your finances. Your passion and purpose will help you live far longer—and will last into perpetuity after you pass away. You'll be able to leave behind a precious "how to fish" guide for your children and grandchildren, rather than just "dumping fish" into their laps. With your finances secure, you can draw a road map to a future full of promise. You can aim at goals loftier than financial affluence. Put yourself in touch with your new vision and you revitalize your physical, mental, emotional, spiritual, and social self.

SET UP YOUR OWN FAMILY BANK

I am a great believer in setting up a family "bank" where the deposits are made not just in dollars but in ideas, knowledge, experiences, and wisdom. This concept has been a tremendous boon to our family and quality of life with our children and grandchildren. If this message resonates with you, I invite you to go to www.MissedFortune.com/FamilyBank to download an explanation of how to establish a family bank. I also provide a sampling of some of the experiences we have captured and deposited in our own family bank. This brief summary will provide powerful insights on how to:

- Train the spotlight on your core assets, such as family, values, health, and heritage.
- Make donations to your family bank, such as your experiences and wisdom.
- Prioritize and schedule time with those who matter most to you.
- Conduct fun and meaningful family vacations with a purpose.
- Teach your children and grandchildren to be responsible and accountable.
- Teach your children and grandchildren to create value and become financially independent for provident living.
- Give back to society and develop a family True Wealth philosophy.
- Count time and capture defining moments on your family balance sheet.
- Use all your assets, tangible and intangible, wisely and optimize them.
- Establish your own family foundation so your passion and purpose lives on.

MAINTAIN CHOICE AND CONTROL

By taking ownership of your retirement, you and your loved ones benefit from social, human, and intellectual assets that you control, as opposed to those financial assets over which we give up choice and control. As human beings, we contribute to the common good by paying taxes, which helps the government pay for civic functions from streetlights and firefighting to programs that help the poor and needy. However, we don't always have as much control as we would like over how the money is spent. In my strategy, by repositioning some of our wealth that otherwise would go to taxes, we have money that we can redirect to charitable, social, and family causes that we *can* choose and control.

ENJOY A LIFE OF PEACE AND ABUNDANCE

I hope that this book has cleared up some of the confusion you may have been feeling as you approach your golden years. And I hope you have gained energy and confidence in realizing there are opportunities for you to better your own future and the future of the generations that come after you. Finally, I hope that you are empowered with new capabilities to enjoy a life of peace and abundance. Among the rewards of maturity is that there is always a last chance to improve your financial assets, as well as to share your hard-earned wisdom. You've heard people say, "Let's turn the world upside down." I say, "Let's turn the world right side up."

REMEMBER THIS:

- Balance working hard by playing hard and never forget to stop to smell the roses; don't just balance your checkbook, *balance your life.*
- Optimize your core assets by preserving your stories and those of your forbears, grandparents, parents, and children in a family-empowered bank into which you deposit memories, family heritage, and wisdom that live on forever.
- Consider giving back to society by establishing your own family foundation that devotes time and money to the causes, institutions, and charities that mean the most to you.
- Please visit www.MissedFortune.com/FamilyBank to download how to establish a family bank and review a sampling of some of the experiences we have captured and deposited in our own family bank.
- Consult with a qualified professional to determine which strategies contained in this book are appropriate for your specific situation. Because tax laws vary from state to state, a professional advisor can take advantage of your unique circumstances. Seek an advisor who is well versed in asset optimization and equity management to help you implement the appropriate strategies properly. Then follow through with your plan or make necessary adjustments as you go to help it reach its full potential. With proper accountability on your part and the help of a professional advisor, you can achieve a high level of financial success.

What You Need to Know About TEFRA, DEFRA, TAMRA, and
Internal Revenue Code Compliance

I T IS IMPORTANT TO HAVE YOUR retirement plans comply
with federal regulations whether they are qualified—that is, if
they are defined-benefit pensions, IRAs and 401(k)s—or nonqualified, such as life insurance. In the 1980s, Congress and/or the Internal Revenue Service made changes in the tax code that affect life
insurance policies used as capital-accumulation investment vehicles.

The Tax Equity and Fiscal Responsibility Act of 1982, referred to
as TEFRA, and the Deficit Reduction Act of 1984, called DEFRA, created a "tax corridor" aimed at making sure people would not abuse
a life insurance contract that permits tax-free death benefits as well
as tax-free accumulation of cash values.

THE TEFRA/DEFRA TAX CORRIDOR

The TEFRA and DEFRA citation, or tax corridor, essentially dictates the minimum death benefit required in order to accommodate the ultimate desired aggregate premium basis—that is, the size
of the bucket, or the total amount you plan to contribute (also referred to as the guideline single premium), based on the insured's
age and gender. To state this another way, if you want to use a cash-
value life insurance policy for tax-free accumulation purposes,

TEFRA and DEFRA rules govern the amount of the minimum death benefit you are required to include in the policy.

For example, if someone wants to purchase a universal life policy with a $100,000 death benefit, the TEFRA/DEFRA corridor would be referenced to determine the amount of money you could invest in premiums without exceeding the definition of a life insurance contract. If the insured is a healthy 50-year-old woman, that amount would be approximately $25,000 to $30,000. Abiding by the TEFRA/DEFRA rules makes the accumulation of cash values and the death benefit not subject to tax under Sections 72(e), 7702, and 101 of the Internal Revenue Code.

Since in my strategy death benefits are a secondary objective, the primary objective is to create a bucket just big enough under the TEFRA/DEFRA tax corridor to hold the amount of money you will likely put into it. By doing so, you are not obligated to fill the bucket to the brim, but you set a maximum allowable contribution within a given time frame. If the premiums paid into this policy reach that limit before the eleventh year, you must stop contributing any additional money or else you exceed the definition of life insurance under those rules. However, the law does not prevent you from opening another bucket (enrolling in a second cash-value life policy, assuming the insured passes the physical exam and is approved by the insurance company).

TAMRA AND THE SEVEN-PAY TEST

By 1988 it was clear that a great amount of money was being transferred out of banks and brokerage accounts into life insurance companies. With their strong lobby, the banks and brokerage firms were able to convince Congress to include another change as part of the Technical and Miscellaneous Revenue Act (TAMRA). The new law still allows a policyholder to pay one large single premium, but a policy bought this way is classified as a Modified Endowment Contract, or MEC. Accumulations in a MEC are still tax-deferred,

and the death benefit is tax-free. But if any money is withdrawn prior to the insured reaching age 59½, that money is subject to a 10 percent penalty just as with an IRA or a 401(k). And when you withdraw money after age 59½, the gain is taxable under LIFO (last in, first out) treatment, just like an annuity.

To conform to TAMRA regulations, a whole life policy that is structured to pay out tax-free distributions for retirement income or any other purposes must pass what is known as the Seven Pay Test. This means a whole life insurance contract cannot be funded any faster than with seven years of relatively equal installments.

The Seven Pay Test is a misnomer when it comes to universal life and causes a great deal of misunderstanding even for life insurance professionals. Because of the TEFRA and DEFRA limits that dictate the amount of death benefits required to meet the definition of a life insurance policy, a universal life policy can be maximum-funded in as little as three years and one day, or four annual installments, by an individual under the approximate age of 50, or in four years and one day (five annual installments) for someone over the approximate age of 50.

The aim of TAMRA was to spread out the premium payments so that the public would be more likely to liquidate their bank or brokerage accounts over the equivalent period—from four to seven annual installments—rather than transferring the entire amount all at once to obtain life insurance that performed more like similar investments. The rationale was that this would lead to a more gentle dip in funds in banks and brokerages.

THE CREATION OF TEMPORARY SIDE BUCKETS

However, the insurance industry responded to TAMRA with temporary side buckets, such as single premium immediate annuities (a SPIA) or advance premium deposit funds. These temporary side buckets have become the legal parking spot for excess funds that would violate TAMRA had they been paid into the main pol-

icy. Insurance companies usually credit these temporary side bucket accounts with interest equal to or greater than what a bank may be paying. The interest is taxable but the side buckets can pour one-quarter or one-fifth of the total money over into the universal life bucket automatically each year until the side bucket is empty at the end of five years and the universal life policy is full and in total compliance with TAMRA.

Despite the creation of these temporary side buckets as a means of accommodating clients who wish to use life insurance as a tax-free retirement alternative, TAMRA has remained in force. The law makes it just complicated enough that some people opt to keep their money in banks and brokerage accounts while filling up their buckets over the allotted period.

In addition, the IRS allows a life insurance policyholder to over-fund an insurance contract in excess of the TAMRA premium and then "perfect" the contract within sixty days of the end of the first policy anniversary. To avoid the policy then being classified as a MEC, thus preserving the tax-free availability of cash values, the policy owner could request a refund of the overage that was paid into the contract in violation of TAMRA, and redeposit it during the first sixty days of the second year.

I believe, as do many financial planners and insurance experts who have taken courses in my strategy, that despite the federal regulations and the length of time needed, universal life insurance contracts remain extremely attractive long-term investments for the purpose of tax-favored retirement income. However, too many life insurance agents do not understand all the ins and outs of the regulations. The result is they are not competent to structure a policy to perform at its optimal level for living benefits rather than just for death benefits.

This is why I urge you to a) use a life insurance professional who is thoroughly versed in how to structure a policy that is both maximum tax-advantaged and also within the various federal guidelines, and b) be patient with performance during the first sev-

eral years that it takes to allow your bucket to fill up to its maximum and still offer reasonable costs and a superior rate of return.

INTERNAL REVENUE CODE COMPLIANCE

When an insurance contract is structured to accommodate serious capital, such as equity funds coming from a mortgage refinance, it is important to comply with the Internal Revenue Code. As a person changes from one residence to another and a new mortgage is obtained on the new home, we don't have to worry about the deductibility of interest on the new mortgage. As explained in Chapter 6, qualified mortgage interest is deductible on the acquisition of a new residence for up to $1 million of indebtedness. We simply need to comply with TEFRA/DEFRA and TAMRA guidelines as we fund the insurance contract using our previous home's equity (to avoid the insurance contract being classified as a MEC). Section 163(h)(3) of the Code and Temporary Regulation 1.163-8T(m)(3) states that qualified residence interest is allowable as a deduction *without regard* to the manner in which such interest expense is allocated. This section of the code should put a taxpayer at ease for deducting interest on home equity indebtedness (up to $100,000) when borrowing on a current residence and using the loan proceeds for any purpose, including investing them into an insurance contract.

In contrast, Section 264(a)(2) of the Internal Revenue Code stipulates that no deduction shall be allowed for "(2) Any amount paid or accrued on indebtedness incurred or continued to purchase or carry a single premium life insurance, endowment, or annuity contract." Section 264(b) states, "For the purposes of subsection (a)(2), a contract shall be treated as a single premium contract—(1) if substantially all the premiums on the contract are paid within a period of four years from the date on which the contract is purchased, or (2) if an amount is deposited with the insurer for payment of a substantial number of future premiums on the contract."

It is unclear how Section 264 relates to a universal life contract versus a single premium life insurance contract. However, to be on the safe side, I recommend that a taxpayer who desires to deduct interest expense from a cash-out refinance on an existing home where the loan proceeds are invested into an insurance contract (although Section 163 may allow deductibility) avoid having the life insurance classified or construed as a single premium contract. By filling the bucket (funding the policy) no sooner than the maximum prescribed premium schedule to comply with TAMRA (which is generally five years with universal life and seven years with whole life), we can avoid falling under the definition of a single premium life insurance contract. Because a person's particular set of circumstances can be unique, I always recommend each person seek competent legal and accounting advice.

I believe it is best that a life insurance contract not be funded solely with the equity from a current home. Remember to use fixed or indexed insurance contracts rather than variable contracts when repositioning home equity. I usually recommend that no more than 40 percent of the total premiums paid into an insurance contract should come from home equity obtained from a refinance of a current home. The remaining 60 percent of premiums should come from other sources, such as repositioned IRA and 401(k) contributions or distributions, or perhaps from repositioned CDs, money markets, and mutual funds. This 60 percent differential could also include redirected annual planned savings meant for capital accumulation.

However, to reemphasize, if a home is sold and a new one is purchased, the equity from the former home may be used capital-gains-tax-free. In that case, the equity could be used solely to fund an insurance contract using a single premium immediate annuity or other side fund to comply with TAMRA. Interest on the new home mortgage would be deductible on up to $1 million of acquisition indebtedness as provided under Section 163. This strategy alone has motivated many couples (who were debating whether to

sell their home and relocate) to sell their homes, take the tax-free gain, and use the equity to generate tax-free retirement income while using mortgage interest deductions on their new home to offset tax liability on their IRA and 401(k) distributions. So if you are looking for a good excuse to sell your home and purchase a new one, maximizing equity management may be the best reason not to hesitate!

Compliance with Sections 163 and 264 of the Internal Revenue Code can be a somewhat complex arrangement; however, a trained professional who understands these parameters and guidelines can structure and fund a life insurance policy to comply. I cannot overemphasize the importance of seeking advice from a competent tax advisor. With proper planning and counsel, modern cash-value life insurance can be designed to accumulate and store cash safely and provide tax-favored living benefits, as well as income-tax-free death benefits, while maintaining liquidity, safety, and achieving an attractive rate of return.

Fig. B.1

STATE INDIVIDUAL INCOME TAXES
(TAX RATES FOR TAX YEAR 2006 — AS OF JANUARY 1, 2006)

State	TAX RATES Low	High	# of Brackets	INCOME BRACKETS Low	High	PERSONAL EXEMPTION Single	Married	Child.	Federal Tax Ded.
ALABAMA	2.0	5.0	3	500 (b)	3,000 (b)	1,500	3,000	300	*
ALASKA	No State Income Tax								
ARIZONA	2.87	5.04	5	10,000 (b)	150,000 (b)	2,100	4,200	2,300	
ARKANSAS (a)	1.0	7.0 (e)	6	3,399	28,500	20 (c)	40 (c)	20 (c)	
CALIFORNIA (a)	1.0	9.3 (x)	6	6,319 (b)	41,477 (b)	87 (c)	174 (c)	272 (c)	
COLORADO	4.63		1	-----Flat rate-----		-----------None----------			
CONNECTICUT	3.0	5.0	2	10,000 (b)	10,000 (b)	12,750 (f)	24,500 (f)	0	
DELAWARE	2.2	5.95	6	5,000	60,000	110 (c)	220 (c)	110 (c)	
FLORIDA	No State Income Tax								
GEORGIA	1.0	6.0	6	750 (g)	7,000 (g)	2,700	5,400	3,000	
HAWAII	1.4	8.25	9	2,000 (b)	40,000 (b)	1,040	2,080	1,040	
IDAHO (a)	1.6	7.8	8	1,159 (h)	23 (h)	3,300 (d)	6,600 (d)	3,300 (d)	
ILLINOIS	3.0		1	-----Flat rate-----		2,000	4,000	2,000	
INDIANA	3.4		1	-----Flat rate-----		1,000	2,000		
IOWA (a)	0.36	8.98	9	1,269	57,106	40 (c)	80(c)	40 (c)	*
KANSAS	3.5	6.45	3	15,000 (b)	30,000 (b)	2,250	4,500	2,250	
KENTUCKY	2.0	6.0	6	3,000	75,000	20 (c)	40 (c)	20 (c)	
LOUISIANA	2.0	6.0	3	12,500 (b)	25,000 (b)	4,500 (i)	9,000 (i)	1,000 (i)	*
MAINE (a)	2.0	8.5	4	4,550 (b)	18,250 (b)	2,850	5,700	2,850	
MARYLAND	2.0	4.75	4	1,000	3,000	2,400	4,800	2,400	
MASSACHUSETTS (a)	5.3	1		-----Flat rate-----		3,575	7,150	1,000	
MICHIGAN (a)	3.9		1	-----Flat rate-----			3,100	6,200	
MINNESOTA (a)	5.35	7.85	3	20,510 (j)	67,360 (j)	3,300 (d)	6,600 (d)	3,300 (d)	
MISSISSIPPI	3.0	5.0	3	5,000	10,000	6,000	12,000	1,500	
MISSOURI	1.5	6.0	10	1,000	9,000	2,100	4,200	1,200	*(s)
MONTANA (a)	1.0	6.9	7	2,300	13,900	1,900	3,800	1,900	*(s)
NEBRASKA (a)	2.56	6.84	4	2,400 (k)	26,500 (k)	103 (c)	206(c)	103(c)	
NEVADA	No State Income Tax								
NEW HAMPSHIRE	State Income Tax is Limited to Dividends and Interest Income Only								
NEW JERSEY	1.4	8.97	6	20,000 (l)	500,000 (l)	1,000	2,000	1,500	
NEW MEXICO	1.7	5.3	4	5,500 (m)	16,000 (m)	3,300 (d)	6,600(d)	3,300(d)	
NEW YORK	4.0	6.85	5	8,000 (n)	500,000 (n)	0	0	1,000	
N. CAROLINA (o)	6.0	8.25	4	12,750 (o)	120,000 (o)	3,300 (d)	6,600 (d)	3,300 (d)	
NORTH DAKOTA	2.1	5.54 (p)	5	29,700 (p)	326,450 (p)	3,300 (d)	6,600 (d)	3,300 (d)	
OHIO (a)	0.712	7.185	9	5,000	200,000	1,300 (q)	2,600 (q)	1,300 (q)	
OKLAHOMA	0.5	6.25 (r)	8	1,000 (b)	10,000 (b)	1,000	2,000	1,000	*(r)
OREGON (a)	5.0	9.0	3	2,650 (b)	6,550 (b)	159 (c)	318 (c)	159 (c)	*(s)
PENNSYLVANIA	3.07			-----Flat rate-----		---------None---------			
RHODE ISLAND	25.0% Federal tax liability (t)			---		---	---	---	
S. CAROLINA (a)	2.5	7.0	6	2,570	12,850	3,300 (d)	6,600 (d)	3,300 (d)	
SOUTH DAKOTA	No State Income Tax								
TENNESSEE	State Income Tax is Limited to Dividends and Interest Income Only.								
TEXAS	No State Income Tax								
UTAH	2.30	7.0	6	863 (b)	4,313 (b)	2,475 (d)	4,950 (d)	2,475 (d)	*(u)
VERMONT (a)	3.6	9.5	5	29,900 (v)	326,450 (v)	3,300 (d)	6,600 (d)	3,300 (d)	
VIRGINIA	2.0	5.75	4	3,000	17,000	900	1,800	900	
WASHINGTON	No State Income Tax								
WEST VIRGINIA	3.0	6.5	5	10,000	60,000	2,000	4,000	2,000	
WISCONSIN	4.6	6.75	4	8,840 (w)	132,580 (w)	700	1,400	400	
WYOMING	No State Income Tax								
DIST. OF COLUMBIA	4.5	9.0	3	10,000	30,000	1,370	2,740	1,370	

(a) 15 states have statutory provision for automatic adjustment of tax brackets, personal exemption or standard deductions to the rate of inflation. Massachusetts, Michigan, Nebraska and Ohio indexes the personal exemption amounts only.

(b) For joint returns, the taxes are twice the tax imposed on half the income.

(c) Tax credits.

(d) These states allow personal exemption or standard deductions as provided in the IRC. Utah allows a personal exemption equal to three-fourths the federal exemptions.

(e) A special tax table is available for low income taxpayers reducing their tax payments.

(f) Combined personal exemptions and standard deduction. An additional tax credit is allowed ranging from 75% to 0% based on state adjusted gross income. Exemption amounts are phased out for higher income taxpayers until they are eliminated for households earning over $56,500.

(g) The tax brackets reported are for single individuals. For married households filing separately, the same rates apply to income brackets ranging from $500 to $5,000; and the income brackets range from $1,000 to $10,000 for joint filers.

(h) For joint returns, the tax is twice the tax imposed on half the income. A $10 filing tax is charge for each return and a $15 credit is allowed for each exemption.

(i) Combined personal exemption and standard deduction.

(j) The tax brackets reported are for single individual. For married couples filing jointly, the same rates apply for income under $29,980 to over $119,100.

(k) The tax brackets reported are for single individual. For married couples filing jointly, the same rates apply for income under $4,000 to over $46,750.

(l) The tax brackets reported are for single individuals. For married couples filing jointly, the tax rates range from 1.4% to 8.97% (with 7 income brackets) applying to income brackets from $20,000 to over $500,000.

(m) The tax brackets reported are for single individuals. For married couples filing jointly, the same rates apply for income under $8,000 to over $24,000. Married households filing separately pay the tax imposed on half the income.

(n) The tax brackets reported are for single individuals. For married taxpayers, the same rates apply to income brackets ranging from $16,000 to $20,000.

(o) The tax brackets reported are for single individuals. For married taxpayers, the same rates apply to income brackets ranging from $21,250 to $200,000. Lower exemption amounts allowed for high income taxpayers. Tax rate scheduled to decrease after tax year 2007.

(p) The tax brackets reported are for single individuals. For married taxpayers, the same rates apply to income brackets ranging from $49,600 to $326,450. An additional $300 personal exemption is allowed for joint returns or unmarried head of households.

(q) Plus an additional $20 per exemption tax credit.

(r) The rate range reported is for single persons not deducting federal income tax. For married persons filing jointly, the same rates apply to income brackets that are twice the dollar amounts. Separate schedules, with rates ranging from 0.5% to 10%, apply to taxpayers deducting federal income taxes.

(s) Deduction is limited to $10,000 for joint returns and $5,000 for individuals in Missouri and Montana, and to $5,000 in Oregon.

(t) Federal Tax Liability prior to the enactment of Economic Growth and Tax Relief Act of 2001.

(u) One half of the federal income taxes are deductible.

(v) The tax brackets reported are for single individuals. For married couples filing jointly, the same rates apply for income under $49,650 to over $326,450.

(w) The tax brackets reported are for single individuals. For married taxpayers, the same rates apply to income brackets ranging from $11,780 to $176,770. An additional $250 exemption is provided for each taxpayer or spouse age 65 or over.

(x) An additional 1% tax is imposed on taxable income over $1 million.

Index

Page numbers of illustrations appear in italics.

AIG Life Brokerage, 258
Amronin, Gene, 151
Andrew, Douglas R. *See also*
    MissedFortune.com
  Brower Quadrant and, 321–22
  Caribbean vacation experience,
    13–15
  elevator speech, 8–9
  Empowered Wealth, LC and, 11
  father's work experience, 21
  vacation cabin, condo, timeshare,
    54, 222–23, 230
  wedding celebrations in Hawaii,
    34–35
annuities, 240, 248–51, 271
  comparison with other plans, *252*
  deferred, 248, 249–50
  fixed, 248, 249
  indexed, 248, 249, 251
  as low risk, 48, 57
  penalty on early withdrawal, 248
  rate of return, 250
  SPIA (single premium immediate),
    248, 249, 298
  survivor benefits, 250–51
  tax-deferred, 99–100, *100*
  tax-favored accumulation, 248
  tax liability, 249, 271
  variable, 248, 249, 250
  withdrawal of funds, LIFO, 248–49
arbitrage, 134–35, *135*
  Federal Reserve Bank and, 151,
    311–13
  separating equity from your home
    and, 147–50, 158–59
ARM (adjustable-rate mortgage),
    120–21, 166–67, 171

assets
  civic, xvii, 319
  contribution, 322
  core assets, 319, 322, 325
  examining for "drag" of
    leveraging, 84
  experience, 322
  financial, xvii, 319, 322
  home equity, 10, 18
  human, xvii, 319
  intellectual, xvii, 319
  lead advisor for optimization plan,
    55–56
  most important, non-financial, 20
  optimizing, *321*, 322
  protecting, 308–10
  quadrant, *322*
  repositioning, 10, 13, 124,
    198–203, 270
  True Wealth, 319–21

Baby Boomer blunders (ten
    mistakes), 19–39
  #1: using short-term investments
    for long-term goals, 23–24
  #2: underestimating years of life,
    24–27
  #3: paying off the mortgage, 27–28
  #4: believing they saved enough,
    28–29, 69–70
  #5: believing tax bracket will lower
    in retirement, 29–30, 73–74, 192
  #6: deferring taxes, 30–31
  #7: IRAs and 402(k)s as retirement
    vehicle, 31–32, 192
  #8: postponing pulling money out
    of tax-deferred accounts, 33
  #9: waiting to enjoy life, 33–34,
    229

Baby Boomer blunders (*cont.*)
   #10 considering retirement as a
      time to coast, 34–35, 304, *304*,
      316
   not saving enough, 19
   overcoming mistakes, 35–38
Baby Boomers
   acting as your own banker, 150–51
   average accumulated savings, 19
   balancing life, 318–19, 325
   becoming a Blazing Boomer, 6–7,
      153
   birth years inclusive of, 1–2
   different from parents, 20–21, 317
   FDIC warning about retirement
      funds, 191
   greater spending power, benefits,
      314–15
   home ownership, percentage, 122
   percentage with little to no
      savings, 19
   post-retirement careers, 34–35,
      305–6
   redefining the future, 317–25
   retirement as the beginning, 301–2
   retirement blunders, 19–39
   retirement concerns, common,
      3–4, 305–7
   running out of time for savings,
      22–23
   as Sandwich Generation, 307
   wealth of, 87
   why lax about retirement
      planning, 22
banks
   arbitrage used by, 134–35, *135*, 154
   borrowing by,134–35
   family-empowered, 226
   foreclosures, 136–37, 156–57
   as investment lodging, 240
   liabilities as assets, 137–38
bonds, 47, 48, *49*, 57, 97–99, 240
Brokamp, Robert, 44
Brower, Lee, 11, 319
*Brower Quadrant, The? The True Wealth
   Phenomenon* (Brower), 320–21
Brower Quadrant Living Experience?,
   xvii, 319–20
Bush, George H. W., 317

capital gains, 94, 124–25
CDs (certificates of deposit), 23–24,
   48, 47, *49*, 97–99, 214, 215, 240,
   241, 298

checking accounts, interest-bearing,
   97–99
college or Cloverdell savings plans,
   308, 316
compound interest. *See* interest
credit cards
   as non-preferred debt, 116
   paying off, 172, 210
credit score, 165, 189
   checking, 169–71
   credit reporting companies,169
   FICO, 169
   free annual report, 170
   general information on Web site,
      170

debt
   acquisition indebtedness, 122–23
   boosting net worth with, 116–17
   borrowing to conserve not
      consume, 62, 120, 135–37
   liabilities as assets, 137–38
   nonpreferred (credit card), 116,
      124, 131
   preferred (tax-deductible), 116,
      122–24, 131

Economic Growth and Tax Relief
   Reconciliation Act, 86
E. F. Hutton, 255
Empowered Wealth, LC, 11, 319
estate planning. *See also* annuities;
      life insurance contracts
   attorney for, 310
   estate tax, 87
   living trust, 310
   taxes on IRAs, 205
   transferring IRAs or 401(k) to heirs,
      205–6

family bank, 226, 323, 325
family foundation, 323, 325
Fannie Mae (Federal National
      Mortgage Association), 165
FDIC (Federal Deposit Insurance
      Corporation), 191
Federal Reserve Bank, 134
   paper on arbitrage for home
      owners, 151, 311–13
FHA (Federal House Authority), 166
financial balance sheet, creating, 57
financial planners, 56. *See also* lead
      advisor
Five Categories of People's Attitude
      to Wealth, *11*

Arrivers, 12, 46, 180, 181
Divers, 12
Strivers, 12, 46, 180
Survivors, 12
Thrivers, 12, 18, 47, 62, 81, 180,
    181, 188
457 plan, 75–76
four forces of flight, 60, 60–61
    drag as safe, positive leverage, 61,
        62, 83, 179, 294, 302, 306
    lift as compound interest, 61, 82,
        84, 141, 179, 184, 281, 302, 306
    thrust as tax-deferred or tax-free
        accumulation, 61, 82, 179–80,
        281, 294, 306
    weight as taxes and inflation, 61
401(k) plan. See also IRA (individual
        retirement account) and 401(k)
        plan
    cap on, 197
    company stock and, 196
    contribution of additional funds,
        196–97
    dangers of, 202
    as defined-contribution plan, 192
    employer-matched contributions,
        195–96
    introduction of, 195
    leaving/changing job and, 202
    penalty for early withdrawal, 196
    restrictions, 195–96
    tax-advantaged status, 195
    tax bracket and increased liability,
        197
    tax-deferred liability on, 196, 245,
        247–48
    vesting, 195, 196
403(b) plan, 75–76
framework for assessing your
        situation, 4–6
Freddie Mac (Federal Home Loan
        Mortgage Corporation), 165

Ginnie Mae (Government National
        Mortgage Association), 165
Goal Cultivator?, 25
Greenspan, Alan, 166

Harman, Pete, 34
home equity loans or lines of credit
        (HELOC), 172, 302
    80/20 mortgage and, 181
    preferred interest and, 119, 119n,
        120

Home Equity Retirement Plan, case
        study, 109–10
home mortgage
    acquisition indebtedness, 122–23,
        168
    amortized or fixed rate, 122, 128,
        159–61, 166, 166–67, 169, 172,
        180–81
    arbitrage and, 134–35, 147–50,
        151, 158–59, 311–13
    ARM, 120–21, 166–67, 235
    biweekly payments, 173
    borrowing to conserve not
        consume, 120
    cash flow, managing and, 122–24,
        148
    costs and types of, 147–50
    example of four couples, different
        ages, offsetting rollouts, 208–17
    example of three cousins,
        mortgage choices and equity
        accumulation, 173–79, 177
    extra principal payments, 9, 20,
        54, 128, 131, 136, 159–61, 160,
        311–13
    first or senior mortgage, 166
    foreclosures, 136–37, 156–57
    importance of keeping a mortgage,
        163–64
    innovative products, 189
    interest on, 116–21, 131, 147–50
        (see also tax breaks, below)
    interest-only, 120–21, 148, 149, 161,
        161, 162, 163–64, 168, 216–17
    junior mortgages, 166
    largest possible as optimal, 302
    money borrowed, not taxable, 116
    negative amortization (deferred
        interest) loan, 120–21, 168–69
    no money down, 125–26
    paying off, 7, 8, 27–28, 138–39,
        140, 153, 158–64, 160, 162, 302
    paying off vs. side fund earnings,
        140
    refinancing, 121, 164, 172, 187,
        187–88, 189, 210, 212
    reverse mortgage, 152–53, 154
    rising rates and, 158
    rule of 72 to calculate rate of
        return, 68, 84
    second residence, 116, 118–20,
        225–27
    selling home with large balance,
        137

home mortgage (*cont.*)
  shopping for best deal, 171–72, 189
  tax breaks, 9, 28, 52, 57, 116,
    118–20, 140, 148, 163, 168, 172,
    175, 189, 302
home mortgage sources, 165-66
home ownership as equity
  appreciation, dramatic, 129, 156
  as asset, 10
  borrowing against, not taxable, 115
  capital gains on sale, new rules,
    124–25
  example of three cousins,
    mortgage choices and equity
    accumulation, 173–79, *177*
  example of using equity in, 36–38
  finding $100,000 in, 23
  freeing equity, mortgage choices,
    147–50
  as greatest resource, 18
  how compound interest helps,
    70–71
  as investment, 48
  investment in side fund,
    qualifications, 271
  leveraging, 81–82
  life insurance contracts for side
    fund, 299
  median new home price in U.S.,
    174
  net worth in the U.S., 155
  as part of estate, 28
  pitcher of water vs. empty glass,
    143–47, *144, 145, 146*, 302
  rate of return on, 142–43, 154,
    155, 180
  risk of disaster loss, 113–15, 128,
    141, 156
  separating equity from, 158–59,
    189, 207, 249, 300, 310
  using to increase liquidity, safety,
    and rate of return, 54–55, 115,
    127–29, 131, 139–42, *140*
home purchase
  80/20 (interest-only/line of credit),
    181
  no money down, 125–26, 176
  rollover of capital gains on sale of
    home and, 124–25
  three examples of building equity,
    180–82
housing market, 129, 156, 157,
  180–82
Huang, Jennifer, 151

inflation, 61
  calculating retirement cost of
    living increases, 69–70
insurance. *See also* life insurance
    contracts
  disaster insurance, 309–10
  health, 309
  homeowner's insurance, 309–10
  long-term health care, 307, 308–9
interest
  compound ("lift), 10, 57, 61, 62,
    62–67, *64, 65,* 82, 84, 141,
    149–50, 154, 179, 184, 281, 302,
    306
  compound and home
    appreciation, 70–71
  difference between annual,
    quarterly, monthly, and daily
    compound interest, *64*
  on home mortgage, 9, 28, 52, 57,
    80–81, 116–21, 140, 163, 168,
    172, 175, 189, 206–8, 302
  on home mortgage, as
    "employment" cost, 147, 148
  lily pond exercise, 71–72
  preferred vs. non-preferred, 116,
    118
  rate reductions, early 2000s, 86
  rising rates, 182–84
  simple interest, 63, 63n, 154
  wealth creation and borrow/invest
    rate, 182–84
interest-only mortgage, 120–21, 173
  80/20 mortgage and, 181
  arbitrage and, 147–49
  to build side fund, 161, *161, 162,*
    163–64, 169
  critics of, 168
  example of, 216–17
  example of and using equity to
    fund retirement savings, 175–76,
    177, 178, 179
  as Option ARM, 168
  true costs, 122
Internet websites
  credit reporting companies, 170
  Federal Trade Commission, 170
  MissedFortune.com, 56, 91–92,
    130, 153, 170–71, 172, 198, 236,
    271, 294–95, 321
  online tax calculators, 91
  TIAA/CREF, 204
investments. *See also specific types*
  annuities, 248–51

bad timing on, 20
best for retirement savings, 242–71
    (*see also* annuities; life insurance
    contracts; mutual funds)
comparison of retirement plans,
    252
covering mortgage with liquid, safe
    side fund, 139–41
examining for compound interest,
    84
home as, 48, 142–43, 154
identify predictable results, 47–48
indexed, 264–68, *267*
indexed universal life, *292–93*
interest rates and inflation, effects
    of, 47
life insurance contracts, 253–70,
    299
liquidity, 48, 87, 115, 126–27, 129,
    141–42, 164, 175, 241–42
LSRR, 126–27, 131, 195, 239–71
LSRR of home ownership, 127–29
millionaire status with initial
    investments of $100,000,
    175,000, and 260,000, 184, *185*,
    186–87, *187*
mutual funds, 242–48, *244*
rate of return, 48,, 142–43, 154,
    155 127, 241, 242
removing money from too soon, 24
reviewing, 39
risk levels, 48
risk-return model, *241*
safety, 48, 51, 113–15, 127, 164,
    241
saleable, *49*
second or vacation home, 221–37
side fund, 298–99 (*see also* side
    fund)
tax-advantaged, 51, 72
tax-deferred, 72–74
taxed dollars invested in
    nonqualifed accounts, 96–97
tax-favorable, 149, 158, 251–52,
    252
tax-free, 80, 163, 240
three lodging places for money,
    48–51, *49*, 57, 157, 240, 303
wrong vehicles for, 20, 23–24
IRA (Individual Retirement Abodes).
    See second or vacation home
IRA (individual retirement account)
    and 401(k) plan. *See also* Roth
    IRA and Roth 401(k)

comparison with other plans, *252*
converting money (*see* strategic
    rollout)
as counterproductive, 8, 54
disadvantages of tax deferring,
    31–32
example of, 176, *177*, 178
IRS penalty for early withdrawal,
    76, 197, 199, 200–201
IRS penalty for not taking
    minimum distribution, 33,
    203–4, *204*
as jog option for retirement,
    100–101, *101*, 111, 252
liberating yourself from, 85–110,
    199–203
life insurance contracts compared
    to, 299
mandatory withdrawal, 76, 203–4
maximum yearly contribution, 76
at MissedFortune.com, 325
pre-tax dollars and, 97
second home compared to,
    227–28, *228*
shrinking income case study,
    107–9
strategic rollout, 33, 73, 79–80,
    198–203, 204, 219, 270, 271,
    303, 310, 316
strings attached, 75–76
taxes due on (tax-deferred), 72–75,
    85, 100–101, *101*, 247–48
transferring to heirs (stretch), 33,
    205–6
withdrawing funds without tax
    consequence, 55, 200–201 (*see
    also* strategic "rollout")

Jobs and Growth Tax Relief
    Reconciliation Act, 86

KFC franchises, 34
kop-jocki, 25

Lappert's Ice Cream shop, 35
Laws of Lifetime Growth (Sullivan),
    19–20
lead advisor, 55–56, 57
leverage, safe, positive, 10, 47, 50, 59
    bank loan or mortgage as, 61
    borrowing to conserve not
        consume, 62, 120, 135–37
    "drag" as, 61, 62, 83, 179, 294,
        302, 306

leverage, safe, positive (*cont.*)
   home equity, 81–82
   safety of principal, 131
   using OPM, 61, 80–81
liabilities, examining for leveraging, 84
life expectancy
   extended and new retirement age,
      2–3
   gap in resources to cover, 2–3
   life insurance policies, endowing
      age, 25
   longer, expectations of, 27, 39
   over one hundred years, 24–25
   tax code tables revised upward
      and, 25
life insurance contracts, *49*, 240,
      253–70
   advantages of, 258, 273
   background on insurance
      investing, 254–55
   as best retirement investment, 299
   cash-value, 256–60, 271
   for college savings, 308
   comparison with other plans, *252*
   cost of life insurance portion, 284
   death benefits of, 257–58, 300
   determining your nest egg, 275–79
   disclosure from NAIC, 289, 289n
   endowing age, 25
   example, 50-year-old couple, plan
      to retire at 65, 274–79
   example, 50-year-old couple, plan
      to retire at 70, 274–75, 291–94
   example, 55-year-old couple, plan
      to retire at 65, 274–75, 280
   example, 60-year-old couple, plan
      to retire at 70, 274–75, 283–89
   excess cash value, 278
   fixed universal life, 261–62
   frequently asked questions, 295–98
   funding phase, 279
   grandfather clauses to protect,
      295–96
   guaranteed cash values, 258
   guideline level or single premiums,
      279
   health issues and, 296–97
   home equity put in, 300
   income in perpetuity, 194, 288–89
   increasing death benefit, 283, 284
   indexed universal life, 245–46,
      263–69, *267*, *292–93*
   "investment grade," *252*, 252,
      268–70

IRS compliance, 296
laws governing, 295–96
LCM case studies at
   MissedFortune.com, 294–95
legal guidelines, 268–69, 281n, 299
level death benefit, 283, 284
life insurance specialist for, 280,
   296
liquidity, 257, 269
as low risk, 48, 57
lump-sum payments, 275–79
Modified Endowment Contract
   (MEC), 282–83, 298
mortality and expense charges,
   277
offset by tax breaks, 258
over-funding, 259–60, 282–83, 300
paid for by tax reduction, 20, 52,
   195
patience and, 300
physical exams, 277
rate of return, 278, 281, 284, 286
ratings of companies, 269
requirements for, 280–82, 281n
retirement income as tax-free, *102*,
   102–5, 254, 255
retirement savings 100-cent dollars
   invested, 103–5, *103*, *104*
stock indexes used for, 266
surrender charges, 297–98
survivor benefits, 278, 284–85,
   290–91
TEAM member to help, 298
term vs. cash-value, 256–57
universal life, 257, 259, 261, *264*,
   276, 281, 283–85, 300
variable life, 257, 260–63
whole life, 257, 260
withdrawing as loan, 286, 288–89,
   300
withdrawing without taxes, 286,
   287
yearly deposit regulations, 277
Lifetime Extender exercise, 25–27,
   43–44
living trust, 310

Manus, Jillian, 306
matching employer plans, 78, 84
Miller, Robert A., 258
millionaire status, 15–16
   creating, initial investments of
      $100,000, 175,000, and 260,000,
      184, *185*, 186–87, *187*

eliminate the barriers to wealth,
    305–7
Missed Fortune (Andrew), 37, 121,
    285, 313
Missed Fortune 101 (Andrew), 7, 36,
    37, 87, 121, 130, 226, 285
MissedFortune.com
    401 Cabin, 236
    AdvisorChecklist at, 56
    Brower book available at, 321
    complimentary Tax Rate
        Schedules, 91–92
    DVD on Seminar Highlights, 153
    family bank, 325
    finding a TEAM professional, 172
    "I'll Bet You Didn't Know This
        About Credit" free booklet, 171
    LCM case studies, 271, 294–95
    online tax bracket calculator,
        198–99
    summary of *Missed Fortune* books,
        130
    Tirone book available at, 170–71
Modified Endowment Contract
    (MEC), 282–83, 298
money market accounts, 23–24, 47,
    48, *49*, 97–99, 240,, 241 298
mortgage insurance, 166
mortgage specialist, 171, 173
mutual funds, 24, 240, 242–48, 271
    401(k) plan in, 245
    growth funds, as high risk, 48, *49*
    index funds, 50
    length of investment, 247
    negative aspects, 245–47
    rate of return, *244*
    recovering from market
        downturns, 245
    risk tolerance and, 243
    tax-deferred, 99–100, *100*
    tax liability, 247–48
    unpredictable results, 47
    Vanguard fund, 244

National Association of Insurance
    Commissioners (NAIC), 262,
    289, 289n
negative amortization (deferred
    interest) loan, 120–21, 168–69, 173
net worth
    assets vs. liabilities and home
        ownership, 143–47, *144*, *145*,
        146, 158

increasing, 9, 13, 116–17
liabilities as assets, 137–38

OPM (Other People's Money), 46, 47.
    See also home mortgage
    bank loan or mortgage as, 61, 125,
        154
    for vacation home, 303
    wasting, by paying off a mortgage,
        138–39
Option ARM (adjustable-rate
    mortgage), 120, 168, 169, 172,
    235
    four ways to pay, 172

pensions
    company plans, failure of, 202
    defined-benefit, 192–95, 235
    defined-contribution, 192, 195–98
        (*see also* 401(k) plan)
    50 percent survivor option, 193
    joint and survivor annuity, 193
    mandatory withdrawal, 203–4, *204*
    single-life only distribution,
        193–95, 235
    "vested," 195, 196
PLAN (Perpetual Life of Asset
    Nurturance?), 8
profit-sharing plan, 75–76

"qualified" retirement plans, 75–78

real estate, *49*, 240. *See also* home
        ownership and equity; rental
        property; second or vacation
        home
    appreciation, dramatic, 129
    bubble, 241
    investments, 50, 157
    investments transferred into,
        49–50
    as IRA (Individual Retirement
        Abodes), 54, 221–37
    as moderate risk, 48, 57
    not leveraged, 99–100, *100*
    safety test, 241
    tax liability, 97
refinancing
    example, 210, 212
    frequency, 121, 164, 172, *187*,
        187–88, 189
rental property, 224
retirement age
    current average, 2

retirement age (*cont.*)
  life expectancy and resource gap,
    2–3
  near future average, 3
  outliving funds, concern about,
    3–4
  underestimating years of life after,
    24–27
retirement income
  increasing net spendable, 9, 13, 74,
    106–7, 179–80
  from insurance contract, *102*,
    102–5, *103*, *104*, 286, *287*,
    288–89, *292–93*
  from IRA and 401(k) plan, 52–54,
    101, 106–7
  outliving funds, concern about,
    3–4, 305
  in perpetuity, 9, 31, 74, 288–89,
    303
  Roth IRA and Roth 401(k), *102*,
    102
  shortfall retiree must cover, 44,
    305
  shrinking IRA/401k case study,
    107–9
  Social Security as, 42–43
  sprint option: 100-cent dollars
    invested and tax-free use, 252
  tax-deferred investment liability,
    99–101, *100*, *101*, 106–7, 192
  taxes paid up front, advantages,
    31, 53–54
  tax-free, 74, *103*, 103–5, *104*,
    106–7, 198
  yearly needs vs. current income,
    29
retirement plans. *See also specific types*
  accumulation stage, 106
  contribution stage, 106
  defined-benefit pension plan,
    75–76, 192–95 (*see also*
    pensions)
  defined-contribution pension plan,
    192, 195–98 (*see also* 401(k)
    plan; pensions)
  examining for "thrust" of tax-free
    accumulation, 84
  examples, four couples, 275–89
  example of four couples, offsetting
    rollouts, 208–17
  four phases of, *32*, *79*, *105*, 105–7,
    202
  homeowner and, 79

life insurance contracts as best, 299
mandatory withdrawal, *204*
matching employer plans, 78
nonqualified alternatives, 78–80,
  192
100-cent dollars used, 52–54,
  100–101, 303
qualified plans, 75–78, 192
reviewing, 219
strategic "rollout," 73, 79–80,
  199–204, 219, 270, 271, 303,
  310, 316
tax-advantaged, 88
taxes due, retired couples, 204
taxes paid up front, advantages,
  53–54
tax-favored accumulation, 175
tax-free, 78–80
transfer stage (as estate), 106
universal life as, 275–79, *276*
withdrawal or distribution stage,
  106, 203–4
retirement savings
  acting as your own banker, 150–51
  Americans with little to none, 19
  amount needed, 22–23
  assessing current, 39
  average accumulated amount, 19
  becoming proactive in acquiring,
    45–46
  conventional advice, 302
  crawl option: taxed dollars
    invested in nonqualifed
    accounts, 96–99, *98*
  examining for compound interest,
    84
  finding $100,000, 23
  four qualities needed in, 46
  four sources of money, 46–47
  investing home equity, gains,
    149–51
  jog option: pre-tax dollars invested
    or tax-free dollars on the back
    end, 100–103, *101*, *102*, 252
  not saving enough, 19, 20
  options, 96–105, 111, 252
  "qualified" plans, 75–78, 97
  second or vacation home as,
    221–37
  sprint option: 100-cent dollars
    invested and tax-free use, *103*,
    103–5, *104*, 111, 270
  tax-deferred, 30–32, 99–101, *100*,
    101, 111, 164, 302

tax-favored accumulation, 52, 59, 62
tax-free, 163, 164, 303
tax-free or taxed as you go, 94, *95*, 96
"thrust" accumulation, 61, 82, 179–80, 281, 294, 306
walk option: tax-deferred savings, 99–100, *100*, 252
reverse mortgage, 152–53, 154
Roth 401(k). *See* Roth IRA and Roth 401(k)
Roth IRA and Roth 401(k), *32*
advantage of, 192
caps on, 77
comparison with other plans, *252*
conversion of regular IRA to, 77
as jog option for savings, *102*, 102–3
maximum yearly contribution, 76
retirement income as tax-free, *102*, 102–3
strings attached, 76–77, 84
waiting period before withdrawal, 77
rule of 72, 67–68, 84

Sanders, Colonel Harland, 34
savings accounts, 96–97
second or vacation home, 20, 54, 221–37, *228*
80/20 mortgage for, 212
"401 cabin" or "401 condo," 222, *226*
appreciation on, 223, 225
boat as, 224
Florida home, example, 231–32
human assets and, 228–29
MissedFortune.com description, 236
mortgage interest, tax-deductible, 116, 118–20, 213, 223–24, 225–27, 237
rate of return compared to IRA, *228*
RV or motor home as, 224, 233–36
third property, allowing as deduction, 226
timeshares or fractional vacation ownership, 229–33
using retirement savings for, 221–37
winter-summer home option, 233–36, 237
"Secrets of Wealthy People" CD, 15–16

SEP IRAs, 212
"7 Social Security Myths" (Brokamp), 44
7 Steps to 720 (Tirone), 170–71
Sialm, Clemens, 151
side fund, *140*, 298–99
interest-only mortgage as seed money, 161, *161*, *162*, 163–64, 169
paying off mortgage vs., 139–41, *140*
qualifications, 271
Social Security, 45
age for collecting full benefits, 43
agency calculations of income replaced by benefits, 44
average monthly benefit, 45
avoiding taxes on, 75
collection of, reliability, 3
contacting for projected benefits, 57
myth, as primary retirement income, 42–43
shortfall retiree must cover, 44, 305
Trust Fund, depletion of, 3, 43–44
stocks, 20, 47, 48, *49*, 57, 97–99, 129, 240
indexes for universal life insurance, 266
liquidity of, 157
losses 2000?2003, 49–50, 86–87
performance, 1990s, 49
recovering from market downturns, 245
rule of 72 to calculate rate of return, 68, 84
S&P 500 Index, 266–67, *267*
tax-deferred, 99–100, *100*
volatility, 240–41
strategic "rollout," 73, 79–80, 198–204, 219, 270, 271, 303, 310, 316
comprehensive plans, available at MissedFortune.com, 271
examples, 208–17
offsetting taxes with mortgage interest deduction, 206–7
potential withdrawn yearly, 271
tax advantage of, 204
Sullivan, Dan, 4, 19, 25

tax advisor, 172
tax bracket, 88–90

tax bracket (*cont.*)
  converting money and, 198–99
  determining your bracket, 39
  lowering with interest deductions,
    116–17
  marginal vs. effective, 90–92
  online calculator, 198–99
  at retirement, 29–30, 85–86, 192
  thresholds raised, 86
  2007 Federal Tax Rate Schedules,
    89
tax breaks
  benefits to the economy, 313–15
  charitable giving, 52
  front end, IRAs and 401(k), 9
  for HELOC, 119, 119n, 120
  home mortgage interest, 9, 27–28,
    52, 57, 116, 118–20, 140, 148,
    163, 168, 172, 175, 189, 206–8,
    302
  legitimate deductions, 90
  offsetting IRA rollout costs, 206–8
  second or vacation home mortgage
    interest, 116, 118–20, 223–24,
    225–27
  using legitimate, 51–52, 57
taxes
  on annuities, 249, 271
  borrowed money, not taxable, 115
  capital gains, 94
  CPA or tax preparer for, 92
  deferred (back end), on retirement
    fund, 9, 30–32, 72–75, *75*, 87,
    111, 192, 197, 204, 302
  estate tax, 87
  expected increase in, 86–88, 111
  form 1040, reviewing, 206, 219
  funds from life insurance
    contracts, 286, *287*, 288–89
  income subject to, 93–94
  increase in liability at retirement,
    9, 197
  IRA and 401(k) transfer to heirs,
    205–6

  IRS penalties for early withdrawal
    from qualified fund, 76, 197,
    199, 200–201
  IRS penalty for not taking
    minimum IRA distribution, 33,
    203–4, *204*
  life insurance contracts, 268–69,
    280, 296
  paid up front, advantages, 31
  recent economic history and,
    86–88
  reform law of 1997, 223
  refunds, 92–93
  on rollout from qualified funds,
    198–99, 204
  savings taxed as you go along, 94,
    95, 96
  on Social Security benefits, 75
  state, 90
  taxable income, calculating, 88–90,
    91
  tax-advantaged retirement plans,
    88
  tax-favored accumulation, 10, 13
  W-4 form, 93
  as "weight," 61
  withholding amount, 93, 123, 148
TEAM (The Equity Alliance Matrix),
  170, 170n, 172, 298
TIAA/CREF, 204
Tirone, Philip, 170–71
"Tradeoff Between Mortgage
  Prepayments and Tax-Deferred
  Retirement Savings, The"
  (Amromin et al), 151, 311–13
True Wealth Transformation?, 37
TSA plan, 75–76

VA (Veterans Administration), 166
Vanguard fund, *244*, 244–45

Wood-Allen, Jenny, 317

About the Author

Douglas R. Andrew has extensive experience in business management, economics, accounting, gerontology (as it relates to the economics of aging), financial and estate planning, and advanced business and tax planning. He is currently the owner and president of Paramount Financial Services, Inc., a comprehensive personal and business financial planning firm with several divisions. Doug helps people find their missed fortune using his asset optimization, equity management, and wealth empowerment strategies. His previous two books, *Missed Fortune* and *Missed Fortune 101*, are national bestsellers.

As a financial strategist and retirement specialist, Doug shows people how to accumulate money on a tax-favored basis to achieve the highest possible net spendable retirement income. Paramount Financial teaches people how to successfully manage equity to enhance its liquidity, safety, and rate of return, as well as maximize tax benefits. Doug also specializes in helping people optimize not only financial assets but also the Core, Experience, and Contribution assets—comprising "True Wealth"—on the family balance sheet. He is most grateful to maximize his personal True Wealth with the greatest treasures of all: his wife of thirty-three years, Sharee, and their six children, with spouses and several grandchildren.

Douglas Andrew is a masterful communicator with the unique ability to take complex strategies and make them simple to under-

stand through the use of powerful metaphors. Doug is a nationally recognized speaker and teaches the Missed Fortune True Wealth Transformation™ strategies in public seminars throughout America, as well as through TeleSeminars and Webinars. For dates and times of these presentations, visit www.MissedFortune.com/semi nars. Doug has developed a nationwide network of financial professionals referred to as The Equity Alliance Matrix (TEAM). TEAM members are trained with more than fifty hours of intensive instruction and study on asset optimization, equity management, and wealth empowerment.

If you would like to contact or be contacted by a TEAM member in your area, please phone the Missed Fortune™ home office tollfree at 1-888-987-5665, e-mail them at info@MissedFortune.com, or contact them through their Web site by visiting www.MissedFor tune.com. If you are a financial services professional, insurance specialist, mortgage specialist, CPA, tax attorney, or real estate agent and would like information on how to become a TEAM member, please contact them in the same manner.